Foundations of 3D Computer Graphics

FOUNDATIONS OF 3D COMPUTER GRAPHICS

Steven J. Gortler

The MIT Press
Cambridge, Massachusetts
London, England

MIT Press books may be purchased at special quantity discounts for business or sales promotional use. For information, please email special_sales@mitpress.mit.edu or write to Special Sales Department, The MIT Press, 55 Hayward Street, Cambridge, MA 02142.

This book was set in Syntax and Times Roman by Westchester Book Group. Printed and bound in the United States of America.

Library of Congress Cataloging-in-Publication Data

Gortler, Steven J. (Steven Jacob), 1966–
Foundations of 3D computer graphics / Steven J. Gortler.
    p.   cm.
Includes bibliographical references and index.
ISBN 978-0-262-01735-0 (hardcover : alk. paper)
1. Computer graphics. 2. Three-dimensional display systems. I. Title.
T385.G658   2012
006.6'93—dc23

                                                        2011040567

10 9 8 7 6 5 4 3 2 1

To A.L.G., F.J.G, and O.S.G.

Contents

Preface

This book developed out of an introductory computer graphics course I have been teaching at Harvard since 1996. Over the years, I have had the pleasure of teaching many amazing students. During class, these students have asked many good questions. In light of these questions, I often realized that some of my explanations in class were a bit sloppy and that I didn't fully understand the topic I had just tried to explain. This would often lead me to rethink the material and change the way I taught it the next time around. Many of these ideas have found their way into this book. Throughout the course of the book, I cover mostly standard material but with an emphasis on understanding some of the more subtle concepts involved.

In this book, we will introduce the basic algorithmic technology needed to produce three-dimensional (3D) computer graphics. We will cover the basic ideas of how 3D shapes are represented and moved around algorithmically. We will cover how a camera can be algorithmically modeled turning this 3D data into a two-dimensional (2D) image made up of a discrete set of dots, or *pixels*, on a screen. Later in the book, we will cover some advanced topics on the basics of color and light representations. We will also briefly introduce some advanced topics on light simulation for producing photo-realistic images, on various ways of dealing with geometric representations, and on producing animated computer graphics.

In this book, we include material that is both above and below the API-hood. Much of the material (especially early on) is stuff you simply need to know to do 3D computer graphics. But we also spend time to explain what is going on inside of OpenGL. This is necessary to understand in order to be a highly competent computer graphics programmer. But also, it is simply fascinating to learn the hows and whys of our amazing computer graphics computational infrastructure.

We will not cover the hardware and compiler aspects of computer graphics in this book. We will also not focus on 2D computer graphics or human–computer interfaces. These topics are all interesting in their own rights but are fairly distinct from the algorithmic side of 3D computer graphics.

In this book, we structure our explanations around OpenGL, a real-time "rasterization-based" rendering environment. We have done this (rather than, say, a "ray tracing–based" environment) because so much of computer graphics is done in this setting. Anyone, for example, who works in 3D video games needs to master this material (and more). We have chosen the OpenGL API (with the GLSL shading language) in particular, as it can be run on a wide variety of computing platforms.

This book is intended for upper-level computer science/math/physics undergraduate students with at least a year of programming under their belts and at least a rudimentary understanding of linear algebra.

For the Professor

In the following paragraphs, I will describe some of the subtle issues that require some care to get right and are often not taught clearly. I hope that students will master these topics from this book.

Chapters 2–4: In computer graphics, we need to think about points and vectors from both a coordinate-free and a coordinate-full approach. We need to use coordinates to obtain a concrete representation ultimately resulting in our rendered images. But it is often important to represent and transform our points with respect to different coordinate systems. As such it is important to

• Distinguish between a geometric point and the coordinates used to represent that point with respect to some frame.

• Use a notation to explicitly keep track of the basis used for a set of coordinates.

• Distinguish in our notation between matrix equations that represent basis changes and matrix expressions that represent geometric transformations being applied to points.

This ultimately leads to what we call the *left-of* rule, which allows us to interpret matrix expressions and understand with respect to which basis a transformation is acting.

It is our hope that by mastering this explicit notational framework, a student can easily figure out how to do complicated transformations. This is in contrast to the "try lots of orderings and inverses of sequences of matrices until the program does the right thing" approach. One loose inspiration for our approach is the manuscript by Tony DeRose [16].

Chapters 5 and 6: We describe an organized framework for dealing with frames in computer graphics and how this translates into simple 3D OpenGL code. In particular, we derive useful ways to move objects around using a "mixed auxiliary frame." This allows us to, say, rotate an object correctly about its own center but in directions that correspond naturally to those on the screen.

Chapter 7: This is a simple and straightforward description of the quaternion representation for rotations. We also derive how properly to combine quaternions and translation vectors to define a rigid-body transformation data type that multiplies and inverts just like matrices.

Chapter 8: This is a simple and straightforward description of the trackball and arcball rotation interface. We also show why the trackball interface is mouse path–invariant.

Chapter 9: We do a quick and dirty introduction to Bezier and Catmull–Rom splines.

Chapters 10–13: In these chapters, we describe how camera projection is modeled using 4 by 4 matrices. We also describe the fixed function operations in OpenGL. We pay special attention to deriving the correct formulas for interpolating the varying variables. Some of the background on affine functions and interpolation is relegated to appendix B. Many of the subtleties here are described nicely in essays by Jim Blinn [5]. In these chapters, we do not cover details about clipping or rasterization algorithms.

Chapters 14 and 15: We give some simple example shaders for diffuse, shiny, and anisotropic materials. We also point to more advanced real-time rendering techniques such as multipass rendering and shadow mapping. These sections are admittedly too brief. Presumably, students pursuing more aggressive rendering projects will need to learn a lot more about the ever-evolving techniques (and tricks) used in modern real-time rendering.

Chapters 16–18: We cover the basics of why filtering is needed to compute discrete images and how basis functions are used to reconstruct continuous ones. In particular, we show how these two concepts need to be combined to do filtering properly during texture mapping (à la Paul Heckbert's M.S. thesis [28]). We do not delve into the details of Fourier analysis here, as we think it would pull us a bit too far off the main narrative (and, in the end, we use box filters anyway).

Chapter 19: We describe the basic theory of human color perception. From a mathematical perspective, we attempt to be clear about the very definition of what a color is and why such things form a linear space. A related treatment to ours can be found in Feynman's lectures [20]. For many of the technical issues of color computations, we rely on the color FAQ of Charles Poynton [58].

Chapter 20: For completeness, we briefly describe ray tracing computations. As this is not the focus of the course, we only touch on the topic.

Chapter 21: As an introduction to advanced topics in photo-realistic rendering, we do a careful introduction to the physical units for describing light and to the reflection, rendering, and measurement equations. One thing we pay close attention to, for example, is why reflection is measured in the particular units used. A good reference on these basics and more is Eric Veach's Ph.D. thesis [71].

Chapter 22: We outline some of the ways that surfaces are modeled and represented in computer graphics. This is a nontechnical discussion that gives a quick introduction to this rich topic. We do go into enough detail to be able to implement Catmull–Rom subdivision surfaces (assuming you have a mesh data structure handy), as these are a quick and easy way to represent a broad family of surfaces.

Chapter 23: We outline some of the ways animation is done in computer graphics. Again, this is a nontechnical discussion that gives a quick introduction to this rich topic.

One nice place to start for this material is Adrien Treuille's course on the CMU website (http://www.cs.cmu.edu/~15869-f10).

Appendix A: We try to get up and running as painlessly as possible with a first OpenGL program. Because we will be using a modern version of OpenGL, there is thankfully not much API left to teach anymore. All OpenGL needs to do is manage the shader programs, vertex buffer objects, and textures. We do not teach any of the deprecated elements of old OpenGL, as they are not used in modern computer graphics programming. Appendix A may be read at any time before chapter 6.

Appendix B: We summarize important facts about affine functions. This is helpful for reading chapter 12 and essential for reading chapter 13.

This book covers a bit more than what would be possible to do in a one-semester course. It does not attempt to be an encyclopedic reference to all of the rich topics in computer graphics theory and practice. Additionally, this book stays close to material in wide use today. We do not cover the many current research results and ideas that may one day become part of standard practice.

The website for readers of the book may be found at www.3dgraphicsfoundations.com, which contains free supplemental content such as code that mirrors and extends the code in the book, errata, and supplemental text for some topics.

Instructors will also find password-protected exercise solutions hosted by the publisher at http://mitpress.mit.edu/foundations.

Aknowledgments

During the development of this book over the past year, I received lots of helpful input from Hamilton Chong, Guillermo Diez-Canas, and Dylan Thurston.

Helpful advice also came from Julie Dorsey, Hugues Hoppe, Zoe Wood, Yuanchen Zhu, and Todd Zickler.

Other comments and assistance came from Gilbert Bernstein, Fredo Durand, Ladislav Kavan, Michael Kazhdan, and Peter-Pike Sloan.

During the development of the course, I was greatly assisted by Xiangfeng Gu, Danil Kirsanov, Chris Mihelich, Pedro Sander, and Abraham Stone.

Over the years, the course has had many talented students acting as teaching assistants. They have contributed in many ways to the evolution of this material and include Brad Andalman, Keith Baldwin, Forrester Cole, Ashley Eden, David Holland, Brad Kittenbrink, Sanjay Mavinkurve, Jay Moorthi, Doug Nachand, Brian Osserman, Ed Park, David Ryu, Razvan Surdulescu, and Geetika Tewari.

Finally, I thank my parents for their years of love and support.

GETTING STARTED

1 Introduction

Computer graphics is an amazing technology success story. The basic ideas, representations, algorithms, and hardware approaches were forged in the 1960s and 1970s and developed to maturity in the following two decades. By the mid-1990s, computer graphics techniques were reasonably mature, but their impact was still somewhat restricted to "high-end" applications such as scientific visualization on supercomputers and expensive flight simulators. It's hard to believe now, but many undergraduate computer science majors had no idea what three-dimensional (3D) computer graphics even was!

The previous decade finally saw the mass commodification of graphics. Every modern PC is capable of producing high-quality computer-generated images, mostly in the form of video games and virtual-life environments. The entire animation industry has been transformed from its high end (e.g., Pixar films) down to daily children's television. For live-action movies, the field of special effects has been completely revolutionized; viewers nowadays don't flinch when they see the most amazing computer-generated special effects—it is simply expected.

In this book, we will introduce the mathematical and algorithmic foundations of computer graphics technology. We cover this material in the context of a programming API (applications programming interface) known as openGL. OpenGL is a cross-platform, graphics programming environment that can be used to build real-time graphics applications such as video games.

1.1 OpenGL

OpenGL began as an API that implemented a very specific sequence of operations used for doing 3D computer graphics. As the underlying hardware became cheaper, more and more flexibility was put into the hardware and exposed to the user by the OpenGL API. Over time, it has become feasible to fully control certain portions of the graphics computation. The user does this by writing small special-purpose programs, called shaders, that are passed to and compiled by the API. In OpenGL, these shaders are written in a C-like special-purpose language called GLSL. As we will describe later, the two main programmable portions are controlled by a *vertex shader* and a *fragment shader*. These specific sections of the computation have been made programmable both because there is great utility in giving the user flexibility in them and because this computation can be done using *single instruction multiple data* (SIMD) parallelism. Data stored with each geometric vertex can be processed independently from the other vertices. Likewise, computation to determine the color of one screen pixel can be performed completely independently from that for the other pixels.

In a modern OpenGL program, much (but not all) of the actual 3D graphics is done by the shaders that you write and are no longer really part of the OpenGL API itself. In this sense, OpenGL is more about organizing your data and your shaders and less about 3D computer graphics. In the rest of this section, we will give an overview of the main processing steps done by OpenGL. But we will also give some high-level descriptions of how the various shaders are typically used in these steps to implement 3D computer graphics.

In OpenGL, we represent our geometry as a collection of triangles. On the one hand, triangles are simple enough to be processed very efficiently by OpenGL, and on the other hand, using collections of many triangles, we can approximate surfaces with complicated shapes (see figure 1.1). If our computer graphics program uses a more abstract geometric representation, it must first be turned into a triangle collection before OpenGL can draw the geometry.

Briefly stated, the computation in OpenGL determines the screen position for each vertex of each of the triangles, figures out which screen dots, called *pixels*, lie within each triangle, and then performs some computation to determine the desired color of that pixel. We now walk through these steps in a bit more detail.

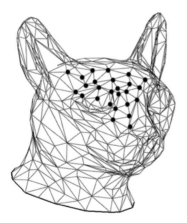

Figure 1.1
A cat head is described by a soup of triangles. Some of the vertices are highlighted with black dots. (From [64], copyright Eurographics and Blackwell Publishing Ltd.)

Each triangle is made up of three vertices. We associate some numerical data with each vertex. Each such data item is called an *attribute*. At the very least, we need to specify the location of the vertex (using two numbers for two dimensional [2D] geometry or three numbers for 3D geometry). We can use other attributes to associate other kinds of data with our vertices that will be used to determine the ultimate appearances of the vertices. For example, we may associate a color (using three numbers representing amounts of red, green, and blue) with each vertex. Other attributes might be used to represent relevant material properties describing, say, how shiny the surface at the vertex is.

Transmitting the vertex data from the central processing unit (CPU) to the graphics hardware (the GPU) is an expensive process, so it is typically done as infrequently as possible. There are specific API calls to transfer vertex data over to OpenGL, which stores these data in a *vertex buffer*.

Once the vertex data have been given to OpenGL, at any subsequent time we can send a *draw* call to OpenGL. This commands OpenGL to walk down the appropriate vertex buffers and draw each vertex triplet as a triangle.

Once the OpenGL draw call has been issued, each vertex (i.e., all of its attributes) gets processed independently by your vertex shader (see figure 1.2). Besides the attribute data, the shader also has access to things called *uniform variables*. These are variables that are set by your program, but you can only set them in between OpenGL draw calls and not per vertex.

The vertex shader is your own program, and you can put whatever you want in it. The most typical use of the vertex shader is to determine the final position of the vertices on the screen. For example, a vertex can have its own abstract 3D position stored as an attribute. Meanwhile, a uniform variable can be used to describe a virtual camera that maps abstract 3D coordinates to the actual 2D screen. We will cover the details of this kind of computation in chapters 2–6 and chapter 10.

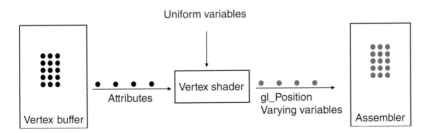

Figure 1.2
Vertices are stored in a vertex buffer. When a draw call is issued, each of the vertices passes through the vertex shader. On input to the vertex shader, each vertex (black) has associated attributes. On output, each vertex (cyan) has a value for gl_Position and for its varying variables.

Once the vertex shader has computed the final position of the vertex on the screen, it assigns this value to the reserved output variable called gl_Position. The x and y coordinates of this variable are interpreted as positions within the drawing window. The lower left corner of the window has coordinates $(-1, -1)$, and the upper right corner has coordinates $(1, 1)$. Coordinates outside of this square represent locations outside of the drawing area.

The vertex shader can also output other variables that will be used by the fragment shader to determine the final color of each pixel covered by the triangle. These outputs are called varying variables because, as we will soon explain, their values can vary as we look at the different pixels within a triangle.

Once processed, these vertices along with their varying variables are collected by the triangle *assembler* and grouped together in triplets.

OpenGL's next job is to draw each triangle on the screen (see figure 1.3). This step is called *rasterization*. For each triangle, it uses the three vertex positions to place the triangle on the screen. It then computes which of the pixels on the screen are inside of this triangle. For each such pixel, the rasterizer computes an *interpolated* value for each of the varying variables. This means that the value for each varying variable is set by blending the three values associated with the triangle's vertices. The blending ratios used are related to the pixel's distance to each of the three vertices. We will cover the exact method of blending in chapter 13. Because rasterization is such a specialized and highly optimized operation, this step has not been made programmable.

Finally, for each pixel, these interpolated data are passed through a fragment shader (see figure 1.4). A fragment shader is another program that you write in the GLSL language and hand off to OpenGL. The job of the fragment shader is to determine the drawn color of the pixel based on the information passed to it as varying and uniform variables. This final color computed by the fragment shader is placed in a part of GPU memory called a *framebuffer*. The data in the framebuffer are then sent to the display, where they are drawn on the screen.

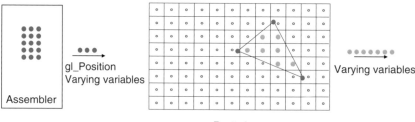

Figure 1.3
The data in gl_Position are used to place the three vertices of the triangle on a virtual screen. The rasterizer figures out which pixels (orange) are inside the triangle and interpolates the varying variables from the vertices to each of these pixels.

In 3D graphics, we typically determine a pixel's color by computing a few equations that simulate the way that light reflects off of the surface of some material. This calculation may use data stored in varying variables that represent the material and geometric properties of the material at that pixel. It may also use data stored in uniform variables that represent the position and color of the light sources in the scene. By changing the program in the fragment shader, we can simulate light bouncing off of different types of materials; this can create a variety of appearances for some fixed geometry, as shown in figure 1.5. We discuss this process in greater detail in chapter 14.

As part of this color computation, we can also instruct the fragment shader to fetch color data from an auxiliary stored image. Such an image is called a *texture* and is pointed to by a uniform variable. Meanwhile, varying variables called *texture coordinates* tell the fragment shader where to select the appropriate pixels from the texture. Using this process called *texture mapping*, one can simulate the "gluing" of some part of a texture image onto each triangle. This process can be used to give high visual complexity to a simple geometric

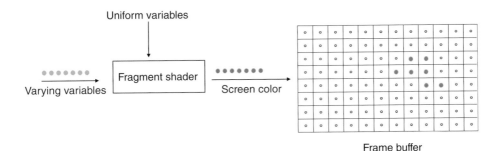

Figure 1.4
Each pixel is passed through the fragment shader, which computes the final color of the pixel (pink). The pixel is then placed in the framebuffer for display.

Figure 1.5
By changing our fragment shader, we can simulate light reflecting off of different kinds of materials.

Figure 1.6
Texture mapping. Left: A simple geometric object described by a small number of triangles. Middle: An auxiliary image called a texture. Right: Parts of the texture are glued onto each triangle giving a more complicated
appearance. (From [65], copyright ACM.)

object defined by only a small number of triangles. See figure 1.6 for such an example. This
is discussed further in chapter 15.

When colors are drawn to the framebuffer, a process called *merging* determines how
the "new" color that has just been output from the fragment shader is mixed in with the
"old" color that may already exist in the framebuffer. When *z-buffering* is enabled, a test is
applied to see whether the geometric point just processed by the fragment shader is closer
to or farther from the viewer than the point that was used to set the existing color in the
framebuffer. The framebuffer is then updated only if the new point is closer. Z-buffering
is very useful in creating images of 3D scenes. We discuss z-buffering in chapter 11. In
addition, OpenGL can also be instructed to blend the old and new colors together using
various ratios. This can be used for example to model transparent objects. This process is
called *alpha blending* and is discussed further in section 16.4 of chapter 16. Because this
merging step involves reading and writing to shared memory (the framebuffer), this step
has not been made programmable, but is instead controlled by various API calls.

In appendix A, we walk through an actual code fragment that implements a simple
OpenGL program that performs some simple 2D drawing with texture mapping. The goal
there is not to learn 3D graphics, but rather to get an understanding of the API itself and
the processing steps used in OpenGL. You will need to go through appendix A in detail at
some point before you get to chapter 6.

Exercises

1.1 To get a feeling for computer graphics of the 1980s, watch the movie *Tron*.

1.2 Play the video game *Battlezone*.

2 Linear

Our first task in learning 3D computer graphics is to understand how to represent points using coordinates and how to perform useful geometric transformations to these points. You very likely have seen similar material when studying linear algebra, but in computer graphics, we often simultaneously use a variety of different coordinate systems, and, as such, we need to pay special attention to the role that these various coordinate systems play. As a result, our treatment of even this basic material may be a bit different than that seen in a linear algebra class.

In this chapter, we will begin this task by looking at vectors and linear transformations. Vectors will be used to represent 3D motion, and linear transformations will be used to apply operations on vectors, such as rotation and scaling. In the following few chapters, we will then investigate affine transformations, which add the ability to translate objects. We will not actually get to the coding process for computer graphics until chapter 6. Our approach will be to first carefully understand the appropriate theory, which will then make it easy to code what we need.

2.1 Geometric Data Types

Imagine some specific geometric point in the real world. This point can be represented with three real numbers,

$$\begin{bmatrix} x \\ y \\ z \end{bmatrix},$$

which we call a *coordinate vector*. The numbers specify the position of the point with respect to some agreed upon coordinate system. This agreed upon coordinate system has some agreed upon origin point and also has three agreed upon directions. If we were to change the agreed upon coordinate system, then we would need a different set of numbers, a different coordinate vector, to describe the same point. So in order to specify the location of an actual point, we need both a coordinate system as well as a coordinate vector. This suggests that we really need to be careful in distinguishing the following concepts: coordinate systems, coordinate vectors, and geometric points.

We start with four types of data, each with its own notation (see figure 2.1).

• A *point* will be notated as $\tilde{p}$ with a tilde above the letter. This is a geometric object, not a numerical one.

• A *vector* will be notated as $\vec{v}$ with an arrow above the letter. This, too, is a non-numerical object. In chapter 3, we will discuss in more detail the difference between vectors and points. The main difference is that points represent places, whereas vectors represent the motion needed to move from point to point.

• A *coordinate vector* (which is a numerical object made up of real numbers) will be represented as **c** with a bold letter.

• A *coordinate system* (which will be a set of at vectors, and so again, non-numeric) will be notated as $\vec{\mathbf{f}}^t$ with a bold letter, arrow, and superscript t. (We use bold to signify a vertical collection, the superscript t makes it a horizontal collection, and the arrow tells us that it is a collection of vectors, not numbers.) There are actually two kinds of coordinate system. A *basis* is used to describe vectors, whereas a *frame* is used to describe points. We use the same notation for all coordinate systems and let the context distinguish the type.

In the next sections, and following chapters, we will define all of these object types and see what operations can be done with them. When thinking about how to manipulate geometry, we will make heavy use of, and do symbolic computation with, both the numerical (coordinate vectors) and the non-numerical (vectors and coordinate systems) objects. Only once we establish all of our necessary conventions in chapter 5 will we be able to drop the non-numerical objects and use the the numerical parts of our calculations in our computer code.

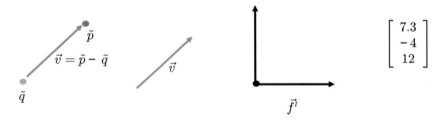

Figure 2.1
Geometric data types: points are shown as dots and vectors as arrows. Vectors connect two dots and do not change when translated. A frame represents a coordinate system and consists of one origin point and a basis of d vectors. A coordinate vector is a triple of real numbers.

2.2 Vectors, Coordinate Vectors, and Bases

Let us start by clearly distinguishing between vectors and coordinate vectors. In this book, a vector will always be an abstract geometric entity that represents motion between two points in the world. An example of such a vector would be "one mile east." A coordinate vector is a set of real numbers used to specify a vector, once we have agreed upon a co-ordinate system.

Formally speaking, a *vector space* V is some set of elements $\vec{v}$ that satisfy certain rules. In particular, one needs to define an addition operation that takes two vectors and maps it to a third vector. One also needs to define the operation of multiplying a real scalar times a vector to get back another vector.

To be a valid vector space, a bunch of other rules must be satisfied, which we will not dwell on too closely here. For example, the addition operation has to be associative and commutative. As another example, scalar multiplication must distribute across vector addition

$$\alpha(\vec{v} + \vec{w}) = \alpha\vec{v} + \alpha\vec{w},$$

and so on [40].

There are many families of objects that have the structure of a vector space. But in this book, we will be interested in the vector space consisting of actual motions between actual geometric points. **In particular, we will not think of a vector as a set of three numbers**.

A coordinate system, or basis, is a small set of vectors that can be used to produce the entire set of vectors using the vector operations. (More formally, we say that a set of vectors $\vec{b}_1 \ldots \vec{b}_n$ is linearly dependent if there exist non-zero scalars $\alpha_1 \ldots \alpha_n$ such that $\sum_i \alpha_i \vec{b}_i = \vec{0}$. If a set of vectors is not linearly dependent, then we call them linearly independent. If $\vec{b}_1 \ldots \vec{b}_n$ are linearly independent and can generate all of V using addition and scalar multiplication, then the set $\vec{b}_i$ is called a basis of V, and we say that n is the dimension of the basis/space.) For free motions in space, the dimension is 3. We also may refer to each of the basis vectors as an *axis*, and in particular we may refer to the first axis as the x axis, the second as the y axis, and the third as the z axis.

We can use a basis as a way to produce any of the vectors in the space. This can be expressed using a set of unique coordinates c_i as follows.

$$\vec{v} = \sum_i c_i \vec{b}_i.$$

We can use vector algebra notation and write this as

$$\vec{v} = \sum_i c_i \vec{b}_i = \begin{bmatrix} \vec{b}_1 & \vec{b}_2 & \vec{b}_3 \end{bmatrix} \begin{bmatrix} c_1 \\ c_2 \\ c_3 \end{bmatrix}. \tag{2.1}$$

The interpretation of the rightmost expression uses the standard rules for matrix–matrix multiplication from linear algebra. Here, each term $c_i \vec{b}_i$ is a real-scalar multiplied by an abstract vector. We can create a shorthand notation for this and write it as

$$\vec{v} = \mathbf{b}^t \mathbf{c},$$

where $\vec{v}$ is a vector, $\mathbf{b}^t$ is a row of basis vectors, and $\mathbf{c}$ is a (column) coordinate vector.

2.3 Linear Transformations and 3 by 3 Matrices

A linear transformation $\mathcal{L}$ is just a transformation from V to V that satisfies the following two properties:

$$\mathcal{L}(\vec{v} + \vec{u}) = \mathcal{L}(\vec{v}) + \mathcal{L}(\vec{u})$$

$$\mathcal{L}(\alpha \vec{v}) = \alpha \mathcal{L}(\vec{v}).$$

We use the notation $\vec{v} \Rightarrow \mathcal{L}(\vec{v})$ to mean that the vector $\vec{v}$ is *transformed* to the vector $\mathcal{L}(\vec{v})$ through $\mathcal{L}$.

The class of linear transformations is exactly the class that can be expressed using matrices. This is because a linear transformation can be exactly specified by telling us its effect on the basis vectors. Let us see how this works:

The two linearity properties described above imply the relationship

$$\vec{v} \Rightarrow \mathcal{L}(\vec{v}) = \mathcal{L}\left(\sum_i c_i \vec{b}_i \right) = \sum_i c_i \mathcal{L}(\vec{b}_i),$$

which we can write in vector algebra notation using equation (2.1) as

$$\begin{bmatrix} \vec{b}_1 & \vec{b}_2 & \vec{b}_3 \end{bmatrix} \begin{bmatrix} c_1 \\ c_2 \\ c_3 \end{bmatrix} \Rightarrow \begin{bmatrix} \mathcal{L}(\vec{b}_1) & \mathcal{L}(\vec{b}_2) & \mathcal{L}(\vec{b}_3) \end{bmatrix} \begin{bmatrix} c_1 \\ c_2 \\ c_3 \end{bmatrix}.$$

Each of the three new vectors $\mathcal{L}(\vec{b}_i)$ is itself an element of V, and each of these vectors can ultimately be written as some linear combination of the original basis vectors. For example, we could write

$$\mathcal{L}(\vec{b}_1) = \begin{bmatrix} \vec{b}_1 & \vec{b}_2 & \vec{b}_3 \end{bmatrix} \begin{bmatrix} M_{1,1} \\ M_{2,1} \\ M_{3,1} \end{bmatrix}$$

for some appropriate set of $M_{j,1}$ values. Doing this for all of our basis vectors, we get

$$\left[\begin{array}{ccc} \mathcal{L}(\vec{b}_1) & \mathcal{L}(\vec{b}_2) & \mathcal{L}(\vec{b}_3) \end{array}\right] = \left[\begin{array}{ccc} \vec{b}_1 & \vec{b}_2 & \vec{b}_3 \end{array}\right] \left[\begin{array}{ccc} M_{1,1} & M_{1,2} & M_{1,3} \\ M_{2,1} & M_{2,2} & M_{2,3} \\ M_{3,1} & M_{3,2} & M_{3,3} \end{array}\right] \quad (2.2)$$

for an appropriate choice of matrix M made up of nine real numbers.

Putting this all together, we see that the operation of the linear transformation operating on a vector can be expressed as:

$$\left[\begin{array}{ccc} \vec{b}_1 & \vec{b}_2 & \vec{b}_3 \end{array}\right] \left[\begin{array}{c} c_1 \\ c_2 \\ c_3 \end{array}\right]$$

$$\Rightarrow \left[\begin{array}{ccc} \vec{b}_1 & \vec{b}_2 & \vec{b}_3 \end{array}\right] \left[\begin{array}{ccc} M_{1,1} & M_{1,2} & M_{1,3} \\ M_{2,1} & M_{2,2} & M_{2,3} \\ M_{3,1} & M_{3,2} & M_{3,3} \end{array}\right] \left[\begin{array}{c} c_1 \\ c_2 \\ c_3 \end{array}\right].$$

In summary, we can use a matrix to transform one vector to another

$$\mathbf{b}^t \mathbf{c} \Rightarrow \mathbf{b}^t M \mathbf{c}$$

(see figure 2.2).

If we apply the transformation to each of the basis vectors, we get a new basis. This can be expressed as

$$\left[\begin{array}{ccc} \vec{b}_1 & \vec{b}_2 & \vec{b}_3 \end{array}\right] \Rightarrow \left[\begin{array}{ccc} \vec{b}_1 & \vec{b}_2 & \vec{b}_3 \end{array}\right] \left[\begin{array}{ccc} M_{1,1} & M_{1,2} & M_{1,3} \\ M_{2,1} & M_{2,2} & M_{2,3} \\ M_{3,1} & M_{3,2} & M_{3,3} \end{array}\right],$$

or for short

$$\vec{\mathbf{b}}^t \Rightarrow \vec{\mathbf{b}}^t M$$

(see figure 2.3).

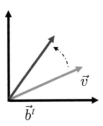

Figure 2.2
A vector undergoes a linear transformation $\vec{v} = \mathbf{b}^t \mathbf{c} \Rightarrow \mathbf{b}^t M \mathbf{c}$. The matrix M depends on the chosen linear transformation.

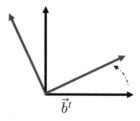

$\vec{b}^t$

Figure 2.3
A basis undergoes a linear transformation $\vec{\mathbf{b}}^t \Rightarrow \vec{\mathbf{b}}^t M$.

And of course, it is valid to multiply a matrix times a coordinate vector,

$$\mathbf{c} \Rightarrow M\mathbf{c}.$$

2.3.1 Identity and Inverse

The identity map leaves all vectors unchanged. Its matrix is the identity matrix

$$I = \begin{bmatrix} 1 & 0 & 0 \\ 0 & 1 & 0 \\ 0 & 0 & 1 \end{bmatrix}.$$

The inverse of a matrix M is the unique matrix M^{-1} with the property $MM^{-1} = M^{-1}M = I$. It represents the inverse transformation on vectors. If a linear transform happens to map more than one input vector to the same output vector, then the transform will not be invertible, and its associated matrix will not have an inverse. In computer graphics, when we choose 3D to 3D linear transforms to move objects around in space (as well as scale them), it will seldom make sense to use a noninvertible transform. So, unless stated, all of the matrices we will be dealing with in this book will have an inverse.

2.3.2 Matrices for Basis Changes

Besides being used to describe a transformation ($\Rightarrow$), a matrix can also be used to describe an equality ($=$) between a pair of bases or pair of vectors. In particular, in equation (2.2), we saw an expression of the form

$$\vec{\mathbf{a}}^t = \vec{\mathbf{b}}^t M \tag{2.3}$$

$$\vec{\mathbf{a}}^t M^{-1} = \vec{\mathbf{b}}^t \tag{2.4}$$

This expresses an equality relationship between the named bases $\vec{\mathbf{a}}^t$ and $\vec{\mathbf{b}}^t$.

Suppose a vector is expressed in a specific basis using a specific coordinate vector: $\vec{v} = \vec{\mathbf{b}}^t \mathbf{c}$. Given equation (2.3), one can write

$$\vec{v} = \vec{\mathbf{b}}^t \mathbf{c} = \vec{\mathbf{a}}^t M^{-1} \mathbf{c}.$$

This is not a transformation (which would use the $\Rightarrow$ notation), but rather an equality (using the $=$ notation). We have simply written the same vector using two bases. The coordinate vector $\mathbf{c}$ represents $\vec{v}$ with respect to $\vec{\mathbf{b}}$, and the coordinate vector $M^{-1}\mathbf{c}$ represents the same $\vec{v}$ with respect to $\vec{\mathbf{a}}$.

2.4   Extra Structure

Vectors in 3D space also come equipped with a *dot product* operation

$$\vec{v} \cdot \vec{w}$$

that takes in two vectors and returns a real number. This dot product allows us to define the squared length (also called squared norm) of a vector

$$\| \vec{v} \|^2 := \vec{v} \cdot \vec{v}.$$

The dot product is related to the angle $\theta \in [0 \ldots \pi]$ between two vectors as

$$\cos(\theta) = \frac{\vec{v} \cdot \vec{w}}{\| \vec{v} \| \| \vec{w} \|}.$$

We say that two vectors are *orthogonal* if $\vec{v} \cdot \vec{w} = 0$.

We say that a basis is *orthonormal* if all the basis vectors are unit length and pairwise orthogonal.

In an orthonormal basis $\vec{\mathbf{b}}'$, it is particularly easy to compute the dot product of two vectors $(\vec{\mathbf{b}}'\mathbf{c}) \cdot (\vec{\mathbf{b}}'\mathbf{d})$. In particular, we have

$$\vec{\mathbf{b}}'\mathbf{c} \cdot \vec{\mathbf{b}}'\mathbf{d} = \left(\sum_i c_i \vec{b}_i \right) \cdot \left(\sum_j d_j \vec{b}_j \right)$$

$$= \sum_i \sum_j c_i d_j (\vec{b}_i \cdot \vec{b}_j)$$

$$= \sum_i c_i d_i,$$

where in the second line we use the fact that the dot product is a bilinear operator, and in the third line we use the orthonormality of the basis.

We say that a 2D orthonormal basis is *right handed* if the second basis vector can be obtained from the first by a 90 degree *counterclockwise* rotation (the order of the vectors in the basis is clearly important here).

We say that a 3D orthonormal basis is right handed if the three (ordered) basis vectors are arranged as in figure 2.4, as opposed to the arrangement of figure 2.5. In particular, in a right-handed basis, if you take your right hand opened flat, with your fingers pointing in the direction of the first basis vector, in such a way that you can curl your fingers so that they

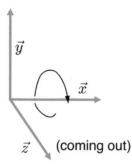

Figure 2.4
A right-handed orthonormal coordinate system. The z axis is coming out of the page. Also shown is the direction of a rotation about the x axis.

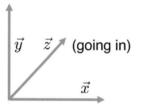

Figure 2.5
A left-handed orthonormal coordinate system. The z axis is going into the page.

point in the direction of the second basis vector, then your thumb will point in the direction of the third basis vector.

In 3D, we also have a *cross-product* operation that takes in two vectors and outputs one vector defined as

$$\vec{v} \times \vec{w} := \| v \| \, \| w \| \, \sin(\theta) \, \vec{n},$$

where $\vec{n}$ is the unit vector that is orthogonal to the plane spanned by $\vec{v}$ and $\vec{w}$ and such that $[\vec{v}, \vec{w}, \vec{n}]$ form a right-handed basis.

In a right-handed orthonormal basis $\vec{\mathbf{b}}^t$, it is particularly easy to compute the cross product of two vectors $(\vec{\mathbf{b}}^t\mathbf{c}) \times (\vec{\mathbf{b}}^t\mathbf{d})$. In particular, its coordinates with respect to $\vec{\mathbf{b}}^t$ can be computed as

$$\begin{bmatrix} c_2d_3 - c_3d_2 \\ c_3d_1 - c_1d_3 \\ c_1d_2 - c_2d_1 \end{bmatrix}.$$

2.5 Rotations

The most common linear transformation we will encounter is a rotation. A rotation is a linear transformation that preserves dot products between vectors and maps a right-handed basis to a right-handed basis. So in particular, applying any rotation to a right-handed orthonormal basis always results in another right-handed orthonormal basis. **In 3D, every rotation fixes an *axis of rotation* and rotates by some angle about that axis.**

We begin by describing the 2D case. We start with a vector.

$$\vec{v} = \left[\begin{array}{cc} \vec{b}_1 & \vec{b}_2 \end{array}\right] \left[\begin{array}{c} x \\ y \end{array}\right].$$

Let us assume $\mathbf{b}^t$ is a 2D right-handed orthonormal basis. Suppose we wish to rotate $\vec{v}$ by θ degrees counterclockwise about the origin: The coordinates $[x', y']^t$ of the rotated vector can be computed as

$$x' = x \cos\theta - y \sin\theta$$

$$y' = x \sin\theta + y \cos\theta.$$

This linear transformation can be written as the following matrix expression:

$$\left[\begin{array}{cc} \vec{b}_1 & \vec{b}_2 \end{array}\right] \left[\begin{array}{c} x \\ y \end{array}\right]$$

$$\Rightarrow \left[\begin{array}{cc} \vec{b}_1 & \vec{b}_2 \end{array}\right] \left[\begin{array}{cc} \cos\theta & -\sin\theta \\ \sin\theta & \cos\theta \end{array}\right] \left[\begin{array}{c} x \\ y \end{array}\right].$$

Likewise, we can rotate the entire basis as

$$\left[\begin{array}{cc} \vec{b}_1 & \vec{b}_2 \end{array}\right]$$

$$\Rightarrow \left[\begin{array}{cc} \vec{b}_1 & \vec{b}_2 \end{array}\right] \left[\begin{array}{cc} \cos\theta & -\sin\theta \\ \sin\theta & \cos\theta \end{array}\right].$$

For the 3D case, let us also assume that we are using a right-handed orthonormal coordinate system. Then, a rotation of a vector by θ degrees around the z axis of the basis is expressed as

$$\left[\begin{array}{ccc} \vec{b}_1 & \vec{b}_2 & \vec{b}_3 \end{array}\right] \left[\begin{array}{c} x \\ y \\ z \end{array}\right]$$

$$\Rightarrow \left[\begin{array}{ccc} \vec{b}_1 & \vec{b}_2 & \vec{b}_3 \end{array}\right] \left[\begin{array}{ccc} c & -s & 0 \\ s & c & 0 \\ 0 & 0 & 1 \end{array}\right] \left[\begin{array}{c} x \\ y \\ z \end{array}\right],$$

where, for brevity, we have used the notation $c := \cos\theta$ and $s := \sin\theta$. As expected, this transformation leaves vectors on the third axis just where they were. On each fixed plane where z is held constant, this transformation behaves just like the 2D rotation just described. The rotation direction can be visualized by grabbing the z axis with your right hand, with the heel of your hand against the $z = 0$ plane; the forward direction is that traced out by your fingertips as you close your hand.

A rotation about the x axis of a basis can be computed as

$$\begin{bmatrix} \vec{b}_1 & \vec{b}_2 & \vec{b}_3 \end{bmatrix} \begin{bmatrix} x \\ y \\ z \end{bmatrix}$$

$$\Rightarrow \begin{bmatrix} \vec{b}_1 & \vec{b}_2 & \vec{b}_3 \end{bmatrix} \begin{bmatrix} 1 & 0 & 0 \\ 0 & c & -s \\ 0 & s & c \end{bmatrix} \begin{bmatrix} x \\ y \\ z \end{bmatrix}.$$

Again, the rotation direction can be visualized by grabbing the x axis with your right hand, with the heel of your hand against the $x = 0$ plane; the forward direction is that traced out by your fingertips as you close your hand (see figure 2.4).

A rotation around the y axis is done using the matrix

$$\begin{bmatrix} c & 0 & s \\ 0 & 1 & 0 \\ -s & 0 & c \end{bmatrix}.$$

In some sense, this is all you need to get any 3D rotation. First of all, the composition of rotations is another rotation. Also, it can be shown that we can achieve *any* arbitrary rotations by applying one x, one y, and one z rotation. The angular amounts of the three rotations are called the *xyz-Euler angles*. Euler angles can be visualized by thinking of a set of *gimbals*, with three movable axes, with three settings to determine the achieved rotation (see figure 2.6).

A more direct way to represent an arbitrary rotation is to pick any unit vector $\vec{k}$ as the *axis of rotation* and directly apply a rotation of θ radians about that axis. Let the coordinates of $\vec{k}$ be given by the unit coordinate vector $[k_x, k_y, k_z]^t$. Then, this rotation can be expressed using the matrix

$$\begin{bmatrix} k_x^2 v + c & k_x k_y v - k_z s & k_x k_z v + k_y s \\ k_y k_x v + k_z s & k_y^2 v + c & k_y k_z v - k_x s \\ k_z k_x v - k_y s & k_z k_y v + k_x s & k_z^2 v + c \end{bmatrix}, \tag{2.5}$$

where, for shorthand, we have introduced the symbol $v := 1 - c$. Conversely, it can be shown that any rotation matrix can be written in this form.

Figure 2.6
By setting the rotation amounts on each of the three axes appropriately, we can place the golden disk in any desired orientation.

We note that 3D rotations behave in a somewhat complicated manner. Two rotations around different axes do not commute with each other. Moreover, when we compose two rotations about two different axes, what we get is a rotation about some third axis!

Later in this book, we will introduce the quaternion representation for rotations, which will be useful for animating smooth transitions between orientations.

2.6 Scales

To model geometric objects, we may find it useful to apply scaling operations to vectors and bases. To scale any vector by factor of α, we can use

$$\begin{bmatrix} \vec{b}_1 & \vec{b}_2 & \vec{b}_3 \end{bmatrix} \begin{bmatrix} x \\ y \\ z \end{bmatrix}$$

$$\Rightarrow \begin{bmatrix} \vec{b}_1 & \vec{b}_2 & \vec{b}_3 \end{bmatrix} \begin{bmatrix} \alpha & 0 & 0 \\ 0 & \alpha & 0 \\ 0 & 0 & \alpha \end{bmatrix} \begin{bmatrix} x \\ y \\ z \end{bmatrix}.$$

To scale differently along the three axis directions, we can use the more general form

$$\begin{bmatrix} \vec{b}_1 & \vec{b}_2 & \vec{b}_3 \end{bmatrix} \begin{bmatrix} x \\ y \\ z \end{bmatrix}$$

$$\Rightarrow \begin{bmatrix} \vec{b}_1 & \vec{b}_2 & \vec{b}_3 \end{bmatrix} \begin{bmatrix} \alpha & 0 & 0 \\ 0 & \beta & 0 \\ 0 & 0 & \gamma \end{bmatrix} \begin{bmatrix} x \\ y \\ z \end{bmatrix}.$$

This kind of operation is useful, for example, to model an ellipsoid given that we already know how to model a sphere.

Exercises

2.1 Which of the following are valid expressions in our notation, and if valid, what is the resulting type?

$\vec{\mathbf{b}}'M, \mathbf{c}M, M^{-1}\mathbf{c}, \vec{\mathbf{b}}'NM^{-1}\mathbf{c}$.

2.2 Given that $\vec{\mathbf{a}}' = \vec{\mathbf{b}}'M$, what are the coordinates of the vector $\vec{\mathbf{b}}'N\mathbf{c}$ with respect to the basis $\vec{\mathbf{a}}'$?

2.3 Let $\vec{0}$ be the zero vector. For any linear transformation $\mathcal{L}$, what is $\mathcal{L}(\vec{0})$?

2.4 Let $\mathcal{T}(\vec{v})$ be the transformation that adds a specific non-zero constant vector $\vec{k}$ to $\vec{v}$: $\mathcal{T}(\vec{v}) = \vec{v} + \vec{k}$. Is $\mathcal{T}$ a linear transformation?

3 Affine

3.1 Points and Frames

It is useful to think of points and vectors as two different concepts. A point is some fixed place in a geometric world, whereas a vector is the motion between two points in the world. We will use two different notations to distinguish points and vectors. A vector $\vec{v}$ will have an arrow on top, and a point $\tilde{p}$ will have a squiggle on top.

If we think of a vector as representing motion between two points, then the vector operations (addition and scalar multiplication) have obvious meaning. If we add two vectors, we are expressing the concatenation of two motions. If we multiply a vector by a scalar, we are increasing or decreasing the motion by some factor. The zero vector is a special vector that represents no motion.

These operations don't really make much sense for points. What should it mean to add two points together (e.g., what is Harvard Square plus Kendall Square)? What does it mean to multiply a point by a scalar? What is 7 times the North Pole? Is there a zero point that acts differently than the others?

There is one operation on two points that does sort of make sense: subtraction. When we subtract one point from another, we should get the motion that it takes to get from the second point to the first one,

$$\tilde{p} - \tilde{q} = \vec{v}.$$

Conversely if we start with a point, and move by some vector, we should get to another point

$$\tilde{q} + \vec{v} = \tilde{p}.$$

It does makes sense to apply a linear transformation to a point. For example we can think of rotating a point around some other fixed origin point. But it also makes sense to translate points (this notion did not make sense for vectors). To represent translations, we need to develop the notion of an *affine transform*. To accomplish this, we use 4 by 4 matrices. These

matrices are not only convenient for dealing with affine transformations here, but also will
be helpful in describing the camera projection operation later on (see chapter 10).

3.1.1 Frames

In an affine space, we describe any point $\tilde{p}$ by first starting from some origin point $\tilde{o}$ and then
adding to it a linear combination of vectors. These vectors are expressed using coordinates
c_i and a basis of vectors

$$\tilde{p} = \tilde{o} + \sum_i c_i \vec{b}_i = \begin{bmatrix} \vec{b}_1 & \vec{b}_2 & \vec{b}_3 & \tilde{o} \end{bmatrix} \begin{bmatrix} c_1 \\ c_2 \\ c_3 \\ 1 \end{bmatrix} = \vec{\mathbf{f}}^t \mathbf{c},$$

where $1\tilde{o}$ is defined to be $\tilde{o}$.

The row

$$\begin{bmatrix} \vec{b}_1 & \vec{b}_2 & \vec{b}_3 & \tilde{o} \end{bmatrix} = \vec{\mathbf{f}}^t$$

is called an *affine frame*; it is like a basis, but it is made up of three vectors and a single
point.

To specify a point using a frame, we use a coordinate 4-vector with four entries, with
the last entry always being a one. To express a vector using an affine frame, we use a
coordinate vector with a zero as the fourth coordinate (i.e., it is simply a sum of the basis
vectors). The use of coordinate 4-vectors to represent our geometry (as well as 4 by 4
matrices) will also come in handy in chapter 10 when we model the behavior of a pinhole
camera.

3.2 Affine Transformations and 4 by 4 Matrices

Similar to the case of linear transformations, we would like to define a notion of affine
transformations on points by placing an appropriate matrix between a coordinate 4-vector
and a frame.

Let us define an *affine matrix* to be a 4 by 4 matrix of the form

$$\begin{bmatrix} a & b & c & d \\ e & f & g & h \\ i & j & k & l \\ 0 & 0 & 0 & 1 \end{bmatrix}.$$

We apply an affine transform to a point $\tilde{p} = \vec{\mathbf{f}}^t \mathbf{c}$ as follows:

$$
\begin{bmatrix} \vec{b}_1 & \vec{b}_2 & \vec{b}_3 & \tilde{o} \end{bmatrix}
\begin{bmatrix} c_1 \\ c_2 \\ c_3 \\ 1 \end{bmatrix}
$$

$$
\Rightarrow \begin{bmatrix} \vec{b}_1 & \vec{b}_2 & \vec{b}_3 & \tilde{o} \end{bmatrix}
\begin{bmatrix} a & b & c & d \\ e & f & g & h \\ i & j & k & l \\ 0 & 0 & 0 & 1 \end{bmatrix}
\begin{bmatrix} c_1 \\ c_2 \\ c_3 \\ 1 \end{bmatrix},
$$

or for short

$$
\vec{\mathbf{f}}^t \mathbf{c} \Rightarrow \vec{\mathbf{f}}^t A \mathbf{c}.
$$

We can verify that the second line of the above describes a valid point, as the multiplication of

$$
\begin{bmatrix} x' \\ y' \\ z' \\ 1 \end{bmatrix}
= \begin{bmatrix} a & b & c & d \\ e & f & g & h \\ i & j & k & l \\ 0 & 0 & 0 & 1 \end{bmatrix}
\begin{bmatrix} x \\ y \\ z \\ 1 \end{bmatrix}
$$

gives us a coordinate 4-vector with a one as the fourth entry. Alternatively, we can see that the multiplication of

$$
\begin{bmatrix} \vec{b}_1' & \vec{b}_2' & \vec{b}_3' & \tilde{o}' \end{bmatrix}
= \begin{bmatrix} \vec{b}_1 & \vec{b}_2 & \vec{b}_3 & \tilde{o} \end{bmatrix}
\begin{bmatrix} a & b & c & d \\ e & f & g & h \\ i & j & k & l \\ 0 & 0 & 0 & 1 \end{bmatrix},
$$

where $0\tilde{o}$ is defined to be $\vec{0}$, gives a valid frame made up of three vectors and a point.

Also note that if the last row of the matrix were not $[0, 0, 0, 1]$, it would generally give us an invalid result.

Similar to the case of linear transform, we can apply an affine transformation to a frame as

$$
\begin{bmatrix} \vec{b}_1 & \vec{b}_2 & \vec{b}_3 & \tilde{o} \end{bmatrix}
\Rightarrow \begin{bmatrix} \vec{b}_1 & \vec{b}_2 & \vec{b}_3 & \tilde{o} \end{bmatrix}
\begin{bmatrix} a & b & c & d \\ e & f & g & h \\ i & j & k & l \\ 0 & 0 & 0 & 1 \end{bmatrix},
$$

or for short

$$
\vec{\mathbf{f}}^t \Rightarrow \vec{\mathbf{f}}^t A.
$$

3.3   Applying Linear Transformations to Points

Suppose we have a 3 by 3 matrix representing a linear transformation. We can embed it into the upper left-hand corner of a 4 by 4 matrix and use this larger matrix to apply the transformation to a point (or frame):

$$\begin{bmatrix} \vec{b}_1 & \vec{b}_2 & \vec{b}_3 & \tilde{o} \end{bmatrix} \begin{bmatrix} c_1 \\ c_2 \\ c_3 \\ 1 \end{bmatrix}$$

$$\Rightarrow \begin{bmatrix} \vec{b}_1 & \vec{b}_2 & \vec{b}_3 & \tilde{o} \end{bmatrix} \begin{bmatrix} a & b & c & 0 \\ e & f & g & 0 \\ i & j & k & 0 \\ 0 & 0 & 0 & 1 \end{bmatrix} \begin{bmatrix} c_1 \\ c_2 \\ c_3 \\ 1 \end{bmatrix}.$$

This has the same effect on the c_i as it did with linear transformations. If we think of the point $\tilde{p}$ as being offset from the origin $\tilde{o}$ by a vector $\vec{v}$, we see that this has the same effect as applying the linear transform to the offset vector. So, for example, if the 3 by 3 matrix is a rotation matrix, this transformation will rotate the point about the origin (see figure 3.1). As we will see later in chapter 4, when applying a linear transformation to a point, the position of the frame's origin plays an important role.

We use the following shorthand for describing a 4 by 4 matrix that just applies a linear transform:

$$L = \begin{bmatrix} l & 0 \\ 0 & 1 \end{bmatrix},$$

where L is a 4 by 4 matrix, l is a 3 by 3 matrix, the upper right zero is a 3 by 1 matrix of zeros, the lower left zero is a 1 by 3 matrix of zeros, and the lower right one is a scalar.

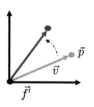

Figure 3.1
A linear transform is applied to a point. This is accomplished by applying the linear transform to its offset vector from the origin.

3.4 Translations

It is very useful to be able to apply a translation transformation to points. Such transformations are not linear (see exercise 2.4). The main new power of the affine transformation over the linear transformations is its ability to express translations. In particular, if we apply the transformation

$$
\begin{bmatrix} \vec{b}_1 & \vec{b}_2 & \vec{b}_3 & \tilde{o} \end{bmatrix}
\begin{bmatrix} c_1 \\ c_2 \\ c_3 \\ 1 \end{bmatrix}
$$

$$
\Rightarrow \begin{bmatrix} \vec{b}_1 & \vec{b}_2 & \vec{b}_3 & \tilde{o} \end{bmatrix}
\begin{bmatrix} 1 & 0 & 0 & t_x \\ 0 & 1 & 0 & t_y \\ 0 & 0 & 1 & t_z \\ 0 & 0 & 0 & 1 \end{bmatrix}
\begin{bmatrix} c_1 \\ c_2 \\ c_3 \\ 1 \end{bmatrix},
$$

we see that its effect on the coordinates is

$$c_1 \Rightarrow c_1 + t_x$$

$$c_2 \Rightarrow c_2 + t_y$$

$$c_3 \Rightarrow c_3 + t_z.$$

For a translation, we use the shorthand

$$
T = \begin{bmatrix} i & t \\ 0 & 1 \end{bmatrix},
$$

where T is a 4 by 4 matrix, i is a 3 by 3 identity matrix, the upper right t is a 3 by 1 matrix representing the translation, the lower left zero is a 1 by 3 matrix of zeros, and the lower right one is a scalar.

Note that if c has a zero in its fourth coordinate, and thus represents a vector instead of a point, then it is unaffected by translations.

3.5 Putting Them Together

Any affine matrix can be factored into a linear part and a translational part:

$$
\begin{bmatrix} a & b & c & d \\ e & f & g & h \\ i & j & k & l \\ 0 & 0 & 0 & 1 \end{bmatrix}
=
\begin{bmatrix} 1 & 0 & 0 & d \\ 0 & 1 & 0 & h \\ 0 & 0 & 1 & l \\ 0 & 0 & 0 & 1 \end{bmatrix}
\begin{bmatrix} a & b & c & 0 \\ e & f & g & 0 \\ h & i & j & 0 \\ 0 & 0 & 0 & 1 \end{bmatrix},
$$

or in shorthand

$$\begin{bmatrix} l & t \\ 0 & 1 \end{bmatrix} = \begin{bmatrix} i & t \\ 0 & 1 \end{bmatrix} \begin{bmatrix} l & 0 \\ 0 & 1 \end{bmatrix} \tag{3.1}$$

$$A = TL. \tag{3.2}$$

Note that as matrix multiplication is not commutative, the order of the multiplication TL matters. An affine matrix can also be factored as $A = LT'$ with a different translation matrix T', but we will not make use of this form.

If L, the linear part of A, is a rotation, we write this as

$$A = TR. \tag{3.3}$$

In this case, we call the A matrix a *rigid body matrix* and its transform a *rigid body transformation*, or RBT. A rigid body transformation preserves dot products between vectors, handedness of a basis, and distance between points.

3.6 Normals

In computer graphics, we often use the normals of surfaces to determine how a surface point should be shaded. So we need to understand how the normals of a surface transform when the surface points undergo an affine transformation described by a matrix A.

One might guess that we could just multiply the normal's coordinates by A. For example, if we rotated our geometry, the normals would rotate in exactly the same way. But using A is, in fact, not always correct. For example, in figure 3.2, we squash a sphere along the y axis. In this case, the actual normals transform by stretching along the y axis instead of squashing. Here, we derive the correct transformation that applies in all cases.

Let us define the *normal* to a smooth surface at a point to be a vector that is orthogonal to the tangent plane of the surface at that point. The tangent plane is a plane of vectors that are defined by subtracting (infinitesimally) nearby surface points, and so we have

Figure 3.2
Left: Shape in blue with normals shown in black. Middle: Shape is shrunk in the y direction and the (unnormalized) normals are stretched in the y direction. Right: Normals are renormalized to give correct unit normals of squashed shape.

$$\vec{n} \cdot (\tilde{p}_1 - \tilde{p}_0) = 0$$

for the normal $\vec{n}$ and two very close points $\tilde{p}_1$ and $\tilde{p}_0$ on a surface. In some fixed orthonormal coordinate system, this can be expressed as

$$\begin{bmatrix} nx & ny & nz & * \end{bmatrix} \left(\begin{bmatrix} x1 \\ y1 \\ z1 \\ 1 \end{bmatrix} - \begin{bmatrix} x0 \\ y0 \\ z0 \\ 1 \end{bmatrix} \right) = 0. \tag{3.4}$$

We use an "$*$" in the fourth slot because it is multiplied by zero and thus does not matter.

Suppose we transform all of our points by applying an affine transformation using an affine matrix A. What vector remains orthogonal to any tangent vector? Let us rewrite equation (3.4) as

$$\left(\begin{bmatrix} nx & ny & nz & * \end{bmatrix} A^{-1} \right) \left(A \left(\begin{bmatrix} x1 \\ y1 \\ z1 \\ 1 \end{bmatrix} - \begin{bmatrix} x0 \\ y0 \\ z0 \\ 1 \end{bmatrix} \right) \right) = 0.$$

If we define $[x', y', z', 1]^t = A[x, y, z, 1]^t$ to be the coordinates of a transformed point and let $[nx', ny', nz', *] = [nx, ny, nz, 1]A^{-1}$, then we have

$$\begin{bmatrix} nx' & ny' & nz' & * \end{bmatrix} \left(\begin{bmatrix} x1' \\ y1' \\ z1' \\ 1 \end{bmatrix} - \begin{bmatrix} x0' \\ y0' \\ z0' \\ 1 \end{bmatrix} \right) = 0,$$

and we see that $[nx', ny', nz']^t$ are the coordinates (up to scale) of the normal of the transformed geometry.

Note that because we don't care about the "$*$" value, we don't care about the fourth column of A^{-1}. Meanwhile, because A is an affine matrix, so is A^{-1}, and thus the fourth row of the remaining three columns are all zeros and can safely be ignored. Thus, using the shorthand

$$A = \begin{bmatrix} l & t \\ 0 & 1 \end{bmatrix},$$

we see that

$$\begin{bmatrix} nx' & ny' & nz' \end{bmatrix} = \begin{bmatrix} nx & ny & nz \end{bmatrix} l^{-1},$$

and transposing the whole expression, we get

$$
\begin{bmatrix} nx' \\ ny' \\ nz' \end{bmatrix} = l^{-t} \begin{bmatrix} nx \\ ny \\ nz \end{bmatrix},
$$

where l^{-t} is the inverse transpose (equiv. transposed inverse) 3 by 3 matrix. Note that if l is a rotation matrix, the matrix is orthonormal, and thus its inverse transpose is in fact the same as l. In this case, a normal's coordinates behave just like a point's coordinates. For other linear transforms, however, the normals behave differently (see figure 3.2). Also note that the translational part of A has no effect on the normals.

Exercise

3.1 I claim that the following operation is a well-defined operation on points: $\alpha_1 \tilde{p}_1 + \alpha_2 \tilde{p}_2$ for real values α_i, as long as $1 = \sum_i \alpha_i$. Show that this can be interpreted using the operations on points and vectors described at the beginning of section 3.1.

4 Respect

4.1 The Frame Is Important

In computer graphics, we simultaneously keep track of a number of different frames. For example, we may have a different frame associated with each object in the scene. The specifics of how we use and organize such frames is described in chapter 5. Because of these multiple frames, we need to be especially careful when using matrices to define transformations.

Suppose we specify a point and a transformation matrix; this does not fully specified the actual mapping. We must also specify what frame we are using. Here is a simple example showing this. Suppose we start with some point $\tilde{p}$ as well as the matrix

$$
\mathbf{S} = \begin{bmatrix} 2 & 0 & 0 & 0 \\ 0 & 1 & 0 & 0 \\ 0 & 0 & 1 & 0 \\ 0 & 0 & 0 & 1 \end{bmatrix}.
$$

Now lets fix a frame $\vec{\mathbf{f}}^t$. Using this basis, the point can be expressed using some appropriate coordinate vector as $\tilde{p} = \vec{\mathbf{f}}^t \mathbf{c}$. If we now use the matrix to transform the point, as described in chapter 3, we get $\vec{\mathbf{f}}^t \mathbf{c} \Rightarrow \vec{\mathbf{f}}^t S \mathbf{c}$. In this case, the effect of the matrix is to transform the point by a scale factor of two from the origin of $\vec{\mathbf{f}}^t$, in the direction of the first (x) axis of $\vec{\mathbf{f}}^t$.

Suppose we instead pick some other frame $\vec{\mathbf{a}}^t$, and suppose that this frame is related to the original one by the matrix equation $\vec{\mathbf{a}}^t = \vec{\mathbf{f}}^t A$. We can express the original point in the new frame with a new coordinate vector $\tilde{p} = \vec{\mathbf{f}}^t \mathbf{c} = \vec{\mathbf{a}}^t \mathbf{d}$, where $\mathbf{d} = A^{-1} \mathbf{c}$.

Now if we use S to perform a transformation on the point represented with respect to $\vec{\mathbf{a}}^t$, we get $\vec{\mathbf{a}}^t \mathbf{d} \Rightarrow \vec{\mathbf{a}}^t S \mathbf{d}$. In this case, we have scaled the same point $\tilde{p}$, but this time we have scaled it from the origin of $\vec{\mathbf{a}}^t$ in the direction of the first (x) axis of $\vec{\mathbf{a}}^t$. This is a different transformation (see figure 4.1). Figure 4.2 shows the same dependence on frame when rotating a point using a fixed matrix R.

The important thing to notice here is that the point is transformed (nonuniform scaling in this case) with respect to the frame that appears immediately to the left of the transformation matrix in the expression. Thus we call this the *left-of rule*. We read

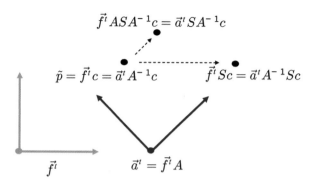

Figure 4.1
The scaling matrix S is used to scale the point $\tilde{p}$ with respect to two different frames. This results in two different answers.

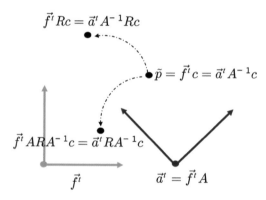

Figure 4.2
The rotation matrix R is used to rotate the point $\tilde{p}$ with respect to two different frames. This results in two different answers.

$$\tilde{p} = \vec{\mathbf{f}}^t \mathbf{c} \Rightarrow \vec{\mathbf{f}}^t S\mathbf{c}$$

as "$\tilde{p}$ is transformed by S with respect to $\vec{\mathbf{f}}^t$." We read

$$\tilde{p} = \vec{\mathbf{a}}^t A^{-1} \mathbf{c} \Rightarrow \vec{\mathbf{a}}^t S A^{-1} \mathbf{c}$$

as "$\tilde{p}$ is transformed by S with respect to $\vec{\mathbf{a}}^t$."

We can apply the same reasoning to transformations of frames themselves. We read

$$\vec{\mathbf{f}}^t \Rightarrow \vec{\mathbf{f}}^t S$$

as "$\vec{\mathbf{f}}^t$ is transformed by S with respect to $\vec{\mathbf{f}}^t$." We read

$$\vec{\mathbf{f}}^t = \vec{\mathbf{a}}^t A^{-1} \Rightarrow \vec{\mathbf{a}}^t S A^{-1}$$

as "$\vec{\mathbf{f}}^t$ is transformed by S with respect to $\vec{\mathbf{a}}^t$."

4.1.1 Transforms Using an Auxiliary Frame

There are many times when we wish to transform a frame $\vec{\mathbf{f}}^t$ in some specific way represented by a matrix M, with respect to some auxiliary frame $\vec{\mathbf{a}}^t$. For example, we may be using some frame to model the planet Earth, and we now wish the Earth to rotate around the Sun's frame.

This is easy to do as long as we know the matrix relating $\vec{\mathbf{f}}^t$ and $\vec{\mathbf{a}}^t$. For example, we may know that

$$\vec{\mathbf{a}}^t = \vec{\mathbf{f}}^t A$$

The transformed frame can then be expressed as

$$\vec{\mathbf{f}}^t \qquad\qquad\qquad\qquad\qquad\qquad\qquad\qquad (4.1)$$

$$= \vec{\mathbf{a}}^t A^{-1}$$

$$\Rightarrow \vec{\mathbf{a}}^t M A^{-1}$$

$$= \vec{\mathbf{f}}^t A M A^{-1}.$$

In the first line of equation (4.1), we rewrite the frame $\vec{\mathbf{f}}^t$ using $\vec{\mathbf{a}}^t$. In the next line, we transform the frame system using the left-of rule; we transform our frame using M with respect to $\vec{\mathbf{a}}^t$. In the final line, we simply rewrite the expression to remove the auxiliary frame.

4.2 Multiple Transformations

We can use this left-of rule to interpret sequences of multiple transformations. Again, recall that, in general, matrix multiplication is not commutative. In the following 2D example, let R be a rotation matrix and T a translation matrix, where the translation matrix has the effect of translating by one unit in the direction of the first axis and the rotation matrix has the effect of rotating by θ degrees about the frame's origin (see figure 4.3).

We will now interpret the following transformation:

$$\vec{\mathbf{f}}^t \Rightarrow \vec{\mathbf{f}}^t T R.$$

We do this by breaking up the transformation into two steps, In the first step,

$$\vec{\mathbf{f}}^t \Rightarrow \vec{\mathbf{f}}^t T = \vec{\mathbf{f}}'^t.$$

This is interpreted as: $\vec{\mathbf{f}}^t$ is transformed by T with respect to $\vec{\mathbf{f}}^t$, and we call the resulting frame $\vec{\mathbf{f}}'^t$.

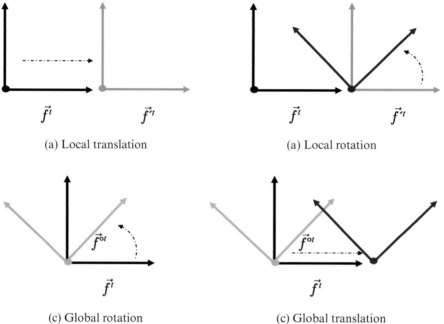

(a) Local translation   (a) Local rotation

(c) Global rotation   (c) Global translation

Figure 4.3
Two ways of interpreting the expression $\vec{\mathbf{f}}^t T R$.

In the second step,

$$\vec{\mathbf{f}}^t T \Rightarrow \vec{\mathbf{f}}^t T R,$$

or equivalently,

$$\vec{\mathbf{f}'}^t \Rightarrow \vec{\mathbf{f}'}^t R.$$

This is interpreted as: $\vec{\mathbf{f}'}^t$ is transformed by R with respect to $\vec{\mathbf{f}'}^t$.

We can also interpret the composed transformations in another valid way. This is done by applying the rotation and translation in the other order. In the first step,

$$\vec{\mathbf{f}}^t \Rightarrow \vec{\mathbf{f}}^t R = \vec{\mathbf{f}}_\circ{}^t,$$

$\vec{\mathbf{f}}^t$ is transformed by R with respect to $\vec{\mathbf{f}}^t$, and we call the resulting frame $\vec{\mathbf{f}}_\circ{}^t$. In the second step,

$$\vec{\mathbf{f}}^t R \Rightarrow \vec{\mathbf{f}}^t T R,$$

$\vec{\mathbf{f}}_\circ{}^t$ is transformed by T with respect to $\vec{\mathbf{f}}^t$.

These are just two different interpretations of the same final composed transformations. (1) Translate with respect to $\vec{\mathbf{f}}^t$ then rotate with respect to the intermediate frame. (2) Rotate with respect to $\vec{\mathbf{f}}^t$ then translate with respect to the original frame $\vec{\mathbf{f}}^t$. At times, it will be more convenient to use the first interpretation, and at other times it may be more convenient to use the second one.

These types of interpretations are often summarized as follows: If we read transformations from left to right, then each transform is done with respect to a newly created "local" frame. If we read the transformations from right to left, then each transform is done with respect to the original "global" frame.

Exercises

4.1 Using the definitions of section 4.2, draw two different sketches illustrating the transformation: $\vec{\mathbf{f}}^t \Rightarrow \vec{\mathbf{f}}^t RT$ (compare with figure 4.3).

4.2 Suppose $\vec{\mathbf{f}}^t$ is an orthonormal frame, and we apply the transform $\vec{\mathbf{f}}^t \Rightarrow \vec{\mathbf{f}}^t ST$, where S is a matrix that applies a uniform scale by a factor of 2, and T translates by 1 along the x axis. How far does the frame's origin move, measured in the original units of $\vec{\mathbf{f}}^t$?

4.3 Given the following two orthonormal frames $\vec{\mathbf{a}}^t$ and $\vec{\mathbf{b}}^t$

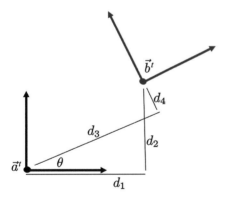

with distances given by the positive quantities d_i. What are the matrices R and T such that $\vec{\mathbf{b}}^t = \vec{\mathbf{a}}^t T R$? What are the matrices R and T such that $\vec{\mathbf{b}}^t = \vec{\mathbf{a}}^t RT$? (Note: Do this without using trigonometric terms in the matrix T.)

4.4 Given the following three frames

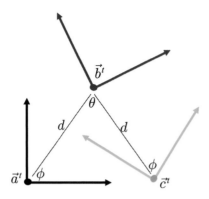

Suppose that $\vec{\mathbf{b}}^t = \vec{\mathbf{a}}^t N$ and $\vec{\mathbf{c}}^t = \vec{\mathbf{a}}^t M$. Express the matrix M using only the symbols N and θ.

5 Frames in Graphics

Now that we have covered the basics of points and matrix transformations, we can describe how they are typically used in computer graphics. We will then discuss various modeling manipulation and imaging operations.

5.1 World, Object, and Eye Frames

When describing the geometry of a scene, we start with a basic right-handed orthonormal frame $\vec{\mathbf{w}}^t$ called the *world frame*. We never alter the world frame. Other frames can then be described with respect to this world frame. If we express the location of some point using coordinates with respect to the world frame, then these will be called *world coordinates*.

Suppose we wish to model, say, a moving car in our scene. We would like to model the geometry of the object using vertex coordinates that do not need to be aware of the global placement of the object in the scene. Likewise, we would like to move the car around the scene without changing any of these coordinates. This is accomplished using object frames.

To every object in the scene we associate a right-handed orthonormal *object frame* $\vec{\mathbf{o}}^t$. We can now express the location of parts of an object using coordinates with respect to the object's coordinate system. These are called *object coordinates* and will be stored in our computer program. To move the entire object, we simply update $\vec{\mathbf{o}}^t$ and do not need to change any of the object coordinates of our points.

The relationship between the object's coordinate system and the world frame is represented by an affine 4 by 4 (rigid body) matrix that we call O. That is,

$$\vec{\mathbf{o}}^t = \vec{\mathbf{w}}^t O.$$

In our computer program, we will store the matrix O, with the understanding that it relates the world frame to the object's coordinate system using the equation above. To move the frame $\vec{\mathbf{o}}^t$, we change the matrix O.

In the real world, when we want to create a 2D picture of a 3D environment, we place a camera somewhere in the scene. The position of each object in the picture is based on its 3D relationship to the camera (i.e., its coordinates with respect to an appropriate basis).

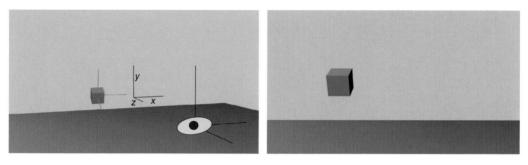

| (a) The frames | (b) The eye's view |

Figure 5.1
The world frame is in red, the object frame is in green, and the eye frame is in blue. The eye is looking down its negative z axis toward the object.

In computer graphics, we achieve this by having a right-handed orthonormal frame $\vec{\mathbf{e}}^t$, called the *eye frame*. We interpret the eye as looking down its negative z axis and making a picture (see figure 5.1). The eye frame is related by some (rigid body) 4 by 4 matrix E,

$$\vec{\mathbf{e}}^t = \vec{\mathbf{w}}^t E.$$

In a computer program, we will explicitly store the matrix E.

Given a point

$$\tilde{p} = \vec{\mathbf{o}}^t \mathbf{c} = \vec{\mathbf{w}}^t O \mathbf{c} = \vec{\mathbf{e}}^t E^{-1} O \mathbf{c},$$

we call $\mathbf{c}$ its object coordinates, $O\mathbf{c}$ its world coordinates, and $E^{-1}O\mathbf{c}$ its *eye coordinates*. We use an o subscript for object coordinates, a w subscript for world coordinates, and an e subscript for eye coordinates. Thus we may write

$$\begin{bmatrix} x_e \\ y_e \\ z_e \\ 1 \end{bmatrix} = E^{-1} O \begin{bmatrix} x_o \\ y_o \\ z_o \\ 1 \end{bmatrix}.$$

Ultimately, it is these eye coordinates that specify where each vertex appears in the rendered image. Thus, as described in chapter 6, our rendering process will need to compute eye coordinates for every vertex.

5.2 Moving Things Around

In an interactive 3D program, we often want to move the objects and the eye around in space using some rigid body transformation. We now discuss how this is commonly done.

5.2.1 Moving an Object

We move an object by appropriately updating its frame, which is represented by updating its matrix O.

Let us say we wish to apply some transformation M to an object frame $\vec{\mathbf{o}}^t$ with respect to some frame $\vec{\mathbf{a}}^t = \vec{\mathbf{w}}^t A$. Then, as in equation (4.1), we have

$$\vec{\mathbf{o}}^t \tag{5.1}$$

$$= \vec{\mathbf{w}}^t O$$

$$= \vec{\mathbf{a}}^t A^{-1} O$$

$$\Rightarrow \vec{\mathbf{a}}^t M A^{-1} O$$

$$= \vec{\mathbf{w}}^t A M A^{-1} O.$$

So we implement this in our code as $O \leftarrow A M A^{-1} O$.

What is a natural choice for $\vec{\mathbf{a}}^t$? The most obvious choice would be to apply the transformation to $\vec{\mathbf{o}}^t$ with respect to $\vec{\mathbf{o}}^t$ itself. Unfortunately, this means that the axes used will be those that correspond to the object itself. "Rightward" will be in the object's rightward direction, which will not correspond with any particular direction in the observed image. We might try to rectify this by instead transforming $\vec{\mathbf{o}}^t$ with respect to $\vec{\mathbf{e}}^t$. This fixes the axis problem but creates another problem. When we rotate the object, it will rotate about the origin of the eye's frame; it will appear to orbit around the eye. But we typically find it more natural to rotate the object about its center, which we think of as the origin of $\vec{\mathbf{o}}^t$ (see figure 5.2).

To fix both of these problems, we can create a new frame that has the origin of the object but the axes of the eye. To do this, let us factor our matrices as follows:

$$O = (O)_T (O)_R$$

$$E = (E)_T (E)_R,$$

where $(A)_T$ is the translational and $(A)_R$ is the rotational factor of A, as in equation (3.3). We can then see that the desired auxiliary frame should be

$$\vec{\mathbf{a}}^t = \vec{\mathbf{w}}^t (O)_T (E)_R. \tag{5.2}$$

This frame is obtained by starting with the world coordinate system and (reading left to right, i.e., successive local interpretation) translating it to the center of the object's frame, and then rotating it about that point to align with the directions of the eye (see figure 5.3).

Thus for this kind of object motion, the matrix A of equation (5.1) should be $A = (O)_T (E)_R$.

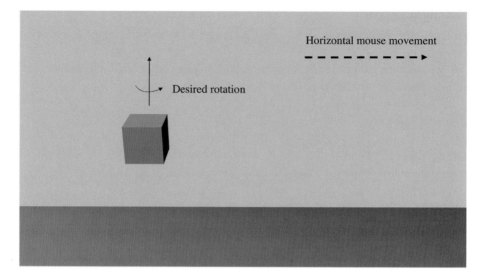

Figure 5.2
When we move the mouse to the right, we want the object to rotate about its own center about the viewer's y axis.

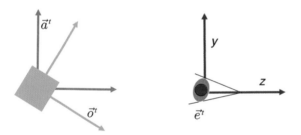

Figure 5.3
The auxiliary frame $\vec{\mathbf{a}}^t$ has the origin of $\vec{o}^t$ with the axes of $\vec{\mathbf{e}}^t$. The x axis extends into the page and has been suppressed.

There is an alternative computation that accomplishes the same effect. Suppose, for example, that we wish to rotate an object around its own center using an axis of rotation $\vec{k}$ that has coordinates $\mathbf{k}$ with respect to $\vec{\mathbf{e}}^t$. (Earlier, we used $\mathbf{k}$ to obtain a matrix M, and together with an appropriate A, we updated $O \leftarrow AMA^{-1}O$.) We can first compute $\mathbf{k}'$, the coordinates of $\vec{k}$ with respect to $\vec{o}^t$. Then plugging $\mathbf{k}'$ into equation (2.5), we can obtain a matrix M' that directly expresses our rotation with respect to $\vec{o}^t$. In this case, we can update the object's matrix as

$$O \leftarrow OM'.\tag{5.3}$$

5.2.2 Moving the Eye

Another operation we may wish to do is move the eye to a different point of view. This involves changing $\vec{\mathbf{e}}^t$, which will be represented in our program by updating the matrix E. Again, we must pick a convenient coordinate system with respect to which our updates will be performed, just like we did for objects.

One choice is to use the same auxiliary coordinate system we just used above. In this case, the eye would orbit around the center of the object.

Another useful choice is to transform $\vec{\mathbf{e}}^t$ with respect to the eye's own frame. This models ego-motion, like turning one's head. This is commonly used to control first-person motion. In this case, the matrix E would be updated as

$$E \leftarrow EM.$$

5.2.3 Lookat

Sometimes (especially for static images) it can be convenient to describe the eye frame, $\vec{\mathbf{e}}^t = \vec{\mathbf{w}}^t E$, directly by specifying the position of the eye $\tilde{p}$, a point $\tilde{q}$ that the eye is looking directly at, and an "up vector" $\vec{u}$ describing the vertical direction of the eye. These points and vector are given by $\mathbf{p}$, $\mathbf{q}$, and $\mathbf{u}$, their coordinates with respect to $\vec{\mathbf{w}}^t$. Given this input, let

$$\mathbf{z} = \texttt{normalize}(\mathbf{q} - \mathbf{p})$$

$$\mathbf{y} = \texttt{normalize}(\mathbf{u})$$

$$\mathbf{x} = \mathbf{y} \times \mathbf{z},$$

where

$$\texttt{normalize}(\mathbf{c}) = \sqrt{c_1^2 + c_2^2 + c_3^2}.$$

Then the matrix E is defined as

$$\begin{bmatrix} x_1 & y_1 & z_1 & p_1 \\ x_2 & y_2 & z_2 & p_2 \\ x_3 & y_3 & z_3 & p_3 \\ 0 & 0 & 0 & 1 \end{bmatrix}.$$

5.3 Scales

Thus far, we have thought of our world as being made up of movable objects, each with its own orthonormal frame represented by its own rigid body matrix $\vec{\mathbf{o}}^t = \vec{\mathbf{w}}^t O$. We have restricted our attention to orthonormal frames so that translation and rotation matrices work as we expect them to.

Of course, for modeling objects, we certainly may want to apply scaling as well. For example, we may want to model an ellipsoid as a squashed sphere. One way to deal with this is to keep a separate scale matrix O' around for the object as well. Then the scaled (non-orthonormal) object frame is $\vec{\mathbf{o}}'^t = \vec{\mathbf{o}}^t O'$. This way, we can still move the object by updating its O matrix as above. To draw the object, we use the matrix $E^{-1}OO'$ to transform the "scaled object coordinates" into eye coordinates.

5.4 Hierarchy

Often, it is convenient to think of an object as being assembled by some fixed or movable subobjects. Each subobject may have its own orthonormal frame, say $\vec{\mathbf{a}}^t$ (and scaled frame as well). Then, we can store the vertex coordinates of the subobject in its own coordinate system. Given this hierarchy, we want the ability to easily model motions of the object as a whole as well as independent motions of the subobjects.

For example, when modeling a robot with moving limbs, we may use an object and scaled object frame to represent the trunk, a subobject frame to represent a rotatable shoulder, and a scaled sub-subobject frame to to represent the upper arm (which moves along with the shoulder) (see figure 5.4).

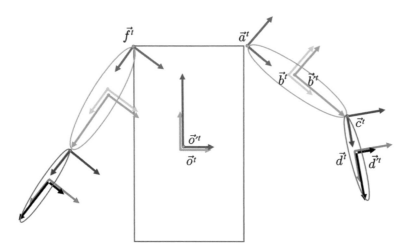

Figure 5.4
In this example, the green frame is the object frame $\vec{\mathbf{o}}^t = \vec{\mathbf{w}}^t O$, and the gray frame is the scaled object frame $\vec{\mathbf{o}}'^t = \vec{\mathbf{o}}^t O'$. The coordinates of a unit cube drawn in $\vec{\mathbf{o}}'^t$ forms a rectangular body. The matrix O can be changed to move the entire robot. The cyan frame $\vec{\mathbf{a}}^t = \vec{\mathbf{o}}^t A$ is the right shoulder frame. The rotational factor of A can be changed to rotate the entire right arm. The red frame $\vec{\mathbf{b}}^t = \vec{\mathbf{a}}^t B$ is the right upper arm frame. The light blue frame $\vec{\mathbf{b}}'^t = \vec{\mathbf{b}}^t B'$ is the scaled right upper arm frame. The coordinates of a unit sphere drawn in $\vec{\mathbf{b}}'^t$ forms the ellipsoidal right upper arm. $\vec{\mathbf{c}}^t = \vec{\mathbf{b}}^t C$ is the right elbow frame. The rotational factor of C can be changed to rotate the right lower arm. $\vec{\mathbf{d}}^t = \vec{\mathbf{c}}^t D$ and $\vec{\mathbf{d}}'^t = \vec{\mathbf{d}}^t D'$ are, respectively, the orthonormal and scaled lower arm frames used to draw the lower arm. The frame $\vec{\mathbf{f}}^t = \vec{\mathbf{o}}^t F$ is the left shoulder frame.

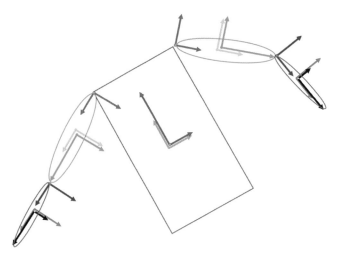

Figure 5.5
To move the entire robot, we update its O matrix.

When we move the whole object, by updating its O matrix, we want all of the subobjects to move along in unison (see figure 5.5). To get this behavior, we represent the subobject's frame using a rigid body matrix that relates it to the object's frame (instead of relating it to the world frame). Thus, we store a rigid body matrix A, which we interpret as defining the relationship $\vec{\mathbf{a}}^t = \vec{\mathbf{o}}^t A$, as well as a scale matrix A' defining its scaled subobject frame as $\vec{\mathbf{a}}'^t = \vec{\mathbf{a}}^t A'$. To reposition the subobject within the object, all we do is update the matrix A. To draw the subobject, we use the matrix $E^{-1} O A A'$, which transforms "scaled subobject coordinates" into eye coordinates. Clearly, this idea can be nested recursively, and we can represent a sub-subobject as $\vec{\mathbf{b}}^t = \vec{\mathbf{a}}^t B$ and a scaled sub-subobject as $\vec{\mathbf{b}}'^t = \vec{\mathbf{b}}^t B'$.

In our robot example, we have used $\vec{\mathbf{a}}^t$ as the right shoulder's frame, $\vec{\mathbf{b}}'^t$ as the right upper arm's frame, and $\vec{\mathbf{c}}^t = \vec{\mathbf{b}}^t C$ as the right elbow frame. $\vec{\mathbf{d}}^t = \vec{\mathbf{c}}^t D$ and $\vec{\mathbf{d}}'^t = \vec{\mathbf{d}}^t D'$ are, respectively, the orthonormal and scaled right lower arm frames. To move the entire robot, we update its O matrix (see figure 5.5). To bend the right arm at the shoulder, we update the A matrix (see figure 5.6). To bend the right arm at the elbow, we update the C matrix (see figure 5.7).

Often, a *matrix stack* data structure can be used to keep track of the matrix representing the currently drawn subobject. In this matrix stack, a push(M) operation creates a new "topmost" matrix, which is just a copy of the previous topmost matrix. It then right multiplies this new top matrix by the argument matrix M. A pop() operation removes the topmost layer of the stack. When "descending" down to a subobject, a push operation is done. When we return from this descent to the parent, this matrix is popped off the stack.

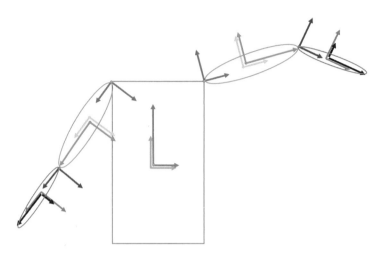

Figure 5.6
To bend the arm at the shoulder, we update the A matrix.

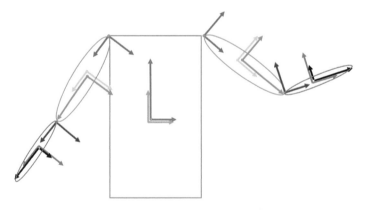

Figure 5.7
To bend the elbow robot, we update its C matrix.

For example, in pseudocode, we may draw the robot above as

```
...
matrixStack.initialize(inv(E));
matrixStack.push(O);
  matrixStack.push(O');
    draw(matrixStack.top(), cube); \\body
  matrixStack.pop(); \\O'

  matrixStack.push(A);
    matrixStack.push(B);
```

```
   matrixStack.push(B');
     draw(matrixStack.top(),sphere); \\upper arm
   matrixStack.pop(); \\B'

   matrixStack.push(C);
     matrixStack.push(C');
       draw(matrixStack.top(),sphere); \\lower arm
     matrixStack.pop(); \\C'
   matrixStack.pop(); \\C

  matrixStack.pop();   \\B
 matrixStack.pop();     \\A

\\current top matrix is inv(E)*O

\\we can now draw another arm
  matrixStack.push(F);
  ...
```

These kinds of hierarchical relations can be hard coded into one's program, as in the above pseudocode, or represented in some linked tree data-structure called a *scene graph*.

Exercises

5.1 Suppose we have a scene with a jet airplane flying in the sky. Suppose the geometry of the airplane is described with respect to the jet's own frame $\vec{\mathbf{j}}^t$, defined as $\vec{\mathbf{j}}^t = \vec{\mathbf{w}}^t J$. Let this frame be centered in the cockpit with its negative z axis facing out the front window. Suppose we wish to render the scene from the point of view of the pilot. Given a point on some other object, $\vec{\mathbf{o}}^t \mathbf{c}$, what is the coordinate vector that we should pass to the renderer to draw this point?

5.2 Suppose we have the robot of figure 5.4. Suppose we want to rotate the shoulder joint with respect to a coordinate system whose origin is at the center of the joint but has axes that align with those of the eye. How would one implement this? (This may be more easily done using the approach of equation 5.3).

6 Hello World 3D

We can now finally describe how the concepts of frames and transformations from the previous chapters are implemented in an interactive 3D graphics setting. Before reading this chapter, you should have already gone through appendix A where we describe how to set up a basic OpenGL program.

6.1 Coordinates and Matrices

To start, it is useful to have Cvec2, Cvec3, Cvec4 data types to represent coordinate vectors. We also need to implement addition of two Cvecs of the same size (u + v) and multiplication with a real scalar, (r * v). In the case of Cvec4, we call the entries x, y, z, w. At this point, the w entry will always be 1 for a point and 0 for a vector.

Next, we need a Matrix4 data type to represent affine matrices. We need to support right-multiplication with a Cvec4, (M * v), multiplication of two Matrix4s, (M * N), the inverse operation inv(M), and the transpose operation transpose(M).

To create useful transformation matrices, we make use of the following operations:

```
Matrix4 identity();
Matrix4 makeXRotation(double ang);
Matrix4 makeYRotation(double ang);
Matrix4 makeZRotation(double ang);
Matrix4 makeScale(double sx,  double sy, double sz);
Matrix4 makeTranslation(double tx, double ty, double tz);
```

(In C++, it is useful to return the identity matrix from default constructor.)

To implement the ideas of sections 3.5 and 5.2.1, we need an operation tranFact(M), which returns a Matrix4 representing just the translational factor of M, as in equation (3.1), as well as linFact(M), which returns a Matrix4 representing just the linear factor of M. That is, M = transFact(M)*linFact(M).

To implement the ideas of section 3.6, we need an operation `normalMatrix(M)`, which simply returns the inverse transpose of the linear factor of M (stored in the upper left of a `Matrix4`).

To implement the ideas of section 5.2.1, we need a function `doMtoOwrtA(M,O,A)`, "do M to O with respect to A," which simply returns $AMA^{-1}O$. We also need the function `makeMixedFrame(O,E)`, which factors both O and E and returns $(O)_T(E)_R$.

6.2 Drawing a Shape

First of all, to do 3D drawing, we need to set a few more state variables in OpenGL:

```
static void InitGLState(){
  glClearColor(128./255., 200./255., 255./255., 0.);
  glClearDepth(0.0);
  glEnable(GL_DEPTH_TEST);
  glDepthFunc(GL_GREATER);
  glEnable(GL_CULL_FACE);
  glCullFace(GL_BACK);
}
```

The detailed meanings of these calls are described later in the book. In the `glClearColor` call, we clear not only the color on the image but also the "z-buffer." We also need to enable depth, or z-buffering, and tell OpenGL that "greater z" means "closer to eye." Z-buffering is discussed in detail in chapter 11. For efficiency, we also tell OpenGL to cull (i.e., not draw) any face that is backfacing to the eye A face is backfacing when its vertices appear in clockwise order as seen in the image. Backface culling is discussed in detail in section 12.2.

Getting back to business now: We use a global variable `Matrix4 objRbt` to represent the rigid body matrix O that relates the object's orthonormal frame to the world frame, as in $\vec{o}^t = \vec{w}^t O$. We use a global variable `Matrix4 eyeRbt` to represent the rigid body matrix E that relates the object's orthonormal frame to the world frame, as in $\vec{e}^t = \vec{w}^t E$.

Let us now look at the following code fragment that draws two triangles and one cube.

The floor is one square made up of two triangles. The cube is made up of six squares (i.e., 12 triangles). For each vertex, we store 3D object coordinates for its position and normal vector. All of this is similar to what is done in appendix A.

```
GLfloat floorVerts[18] =
  {
    -floor_size, floor_y, -floor_size,
     floor_size, floor_y,  floor_size,
     floor_size, floor_y, -floor_size,
    -floor_size, floor_y, -floor_size,
    -floor_size, floor_y,  floor_size,
```

```
       floor_size, floor_y,  floor_size
  };
GLfloat floorNorms[18] =
  {
     0,1,0,
     0,1,0,
     0,1,0,
     0,1,0,
     0,1,0,
     0,1,0
  };

GLfloat cubeVerts[36*3]=
  {
     -0.5, -0.5, -0.5,
     -0.5, -0.5, +0.5,
     +0.5, -0.5, +0.5,

     // 33 more vertices not shown
  };

// Normals of a cube.
GLfloat cubeNorms[36*3] =
  {
     +0.0, -1.0, +0.0,
     +0.0, -1.0, +0.0,
     +0.0, -1.0, +0.0,

       // 33 more vertices not shown
  };
```

We now initialize the vertex buffer objects (VBOs), which are handles to collections of vertex data, such as vertex positions and normals.

```
static GLuint floorVertBO, floorNormBO, cubeNormBO, cubeNormBO;

static void initVBOs(void){
  glGenBuffers(1,&floorVertBO);
  glBindBuffer(GL_ARRAY_BUFFER,floorVertBO);
  glBufferData(
      GL_ARRAY_BUFFER,
      18*sizeof(GLfloat),
      floorVerts,
      GL_STATIC_DRAW);
```

```
glGenBuffers(1,&floorNormBO);
glBindBuffer(GL_ARRAY_BUFFER,floorNormBO);
glBufferData(
     GL_ARRAY_BUFFER,
     18*sizeof(GLfloat),
     floorNorms,
     GL_STATIC_DRAW);

glGenBuffers(1,&cubeVertBO);
glBindBuffer(GL_ARRAY_BUFFER,cubeVertBO);
glBufferData(
     GL_ARRAY_BUFFER,
     36*3*sizeof(GLfloat),
     cubeVerts,
     GL_STATIC_DRAW);


glGenBuffers(1,&cubeNormBO);
glBindBuffer(GL_ARRAY_BUFFER,cubeNormBO);
glBufferData(
     GL_ARRAY_BUFFER,
     36*3*sizeof(GLfloat),
     cubeNorms,
     GL_STATIC_DRAW);


}
```

We draw an object using its position and normal VBOs as

```
void drawObj(GLuint vertbo, GLuint normbo, int numverts){

  glBindBuffer(GL_ARRAY_BUFFER,vertbo);
  safe_glVertexAttribPointer(h_aVertex);
  safe_glEnableVertexAttribArray(h_aVertex);

  glBindBuffer(GL_ARRAY_BUFFER,normbo);
  safe_glVertexAttribPointer(h_aNormal);
  safe_glEnableVertexAttribArray(h_aNormal);

  glDrawArrays(GL_TRIANGLES,0,numverts);

  safe_glDisableVertexAttribArray(h_aVertex);
  safe_glDisableVertexAttribArray(h_aNormal);
}
```

We are now able to look at our display function.

```
static void display(){
  safe_glUseProgram(h_program_);
  glClear(GL_COLOR_BUFFER_BIT | GL_DEPTH_BUFFER_BIT);

  Matrix4 projmat = makeProjection(frust_fovy, frust_ar,
                                   frust_near, frust_far);
  sendProjectionMatrix(projmat);

  Matrix4 MVM = inv(eyeRbt);
  Matrix4 NMVM = normalMatrix(MVM);
  sendModelViewNormalMatrix(MVM,NMVM);

  safe_glVertexAttrib3f(h_aColor, 0.6, 0.8, 0.6);
  drawObj(floorVertBO,floorNormBO,6);

  MVM = inv(eyeRbt) * objRbt;
  NMVM = normalMatrix(MVM);
  sendModelViewNormalMatrix(MVM,NMVM);

  safe_glVertexAttrib3f(h_aColor, 0.0, 0.0, 1.0);
  drawObj(cubeVertBO,cubeNormBO,36);

  glutSwapBuffers();
  if (glGetError() != GL_NO_ERROR){
    const GLubyte *errString;
    errString=gluErrorString(errCode);
    printf("error: %s\n", errString);
  }
}
```

makeProjection returns a special kind of matrix that describes the internals of a "virtual camera." The camera is determined by several parameters, a field of view, window aspect ratio, as well as so-called near and far z-values. sendProjectionMatrix sends this "camera matrix" to the vertex shader and places it in a variable named uProjMatrix. We will learn more about this matrix in later chapters, but for now, you can just find the code on the book's website.

In our program, the vertex coordinates stored in a VBO are object coordinates of the vertices. Because the renderer will eventually need eye coordinates, we send the matrix $E^{-1}O$ to the API as well. This matrix is often called MVM, or *modelview matrix*. (To draw the floor, we use $O = I$.) The vertex shader (described later) will take these vertex data and perform the multiplication $E^{-1}O\mathbf{c}$ producing the eye coordinates used in rendering. Similarly, all of the coordinates for normals need to be multiplied by an associated *normal matrix*, which allows us to transform them from object to eye coordinates.

Our procedure `sendModelViewNormalMatrix(MVM,NMVM)` sends both the MVM and normal matrix to the vertex shader and places them in the variables named `uModelViewMatrix` and `uNormalMatrix`.

An aside: In computer graphics, the normal vector attached to a vertex of a triangle, and then used for shading, does not have to be the true geometric normal of the flat triangle. For example, if we are drawing a sphere shape using a triangle mesh to approximate it, we may want to have three distinct normals for the three vertices of one triangle to better match the shape of the sphere (see figure 6.1). This will lead to a smoother and less tessellated appearance in the shaded image. If we want the faces to appear flat, such as with the faces of a cube, then we would pass the actual geometric normals of each triangle to OpenGL.

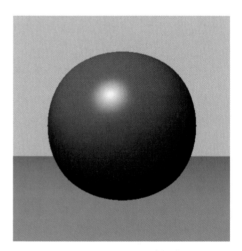

(a) Flat normals   (b) Smooth normals

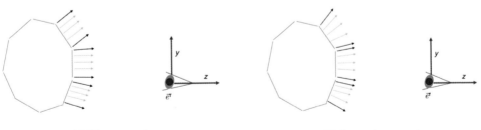

(c) Flat normals   (d) Smooth normals

Figure 6.1
In graphics, we are free to specify any normals we wish at vertices. These normals (like all attribute variables) are interpolated to all points inside the triangle. In our fragment shader, we may use these interpolated normals to simulate lighting and determine the color. When the triangle's true normals are given, then we get a faceted appearance. If we specify normals to approximate some underlying smooth shape, we obtain a smooth rendering.

The call to `safe_glVertexAttrib3f` passes three floats to the vertex shader variable "pointed to" by the handle `h_aColor`. Because of the way we have initialized our shaders, this handle "points to" an attribute variable in the vertex shader named `aColor`. The setting of any attribute variable remains in effect until it is changed by another `safe_glVertexAttrib3f` call. Thus until changed, it will be bound to each subsequent vertex. The data sent to `aColor` can be interpreted in any way we want by our vertex shader. In our case, we will interpret these data as the "rgb-color" coordinates of the vertex.

6.3 The Vertex Shader

Our vertex shader takes the object coordinates of every vertex position and turns them into eye coordinates, as described in section 5.1. It likewise transforms the vertex's normal coordinates.

Here is the complete code of the vertex shader:

```
#version 330

uniform Matrix4 uModelViewMatrix;
uniform Matrix4 uNormalMatrix;
uniform Matrix4 uProjMatrix;

in vec3 aColor;
in vec4 aNormal;
in vec4 aVertex;

out vec3 vColor;
out vec3 vNormal;
out vec4 vPosition;

void main()
{
  vColor = aColor;
  vPosition = uModelViewMatrix * aVertex;
  vec4 normal = vec4(aNormal.x, aNormal.y, aNormal.z, 0.0);
  vNormal = vec3(uNormalMatrix * normal);
  gl_Position = uProjMatrix * vPosition;
}
```

This shader is quite simple to understand. It passes its color variable `aColor` on to the output `vColor` unchanged. It performs one matrix–vector multiplication to turn the object coordinates into eye coordinates and sends these as output.

It also performs one matrix–vector multiplication to turn the object coordinates of the normal into eye coordinates and sends these as output.

Finally, it uses the special (and not yet fully explained) camera projection matrix to get a new kind of coordinates called *clip coordinates* of the vertex and sends these as output to gl_Position. In this case, and unlike the simpler code we saw in appendix A, gl_Position is actually a 4-vector. In chapters 10–12, we will further discuss exactly how the clip coordinate data are used to place the vertex on the screen.

6.4 What Happens Next

The details of what OpenGL does next with the output of the vertex shader will be described in later chapters. Almost every paragraph below will need to be expanded into a full chapter to understand fully what is going on. But for now, here are the main things we need to know.

The clip coordinates are used by the renderer to determine where to place the vertex on the screen, and thus where the triangle will be drawn. Once OpenGL gets the clip coordinates of three vertices forming a triangle, it calculates which pixels on the screen fall inside of the triangle. For each of these pixels, it determines how "far away" this pixel is from each of the three vertices. This is used to determine how to blend or *interpolate* the varying variables of the three vertices.

The interpolated variables at each pixel are then used by a user-written fragment shader, which is called independently for each pixel. Here is the simplest possible fragment shader:

```
in vec3 vColor;

out fragColor;

void main()
{
   fragColor = vec4(vColor.x, vColor.y, vColor.z, 1.0);
}
```

It simply takes the interpolated color data for the pixel and sends it to the output variable fragColor. This is then sent to the screen as the pixel's color. (The fourth value of 1.0 is called the alpha, or opacity value, and will not concern us yet.) The clip coordinates are also used to determine how far the triangle is from the screen. When z-buffering is enabled, this information is used to determine, at each pixel, which triangle is closest and thus drawn. Because this decision is made on a pixel by pixel basis, even complicated arrangements of interpenetrating triangles will be drawn correctly.

Note that when using the above fragment shader, we did not use the varying variables vPosition and vNormal and in this case did not really have to send them as output in the vertex shader. Here is a slightly more complicated and more realistic shader that does use these data:

```
#version 330

uniform vec3 uLight;
in vec3 vColor;
in vec3 vNormal;
in vec4 vPosition;

out fragColor;

void main()
{
  vec3 toLight = normalize(uLight - vec3(vPosition));
  vec3 normal = normalize(vNormal);
  float diffuse = max(0.0, dot(normal, toLight));
  vec3 intensity = vColor * diffuse;
  fragColor = vec4(intensity.x, intensity.y, intensity.z, 1.0);
}
```

Here we assume that uLight are the eye coordinates of a point light source and that these data have been appropriately passed to the shaders from our main program using the appropriate safe_glVertexUniform3f call. The data in vNormal and vPosition, like those of vColor, are interpolated from the vertex data. Because of the way the interpolation is done, the data in vPosition correctly represent the eye coordinates of the geometric point inside the triangle that is seen at this pixel. The rest of the code does a simple calculation, computing various vectors and taking dot products. The goal is to simulate the reflectance of a diffuse, or matte (as opposed to shiny), material. We will revisit the details of this computation in chapter 14.

6.5 Placing and Moving with Matrices

Going back to our original code, all that remains is to initialize the eyeRbt and objRbt variables and also explain how we may update them. In this simple case, we might start off with

```
Matrix4 eyeRbt = makeTranslation(Cvec3(0.0, 0.0, 4.0));
Matrix4 objRbt = makeTranslation(Cvec3(-1,0,-1))*
                 makeXRotation(22.0);
```

In this case, all of our frames start out with axes aligned with the world frame's. The eye's frame is translated by $+4$ with respect to the world's z axis. Recall that our "camera" is, by definition, looking down the eye's negative z axis, thus the eye is now looking toward the world's origin. The object's frame is translated a bit back and to "the left" in the world's frame and rotated about its x axis (see figure 5.1).

Let us now allow the user to move the object. Recall that in the motion callback function described in appendix A, we calculated the horizontal deltax mouse displacement while the left mouse was held down. Vertical displacement can likewise be computed.

We can now add the following lines to the motion function to move the object.

```
Matrix4 M =  makeXRotation(deltay) * makeYRotation(deltax);
Matrix4 A = makeMixedFrame(objRbt,EyeRbt);
objRbt = doMtoOwrtA(M, objRbt, A);
```

We can also augment the motion function to use mouse motion, while the right button is held down, to translate the object using

```
M= makeTranslation(Cvec3(deltax, deltay, 0) * 0.01)
```

We can use mouse motion, while the middle button is held down, to translate the object nearer and farther using

```
M=makeTranslation(Cvec3(0, 0, -deltay) * 0.01)
```

If we wish to move the eye using the auxiliary frame, then we use the code

```
eyeRbt = doMtoOwrtA(inv(M), eyeRbt, A).
```

If we wish to perform ego motion, as if we are turning our head, then we may use the code

```
eyeRbt = doMtoOwrtA(inv(M), eyeRbt, eyeRbt).
```

In either of these last two cases, we invert the M so that the mouse movements produce the image movements in more desired directions.

Exercises

6.1 In this chapter, we have explained the basics of an OpenGL 3D "Hello World" program. At the book's website, we have some basic starter code, including the necessary Cvec and Matrix4 classes. Download and compile this program.

6.2 Add code to allow the user to move the blue cube with respect to the auxiliary coordinate frame of equation (5.2). The mouse motion should be interpreted as follows:

• Left button: moving the mouse right/left rotates around the y-direction.
• Left button: moving the mouse up/down rotates around the x-direction.
• Right button: moving the mouse right/left translates in the x-direction.
• Right button: moving the mouse up/down translates in the y-direction.

- Middle button (or both left and right buttons down): moving the mouse up/down translates in the z-direction.

6.3 Use the "o" key to let the user toggle between the blue cube and red cube. This lets the user manipulate either object.

6.4 Use the "o" key to let the user toggle between the blue cube, the red cube, and the eye to let the user manipulate either object or the eye. For the eye motion, apply all transformations with respect to $\vec{e}^t$ (ego motion) and invert the signs of the translations and rotations.

6.5 Replace each of the cubes with a tessellated sphere. To tessellate a sphere, parameterrize each point on the unit sphere with angular coordinates $\theta \in [0 \ldots \pi]$ and $\phi \in [0 \ldots 2\pi]$. Define the object coordinates of each point using

$$x = \sin\theta \cos\phi$$

$$y = \sin\theta \sin\phi$$

$$z = \cos\theta.$$

6.6 (Lengthy) Replace each of the cubes with a simple robot. Each robot will have movable joints at the shoulders, elbows, hips, and knees. Use the numeral keys to let the user pick the relevant joint. Let the shoulder and hip have full 3D rotational degrees of freedom. Let the elbow have just two rotational degrees of freedom and the knee just one rotational degree of freedom. For joints with 1 or 2 degrees of freedom, you should store these as Euler angles corresponding to rotations about the appropriate (e.g., x or z) axes. The body parts should be drawn as nonuniformly scaled cubes or spheres.

6.7 The user should be allowed to press "p" and then use the mouse to left click on a desired robot part. The determination of which part the user clicked on is called "picking." After picking a part, the user should then be allowed to use the mouse to rotate the part about its joint.

To do picking, we follow these steps: when "p" is pressed, the next left mouse click will trigger the following. The current scene is rendered, but this time, instead of drawing the usual colors into the color back buffer, you will assign each part to be drawn with its own unique color into the buffer. Because each part's color is unique, it will serve as an ID for the part. Drawing this ID-tagged scene will involve using a fragment shader that does not do lighting calculations but instead directly returns its input color. After rendering the scene, call `glFlush()`, and then read the ID from the back buffer using a call to `glReadPixels` to determine which part was selected by the mouse. To set the back buffer as the read target, use `glReadBuffer(GL_BACK)` at some point before the `glReadPixels` call. Also, in your initialization code, you should call `glPixelStorei(GL_UNPACK_ALIGNMENT, 1)`, so you can correctly access the pixel data.

• If the mouse click was over a robot's part, then the chosen robot part is selected.
• If the mouse click was over a robot's main body, the entire robot is selected.
• If the mouse click was not over any robot, then the eye is selected for manipulation.

Once picking is done, subsequent mouse motion with the mouse button depressed should manipulate the selected object or joint.

II ROTATIONS AND INTERPOLATION

7   Quaternions (a Bit Technical)

In this chapter, we will explore the quaternion representation of rotations as an alternative to rotation matrices

$$R = \begin{bmatrix} r & 0 \\ 0 & 1 \end{bmatrix}.$$

Our main use for quaternions will be to aid us in interpolating between orientations in a natural way. This will be useful for animating objects as they fly through space. If we are not planning on interpolating rotations for our particular application, then this representation may not be necessary.

7.1   Interpolation

Let us suppose we have a desired object frame for "time=0," $\vec{\mathbf{o}}_0^t = \vec{\mathbf{w}}^t R_0$, and a desired object frame for "time=1," $\vec{\mathbf{o}}_1^t = \vec{\mathbf{w}}^t R_1$, where R_0 and R_1 are 4 by 4 rotation matrices. Suppose we wish to find a sequence of frames $\vec{\mathbf{o}}_\alpha^t$, for $\alpha \in [0 \dots 1]$, that naturally rotates from $\vec{\mathbf{o}}_0^t$ to $\vec{\mathbf{o}}_1^t$.

One idea would be to define $R_\alpha := (1 - \alpha)R_0 + (\alpha)R_1$ and then set $\vec{\mathbf{o}}_\alpha^t = \vec{\mathbf{w}}^t R_\alpha$. The problem is that, under matrix linear interpolation, each vector simply moves along a straight line (see figure 7.1). In this case, the intermediate R_α are not rotation matrices; this is clearly unacceptable. Moreover (especially in 3D), it is not very easy to remove this squashing by somehow finding a true rotation matrix that approximates this interpolated matrix.

Another idea, not worth pursuing too deeply, is somehow to factor both R_0 and R_1 into three so-called Euler angles (see section 2.5). These three scalar values could each be linearly interpolated using α. The interpolated Euler angles could then be used to generate intermediate rotations. It turns out that when interpolating Euler angles, the sequence of interpolated rotations is not particularly natural in any physical or geometric way. For example, it is not invariant to basis changes (defined later).

What we would really like to do is first to create a single transition matrix $R_1 R_0^{-1}$. This matrix can, as any rotation matrix, be thought of as a rotation of some θ degrees about

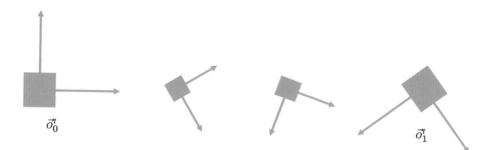

Figure 7.1
Linear interpolation of the R_i matrices simply moves vectors along straight lines and does not model rotation.

some axis $[k_x, k_y, k_z]^t$, as in equation (2.5). Let us now imagine that we had an operation $(R_1 R_0^{-1})^\alpha$ that gave us a rotation about $[k_x, k_y, k_z]^t$ by $\alpha \cdot \theta$ degrees instead. Then it would be natural to define

$$R_\alpha := (R_1 R_0^{-1})^\alpha R_0 \tag{7.1}$$

and set

$$\vec{\mathbf{o}}'_\alpha = \vec{\mathbf{w}}^t R_\alpha.$$

Doing so, we would get a sequence of frames that rotates more and more about a single axis, as we increase α, until it reaches its desired resting pose. Clearly, at the beginning we have $\vec{\mathbf{w}}^t (R_1 R_0^{-1})^0 R_0 = \vec{\mathbf{w}}^t R_0 = \vec{\mathbf{o}}_0$, and at the end we have $\vec{\mathbf{w}}^t (R_1 R_0^{-1})^1 R_0 = \vec{\mathbf{w}}^t R_1 = \vec{\mathbf{o}}_1$, as desired.

The hard part here is to factor a transition rotation matrix, like $R_1 R_0^{-1}$, into its axis/angle form. The idea behind the quaternion representation is to keep track of the axis and angle at all times so that no such factoring is needed. Importantly, the quaternion representation does this in such a way that still allows us to do all of the necessary manipulations that we can do with rotation matrices.

7.1.1 Cycles
We need to clarify one detail here. The matrix $R_1 R_0^{-1}$ can, in fact, be thought of as a rotation of some $\theta + n2\pi$ degrees for any integer n. When looking at the effect of this rotation acting as a linear transform on a vector, these extra factors of 2π are irrelevant. But when defining a power operator that gives us "a sequence of frames that rotate more and more about a single axis, until it reaches its desired resting pose," we need to decide how to choose a value of n given the matrix $R_1 R_0^{-1}$. For interpolation, the natural choice is to choose n such that $|\theta + n2\pi|$ is minimal. In particular, this means that, for this choice of n, we have $\theta + n2\pi \in [-\pi \ldots \pi]$. Additionally, this choice is unambiguous (except in the case that

$\theta = \pi + n2\pi$, in which case we would need to choose arbitrarily between $-\pi$ and π). Indeed, this choice of n will come up later in section 7.4.

7.1.2 Invariance

There are many natural things about the single-axis, constant angular velocity motion of equation (7.1). For one thing, an object flying through space with no forces acting on it has its center of mass follow a straight line, and its orientation spins along a fixed axis. Additionally, this kind of orientation interpolation satisfies both left and right invariance, which we will now explain.

Suppose we have an alternate world frame $\vec{\mathbf{w}}^{\prime t}$ such that $\vec{\mathbf{w}}^t = \vec{\mathbf{w}}^{\prime t} R_l$ with R_l being some fixed "left" rotation matrix. Using this frame, we can re-express our original interpolation problem as one of interpolating between $\vec{\mathbf{o}}_0 := \vec{\mathbf{w}}^{\prime t} R_l R_0$ and $\vec{\mathbf{o}}_1 := \vec{\mathbf{w}}^{\prime t} R_l R_1$. We say that our interpolation satisfies left invariance if this re-expression does not change the interpolated answer: if the original interpolation gave us $\vec{\mathbf{o}}_\alpha = \vec{\mathbf{w}}^t R_\alpha$, with some R_α, then the re-expressed interpolation problem gives us $\vec{\mathbf{w}}^{\prime t} R_l R_\alpha$, which thus results in the exact same $\vec{\mathbf{o}}_\alpha^t$ (see figure 7.2). In other words, an interpolation scheme is left invariant if it depends only on the geometry of the frames $\vec{\mathbf{o}}_0$ and $\vec{\mathbf{o}}_1$, not on the choice of world frame and the resulting R_0 and R_1. Left invariance is a very natural property to desire; there are very few cases where it makes any sense for the interpolation to depend on the choice of world frame.

We can see that the interpolation using equation (7.1) satisfies left invariance as follows. The "transition" affine transform that maps one frame, $\vec{\mathbf{o}}_0^t$, into another, $\vec{\mathbf{o}}_1^t$, is always unique.

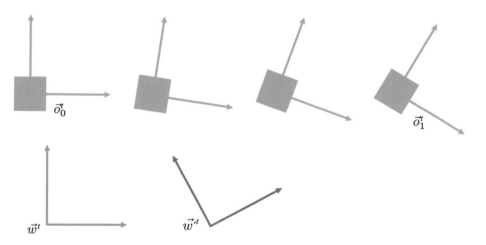

Figure 7.2
The interpolation satisfies left invariance if it does not change as we replace $\vec{\mathbf{w}}^t$ with $\vec{\mathbf{w}}^{\prime t}$. (Here we are only dealing with rotations, and the translations are just added for visual clarity.)

In our case, because our frames are both right handed, orthonormal, and share an origin, this transform must be a rotation. Meanwhile, the power operator on rotations that we just defined (namely, keep the axis but scale the angle) is an intrinsic geometric operation and can be described without reference to any coordinates. Thus, this interpolation scheme does not depend on the choice of world frame and is left invariant.

Right invariance, in contrast, means that the interpolation *of an object* does change, even if we change the object frame being used. In particular, suppose we fix a "right" rotation matrix R_r, and use this to define new object frames for time=0 and time=1: $\vec{\mathbf{o}}'^t_0 = \vec{\mathbf{o}}^t_0 R_r$ and $\vec{\mathbf{o}}'^t_1 = \vec{\mathbf{o}}^t_1 R_r$. Because we don't want our object's pose itself to change, we appropriately reassign the object coordinates of all of its vertices using $\mathbf{c}' = R_r^{-1}\mathbf{c}$. We say that our interpolation satisfies right invariance if this change of object basis has no impact on the interpolation of the rotating object itself. In other words, if the original interpolation gave us $\vec{\mathbf{o}}_\alpha = \vec{\mathbf{w}}^t R_\alpha$, with some R_α, then the new interpolation gives us $\vec{\mathbf{w}}^t R_\alpha R_r$. Thus, the object's interpolation (using the new object coordinates $\mathbf{c}'$) are unchanged (see figure 7.3). Right invariance is a reasonably natural property. But we will see later that when we also include translations along with our rotations, we may want the interpolation to depend on the choice of the object frame's origin.

We can directly see that the interpolation using equation (7.1) satisfies right invariance as

$$\left[(R_1 R_r)(R_r^{-1} R_0^{-1})\right]^\alpha R_0 R_r = (R_1 R_0^{-1})^\alpha R_0 R_r = R_\alpha R_r.$$

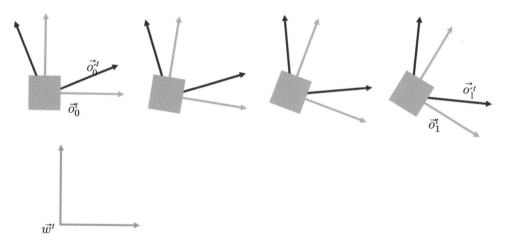

Figure 7.3
Here we change to new object frames (blue) but draw the same square at time=0 and time=1 using new object coordinates. If the interpolation satisfies right invariance, we will get the same animation of the square.

7.2 The Representation

A *quaternion* is simply a four-tuple of real numbers, on which we will soon define suitable operations.

We write a quaternion as

$$\left[\begin{array}{c} w \\ \hat{\mathbf{c}} \end{array} \right],$$

where w is a scalar and $\hat{\mathbf{c}}$ is a coordinate 3-vector. We have added the "hat" notation to $\hat{\mathbf{c}}$ to distinguish it from a coordinate 4-vector.

To represent a rotation of θ degrees about a unit length axis $\hat{\mathbf{k}}$, we use the quaternion

$$\left[\begin{array}{c} \cos(\frac{\theta}{2}) \\ \sin(\frac{\theta}{2})\hat{\mathbf{k}} \end{array} \right].$$

The division by 2 looks a bit surprising, but it makes the quaternion operations, described later, work out properly. Note that a rotation of $-\theta$ degrees about the axis $-\hat{\mathbf{k}}$ gives us the same quaternion. A rotation of $\theta + 4\pi$ degrees about an axis $\hat{\mathbf{k}}$ also gives us the same quaternion. So far, so good. Oddly, a rotation of $\theta + 2\pi$ degrees about an axis $\hat{\mathbf{k}}$, which in fact is the same rotation, gives us the negated quaternion

$$\left[\begin{array}{c} -\cos(\frac{\theta}{2}) \\ -\sin(\frac{\theta}{2})\hat{\mathbf{k}} \end{array} \right].$$

This oddity will complicate matters a bit later on when we define the power operator.

The quaternions

$$\left[\begin{array}{c} 1 \\ \hat{\mathbf{0}} \end{array} \right], \left[\begin{array}{c} -1 \\ \hat{\mathbf{0}} \end{array} \right]$$

represent the identity rotation matrix.

The quaternions

$$\left[\begin{array}{c} 0 \\ \hat{\mathbf{k}} \end{array} \right], \left[\begin{array}{c} 0 \\ -\hat{\mathbf{k}} \end{array} \right]$$

represent a 180-degree rotation about $\hat{\mathbf{k}}$.

Any quaternion of the form

$$\left[\begin{array}{c} \cos(\frac{\theta}{2}) \\ \sin(\frac{\theta}{2})\hat{\mathbf{k}} \end{array} \right]$$

has a norm (square root of sum of squares of the four entries) of 1. Conversely, any such *unit* norm quaternion can be interpreted (along with its negation) as a unique rotation matrix.

7.3 Operations

Multiplication of a (not necessarily unit norm) quaternion by a scalar is defined as

$$\alpha \begin{bmatrix} w \\ \hat{\mathbf{c}} \end{bmatrix} = \begin{bmatrix} \alpha w \\ \alpha \hat{\mathbf{c}} \end{bmatrix}.$$

Multiplication between two (not necessarily unit norm) quaternions is defined using the following strange looking operation

$$\begin{bmatrix} w_1 \\ \hat{\mathbf{c}}_1 \end{bmatrix}\begin{bmatrix} w_2 \\ \hat{\mathbf{c}}_2 \end{bmatrix} = \begin{bmatrix} (w_1 w_2 - \hat{\mathbf{c}}_1 \cdot \hat{\mathbf{c}}_2) \\ (w_1 \hat{\mathbf{c}}_2 + w_2 \hat{\mathbf{c}}_1 + \hat{\mathbf{c}}_1 \times \hat{\mathbf{c}}_2) \end{bmatrix}, \tag{7.2}$$

where $\cdot$ and $\times$ are the dot and cross product on 3D coordinate vectors. This strange multiplication possesses the following useful property: if $[w_i, \hat{\mathbf{c}}_i]^t$ represents the rotation matrix R_i, then the product $[w_1, \hat{\mathbf{c}}_1]^t [w_2, \hat{\mathbf{c}}_2]^t$ represents the rotation matrix $R_1 R_2$. This can be verified through a series of not particularly intuitive calculations.

The multiplicative inverse of a unit norm quaternion is

$$\begin{bmatrix} \cos(\frac{\theta}{2}) \\ \sin(\frac{\theta}{2})\hat{\mathbf{k}} \end{bmatrix}^{-1} = \begin{bmatrix} \cos(\frac{\theta}{2}) \\ -\sin(\frac{\theta}{2})\hat{\mathbf{k}} \end{bmatrix}.$$

This quaternion simply rotates by $-\theta$ around the same axis. (Inverses can also be defined for non-unit norm quaternions, but we will not need this.)

Importantly, we can use quaternion multiplication to apply a rotation to a coordinate vector. Suppose we have the 4-coordinate vector $\mathbf{c} = [\hat{\mathbf{c}}, 1]^t$, and we left multiply it by a 4 by 4 rotation matrix R to get

$$\mathbf{c}' = R\mathbf{c},$$

where the resulting 4-coordinate vector is of the form $\mathbf{c}' = [\hat{\mathbf{c}}', 1]^t$. To do this with quaternions, let R be represented with the unit norm quaternion

$$\begin{bmatrix} \cos(\frac{\theta}{2}) \\ \sin(\frac{\theta}{2})\hat{\mathbf{k}} \end{bmatrix}.$$

Let us take the 3-coordinate vector $\hat{\mathbf{c}}$ and use it to create the non-unit norm quaternion

$$\begin{bmatrix} 0 \\ \hat{\mathbf{c}} \end{bmatrix}.$$

Next, we perform the following triple quaternion multiplication:

$$
\begin{bmatrix} \cos(\frac{\theta}{2}) \\ \sin(\frac{\theta}{2})\hat{\mathbf{k}} \end{bmatrix}
\begin{bmatrix} 0 \\ \hat{\mathbf{c}} \end{bmatrix}
\begin{bmatrix} \cos(\frac{\theta}{2}) \\ \sin(\frac{\theta}{2})\hat{\mathbf{k}} \end{bmatrix}^{-1}.
\tag{7.3}
$$

It can again be verified through a series of not particularly intuitive calculations that the result of this triple quaternion product is in fact a quaternion of the form

$$
\begin{bmatrix} 0 \\ \hat{\mathbf{c}}' \end{bmatrix},
$$

where $\hat{\mathbf{c}}'$ is the 3-coordinate vector of the desired answer.

Thus, quaternions on the one hand explicitly encode the rotation axis and angle and on the other hand possess operations that allow us easily to manipulate them like rotations.

7.4   Power

Given a unit norm quaternion representing a rotation, we can raise it to the power α as follows. We first extract the unit axis $\hat{\mathbf{k}}$ by normalizing the three last entries of the quaternion. Next, we extract θ using the `atan2` function. This gives us a unique value $\theta/2 \in [-\pi \ldots \pi]$, and thus a unique $\theta \in [-2\pi \ldots 2\pi]$. Then we define

$$
\begin{bmatrix} \cos(\frac{\theta}{2}) \\ \sin(\frac{\theta}{2})\hat{\mathbf{k}} \end{bmatrix}^{\alpha}
=
\begin{bmatrix} \cos(\frac{\alpha\theta}{2}) \\ \sin(\frac{\alpha\theta}{2})\hat{\mathbf{k}} \end{bmatrix}.
$$

As α goes from 0 to 1, we get a series of rotations with angles going between 0 and θ.

If $\cos(\frac{\theta}{2}) > 0$, we get $\theta/2 \in [-\pi/2 \ldots \pi/2]$, and thus $\theta \in [-\pi \ldots \pi]$. In this case, when we use $\alpha \in [0 \ldots 1]$ to interpolate between two orientations, we will be interpolating the "short way" between the orientations. Conversely, if $\cos(\frac{\theta}{2}) < 0$, then $|\theta| \in [\pi \ldots 2\pi]$, and we will be interpolating the "long way" (greater than 180 degrees). In general, it is more natural to interpolate the short way between two orientations, and so when given a quaternion with negative first coordinate, we always negate the quaternion before applying the power operation.

7.4.1   Slerp and Lerp

Putting all this together, if we want to interpolate between two frames that are related to the world frame through the rotation matrices R_0 and R_1, and if these two matrices correspond to the two quaternions

$$
\begin{bmatrix} \cos(\frac{\theta_0}{2}) \\ \sin(\frac{\theta_0}{2})\hat{\mathbf{k}}_0 \end{bmatrix},
\begin{bmatrix} \cos(\frac{\theta_1}{2}) \\ \sin(\frac{\theta_1}{2})\hat{\mathbf{k}}_1 \end{bmatrix},
$$

then we simply need to compute the quaternion:

$$\left(\begin{bmatrix} \cos(\frac{\theta_1}{2}) \\ \sin(\frac{\theta_1}{2})\hat{\mathbf{k}}_1 \end{bmatrix} \begin{bmatrix} \cos(\frac{\theta_0}{2}) \\ \sin(\frac{\theta_0}{2})\hat{\mathbf{k}}_0 \end{bmatrix}^{-1} \right)^{\alpha} \begin{bmatrix} \cos(\frac{\theta_0}{2}) \\ \sin(\frac{\theta_0}{2})\hat{\mathbf{k}}_0 \end{bmatrix}. \tag{7.4}$$

This interpolation operation is often called *spherical linear interpolation* or just *slerping* for the following reason. Unit norm quaternions are simply 4-tuples of real numbers with sum-of-squares equal to one; thus, we can think of these geometrically as points on the unit sphere in $\mathbb{R}^4$. It can be shown (see later) that if you start with two unit norm quaternions and then interpolate them using equation (7.4), the resulting path in $\mathbb{R}^4$, in fact, corresponds exactly to a great arc connecting these two points on the unit sphere. Moreover, the interpolation proceeds along this path with arc length proportional to α.

In any dimension n, a trigonometric argument can be used to show that spherical linear interpolation between any two unit vectors, $\vec{v}_0$ and $\vec{v}_1$, can be calculated as

$$\frac{\sin[(1-\alpha)\Omega]}{\sin(\Omega)}\vec{v}_0 + \frac{\sin(\alpha\Omega)}{\sin(\Omega)}\vec{v}_1, \tag{7.5}$$

where Ω is the angle between the vectors in $\mathbb{R}^n$. Thus, applying this to our two unit quaternions in $\mathbb{R}^4$, we see that we can replace equation (7.4) with the equivalent interpolant

$$\frac{\sin[(1-\alpha)\Omega]}{\sin(\Omega)} \begin{bmatrix} \cos(\frac{\theta_0}{2}) \\ \sin(\frac{\theta_0}{2})\hat{\mathbf{k}}_0 \end{bmatrix} + \frac{\sin(\alpha\Omega)}{\sin(\Omega)} \begin{bmatrix} \cos(\frac{\theta_1}{2}) \\ \sin(\frac{\theta_1}{2})\hat{\mathbf{k}}_1 \end{bmatrix}, \tag{7.6}$$

where Ω is the angle between the initial and final quaternions in $\mathbb{R}^4$. Later, we sketch the steps needed to verify the equivalence of equations (7.4) and (7.6). Note that as with equation (7.4), in order to select "the short interpolation" of less than 180 degrees, we must negate (any) one of the two quaternions if the four-dimensional dot product between the two quaternions is negative.

From this point of view, we see that we can approximate equation (7.4), and thus equation (7.6), with the simpler linear interpolation in $\mathbb{R}^4$. That is, we can simply compute

$$(1-\alpha) \begin{bmatrix} \cos(\frac{\theta_0}{2}) \\ \sin(\frac{\theta_0}{2})\hat{\mathbf{k}}_0 \end{bmatrix} + (\alpha) \begin{bmatrix} \cos(\frac{\theta_1}{2}) \\ \sin(\frac{\theta_1}{2})\hat{\mathbf{k}}_1 \end{bmatrix}.$$

Because this interpolant is no longer a unit norm quaternion, we must then normalize the result, but this is easy to do. Importantly, this interpolation process, which is called *lerping*, traces out the same path of quaternions that the more complicated slerp does (rotating through a single fixed axis), though its rotation angle no longer moves evenly with α (see figure 7.4).

The lerp operation is both left and right invariant. For example, left invariance follows from

$$(1-\alpha)\begin{bmatrix} w_l \\ \hat{\mathbf{c}}_l \end{bmatrix}\begin{bmatrix} w_0 \\ \hat{\mathbf{c}}_0 \end{bmatrix} + (\alpha)\begin{bmatrix} w_l \\ \hat{\mathbf{c}}_l \end{bmatrix}\begin{bmatrix} w_1 \\ \hat{\mathbf{c}}_1 \end{bmatrix}$$

$$= \begin{bmatrix} w_l \\ \hat{\mathbf{c}}_l \end{bmatrix}\left((1-\alpha)\begin{bmatrix} w_0 \\ \hat{\mathbf{c}}_0 \end{bmatrix} + (\alpha)\begin{bmatrix} w_1 \\ \hat{\mathbf{c}}_1 \end{bmatrix}\right)$$

as scalar multiplication commutes across quaternion multiplication, and quaternion multiplication distributes over sums. Similarly, we can directly see from its form that equation (7.6) is also both left and right invariant. The only tricky part is going through the calculations that show that the angle, Ω, is left and right invariant.

Lerp can be implemented more efficiently than slerp. More importantly, it generalizes quite easily to the case of blending between n different rotations. We can simply blend the quaternions in $\mathbb{R}^4$, and then normalize the result. Such n-way blends can be useful when constructing splines of rotations (see section 9.3) and when performing skinning for animation (see section 23.1.2). There are also methods that perform n-way blending

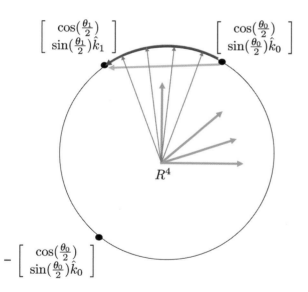

Figure 7.4
Our rotation interpolation can be interpreted as taking a constant speed path along a great arc (brown) connecting two quaternions on the unit sphere in $\mathbb{R}^4$. This can be approximated by taking a constant speed linear path (green) inside of the unit sphere, followed by normalization (cyan). The normalized linear interpolation follows the same path on the unit sphere in $\mathbb{R}^4$, but does not have constant speed on the great arc. Note that in order to choose the shorter rotation we must negate any of one of the two quaternions if that would form a smaller path on the sphere.

intrinsically on the sphere, though such methods do not come with a constant time evaluation method [10].

Equivalence of Power-Based and Sphere-Based Slerps (Optional)   Here we sketch the steps needed to establish the equivalence between the power-based and sphere-based interpolations on rotations.

• It can be argued (as we just did above) that equation (7.6) is left invariant. Note that we already established left invariance earlier for equation (7.4). Because of the left invariance of both interpolation methods, we can, without loss of generality, just consider the case where R_0 is the identity.

• Assuming R_0 is the identity, the power-based interpolant of equation (7.4) gives us $(R_1)^\alpha$, which is

$$
\begin{bmatrix}
\cos(\frac{\alpha\theta_1}{2}) \\
\sin(\frac{\alpha\theta_1}{2})\hat{\mathbf{k}}_1
\end{bmatrix}.
\tag{7.7}
$$

• Because R_0 is the identity, the initial quaternion is $[1, \hat{\mathbf{0}}]^t$. Plugging this into equation (7.6), we can verify that this also agrees with equation (7.7).

• A trigonometric argument can be used to show that equation (7.6) corresponds geometrically to interpolation along the surface of a sphere.

7.5 Code

A quaternion class can be encoded very simply.

We define `Quat` as a four-tuple of reals. We then define the multiplication (`q1 * q2`) as in equation (7.2). Given a unit norm quaternion, `Quat q`, we define `inv(q)`. Given a unit norm quaternion, `Quat q`, and a `Cvec4 c`, we define (`q * c`), which applies the rotation to the coordinate vector **c**, as in equation (7.3), and returns the coordinate vector **c'**.

We also write code to implement the `MakeRotation` functions as we had for matrices.

Given a unit norm quaternion `q` and a real number `alpha`, we define the power operator: `pow(q,alpha)`. Given two quaternions `q0` and `q1`, we can define the interpolating quaternion: `slerp(q0,q1,alpha)`. Remember that when implementing slerp, we need to negate the quaternion (`q1 * inv(q0)` before calling `pow` if its first coordinate is negative in order to interpolate the "short way."

7.6 Putting Back the Translations

Thus far, we have discussed how quaternions are useful for representing rotations but have ignored translations. Now we will discuss how to use quaternions in concert with translation vectors to represent rigid body transformations.

A rigid body transformation, or RBT, can be described by composing a translation and a rotation.

$$A = TR$$

$$\begin{bmatrix} r & t \\ 0 & 1 \end{bmatrix} = \begin{bmatrix} i & t \\ 0 & 1 \end{bmatrix} \begin{bmatrix} r & 0 \\ 0 & 1 \end{bmatrix}.$$

Thus, we can represent this as an object:

```
class RigTform{
  Cvec4 t;
  Quat r;
};
```

Remember that because t represents a translation vector, its fourth coordinate is 0.

7.6.1 Interpolation

Given two RBTs $O_0 = (O_0)_T(O_0)_R$ and $O_1 = (O_1)_T(O_1)_R$, we can interpolate between them by first linearly interpolating the two translation vectors to obtain the translation T_α, then slerping between the rotation quaternions to obtain the rotation R_α, and finally setting the interpolated RBT O_α to be $T_\alpha R_\alpha$. If $\vec{\mathbf{o}}_0^t = \vec{\mathbf{w}}^t O_0$ and $\vec{\mathbf{o}}_1^t = \vec{\mathbf{w}}^t O_1$, we can then set $\vec{\mathbf{o}}_\alpha^t = \vec{\mathbf{w}}^t O_\alpha$. Under this interpolation, the origin of $\vec{\mathbf{o}}^t$ travels in a straight line with constant velocity, and the vector basis of $\vec{\mathbf{o}}^t$ rotates with constant angular velocity about a fixed axis. As we already said, this is very natural, as an object flying through space with no forces acting on it has its center of mass follow a straight line, and its orientation spins along a fixed axis. Additionally, this unique geometric interpolant between $\vec{\mathbf{o}}_0^t$ and $\vec{\mathbf{o}}_1^t$ can be expressed with reference to any specific coordinates. Therefore, it does not depend on the choice of world frame and must be left invariant.

It is important to note that this RBT interpolant is not right invariant. If you change the object frames and interpolate between them using this method, the **new** origin will travel in a straight line, whereas the old origin will trace out a curved path (see figure 7.5). Thus, this method makes the most sense where there is a meaningful notion of "center" for the object being interpolated. In cases where there is no such center, the most natural answer is less obvious (but see, e.g., [35]).

7.6.2 Operations

Going back to our drawing code of section 6.2, we can now represent the eyeRBT and objRBT RBTs using the RigTform data type instead of Matrix4.

To create useful rigid body transformations, we need the following operations:

```
RigTForm identity();
RigTForm makeXRotation(const double ang);
```

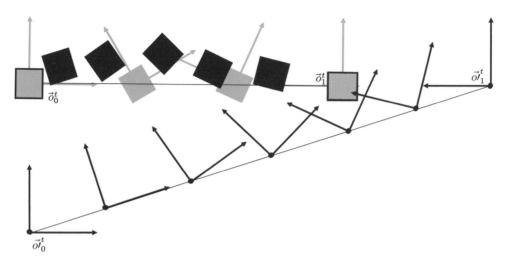

Figure 7.5
Here we change the object frames (from green to blue) but draw the same square at time=0 and time=1 using new object coordinates. Our RBT interpolation does not satisfy right invariance. For intermediate α, the blue square diverges from the green square.

```
RigTForm makeYRotation(const double ang);
RigTForm makeZRotation(const double ang);
RigTForm makeTranslation(const double tx,
            const double ty, const double tz);
```

We need to code the product of a `RigTForm` A and a `Cvec4` c, which returns `A.r * c + A.t`.

Next, we need to code the product of two `RigTForm`. To understand how to do this, let us look at the product of two such rigid body transformations.

$$\begin{bmatrix} i & t_1 \\ 0 & 1 \end{bmatrix}\begin{bmatrix} r_1 & 0 \\ 0 & 1 \end{bmatrix}\begin{bmatrix} i & t_2 \\ 0 & 1 \end{bmatrix}\begin{bmatrix} r_2 & 0 \\ 0 & 1 \end{bmatrix}$$

$$=\begin{bmatrix} i & t_1 \\ 0 & 1 \end{bmatrix}\begin{bmatrix} r_1 & r_1 t_2 \\ 0 & 1 \end{bmatrix}\begin{bmatrix} r_2 & 0 \\ 0 & 1 \end{bmatrix}$$

$$=\begin{bmatrix} i & t_1 \\ 0 & 1 \end{bmatrix}\begin{bmatrix} i & r_1 t_2 \\ 0 & 1 \end{bmatrix}\begin{bmatrix} r_1 & 0 \\ 0 & 1 \end{bmatrix}\begin{bmatrix} r_2 & 0 \\ 0 & 1 \end{bmatrix}$$

$$=\begin{bmatrix} i & t_1 + r_1 t_2 \\ 0 & 1 \end{bmatrix}\begin{bmatrix} r_1 r_2 & 0 \\ 0 & 1 \end{bmatrix}.$$

From this we see that the result is a new rigid transform with translation $t_1 + r_1 t_2$ and rotation $r_1 r_2$.

Next, we need to code the inverse operator for this data type. If we look at the inverse of a rigid body transformation, we see that

$$\left(\begin{bmatrix} i & t \\ 0 & 1 \end{bmatrix} \begin{bmatrix} r & 0 \\ 0 & 1 \end{bmatrix} \right)^{-1}$$

$$= \begin{bmatrix} r & 0 \\ 0 & 1 \end{bmatrix}^{-1} \begin{bmatrix} i & t \\ 0 & 1 \end{bmatrix}^{-1}$$

$$= \begin{bmatrix} r^{-1} & 0 \\ 0 & 1 \end{bmatrix} \begin{bmatrix} i & -t \\ 0 & 1 \end{bmatrix}$$

$$= \begin{bmatrix} r^{-1} & -(r^{-1}t) \\ 0 & 1 \end{bmatrix}$$

$$= \begin{bmatrix} i & -(r^{-1}t) \\ 0 & 1 \end{bmatrix} \begin{bmatrix} r^{-1} & 0 \\ 0 & 1 \end{bmatrix}.$$

Thus, we see that the result is a new rigid body transformation with translation $-(r^{-1}t)$ and rotation r^{-1}.

Given this infrastructure, we can now recode the function doMtoOwrtA(RigTForm M, RigTform O, RigTForm A) using our new data type.

Finally, to communicate with the vertex shader using 4 by 4 matrices, we need a procedure Matrix4 makeRotation(quat q), which implements equation (2.5). Then, the matrix for a rigid body transformation can be computed as

```
matrix4 makeTRmatrix(const RigTform& rbt){
  matrix4 T = makeTranslation(rbt.t);
  matrix4 R = makeRotation(rbt.r);
  return  T * R;
}
```

Thus, our drawing code starts with

```
Matrix4 MVM = makeTRmatrix(inv(eyeRbt) * objRbt);
\\ can right multiply scales here
Matrix4 NMVM = normalMatrix(MVM);
sendModelViewNormalMatrix(MVM,NMVM);
```

Note that the way we have structured our computation, we will not need any code that takes a Matrix4 and converts it to a Quat.

Other than switching from the Matrix4 data type to the RigTForm type, the rest of our code, which keeps track of the various rigid body frames, does not need to be altered. In this new implementation, a scale is still represented by a Matrix4.

Exercises

7.1 On the book's website, we have code implementing much of a Quat class. Use this code to create a rigid body transformation class. Use this class instead of the Matrix4 class to represent rigid body transformations in your OpenGL code from exercise 6.6.

7.2 Implement the power operator for the Quat class and test it by linearly interpolating a cube between two orientations.

8 Balls: Track and Arc

In an interactive computer graphics application, we often track the mouse and use this to specify object motion. Translations are reasonably straightforward to handle. In section 6.5, when the left mouse button was held down, we interpreted left/right mouse motion as x translation and up/down motion as y translation (all with respect to the eye's frame). When the right mouse button was held down, we interpreted up/down motion as z translation.

Rotations are a bit less obvious: There are many ways to link mouse motions to rotations, and each of them has a slightly different feel for the user. Earlier, in section 6.5, we described a simple interface of interpreting mouse displacement as some specific sequence of rotations about the x and y axis. In this section, we will describe two more-sophisticated interfaces: arcball and trackball. The main advantage of the trackball interface is that it should feel like moving a physical sphere in space. The main advantage of the arcball interface is that if the user starts moving the mouse at one point and finishes at another point, the final rotation will not depend on the path the mouse took in between.

Let us assume that we are moving an object with respect to the frame $\vec{\mathbf{a}}^t = \vec{\mathbf{w}}^t(O)_T(E)_R$, as we did in section 5.2.1. The user clicks on the screen and drags the mouse. We wish to interpret this user motion as some rotation M that is applied to $\vec{\mathbf{o}}^t$ with respect to $\vec{\mathbf{a}}^t$. In this chapter, we will describe two different methods, trackball and arcball, for computing a value of M.

8.1 The Interfaces

We imagine a sphere of some chosen radius that is centered at $\tilde{o}$, the origin of $\vec{\mathbf{o}}^t$. Often, it is useful actually to draw this sphere in wireframe surrounding the object so that the user can better feel what is happening. Suppose the user clicks on the screen at some pixel s_1 over the sphere in the image; we can interpret this as the user selecting some 3D point $\tilde{p}_1$ on the sphere. Suppose the user then moves the mouse to some other pixel s_2 over the sphere; we interpret this as a second point $\tilde{p}_2$ on the sphere.

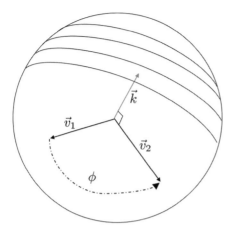

Figure 8.1
The setup for trackball and arcball. Two selected points on the surface of a sphere give us two vectors. These in turn give us an angle and axis.

Given these two points, define the two vectors $\vec{v}_1$, $\vec{v}_2$ as the unit length vectors in the directions of the vectors $\tilde{p}_1 - \tilde{o}$ and $\tilde{p}_2 - \tilde{o}$, respectively. Define the angle $\phi = \arccos(\vec{v}_1 \cdot \vec{v}_2)$ and the axis $\vec{k} = \text{normalize}(\vec{v}_1 \times \vec{v}_2)$ (see figure 8.1).

In the trackball interface, we define M as the rotation of ϕ degrees about the axis $\vec{k}$. In the arcball interface, we define M as the rotation of 2ϕ degrees about the axis $\vec{k}$. Using quaternion operations, the rotation of 2ϕ degrees about the axis $\vec{k}$ can be represented by the quaternion

$$
\begin{bmatrix} \cos(\phi) \\ \sin(\phi)\hat{\mathbf{k}} \end{bmatrix} = \begin{bmatrix} \hat{\mathbf{v}}_1 \cdot \hat{\mathbf{v}}_2 \\ \hat{\mathbf{v}}_1 \times \hat{\mathbf{v}}_2 \end{bmatrix} = \begin{bmatrix} 0 \\ \hat{\mathbf{v}}_2 \end{bmatrix} \begin{bmatrix} 0 \\ -\hat{\mathbf{v}}_1 \end{bmatrix},
\tag{8.1}
$$

where $\hat{\mathbf{k}}$, $\hat{\mathbf{v}}_1$, and $\hat{\mathbf{v}}_2$ are the coordinate 3-vectors representing the vectors $\vec{k}$, $\vec{v}_1$, and $\vec{v}_2$ with respect to the frame $\vec{\mathbf{a}}^t$.

8.2 Properties

The trackball interface is quite natural: It feels like the user is simply grabbing a physical point on a sphere and dragging it around. But there is an unexpected consequence: If the user first moves her mouse on the screen from s_1 to s_2, and then from s_2 to s_3, the composed trackball rotations will be different from the result of moving the mouse directly from s_1 to s_3! In both cases, the point $\tilde{p}_1$ will be rotated to $\tilde{p}_3$, but the two results can differ by some "twist" about the axis $\tilde{o} - \tilde{p}_3$. This path dependence also exists in our simple rotation interface in section 6.5.

The arcball interface has somewhat opposite properties. On the one hand, the object appears to spin twice as fast as expected. But, on the other hand, the arcball interface is indeed path independent. We can see this easily using the quaternion operations of equation (8.1). If we compose two arcball rotations, corresponding to motion from $\tilde{p}_1$ to $\tilde{p}_2$ followed by motion from $\tilde{p}_2$ to $\tilde{p}_3$, we get

$$
\begin{bmatrix} \hat{\mathbf{v}}_2 \cdot \hat{\mathbf{v}}_3 \\ \hat{\mathbf{v}}_2 \times \hat{\mathbf{v}}_3 \end{bmatrix}
\begin{bmatrix} \hat{\mathbf{v}}_1 \cdot \hat{\mathbf{v}}_2 \\ \hat{\mathbf{v}}_1 \times \hat{\mathbf{v}}_2 \end{bmatrix}.
$$

This is because both rotations are applied with respect to the frame $\vec{\mathbf{a}}^t$, which in fact is unchanged. Using the decomposition of equation (8.1), we see that this is equal to

$$
\begin{bmatrix} 0 \\ \hat{\mathbf{v}}_3 \end{bmatrix}
\begin{bmatrix} 0 \\ -\hat{\mathbf{v}}_2 \end{bmatrix}
\begin{bmatrix} 0 \\ \hat{\mathbf{v}}_2 \end{bmatrix}
\begin{bmatrix} 0 \\ -\hat{\mathbf{v}}_1 \end{bmatrix}
=
\begin{bmatrix} 0 \\ \hat{\mathbf{v}}_3 \end{bmatrix}
\begin{bmatrix} 0 \\ -\hat{\mathbf{v}}_1 \end{bmatrix}
=
\begin{bmatrix} \hat{\mathbf{v}}_1 \cdot \hat{\mathbf{v}}_3 \\ \hat{\mathbf{v}}_1 \times \hat{\mathbf{v}}_3 \end{bmatrix},
$$

which is exactly what we would have gotten had we moved directly from $\tilde{p}_1$ to $\tilde{p}_3$.

8.3 Implementation

Trackball and arcball can be directly implemented using either 4 by 4 matrices or quaternions to represent the transformation M.

Because all of the operations depend only on vectors and not on points, the origin of the coordinate system is unimportant, and we can work in any coordinates system that shares the axes of $\vec{\mathbf{a}}^t$; in particular, we can use eye coordinates.

One slightly tricky part is computing the coordinates of the point on the sphere corresponding to a selected pixel (this is essentially ray-tracing, which is covered in chapter 20). One simple way to get approximately the correct behavior is to work in "window coordinates." In this case, we think of a 3D space where the x axis is the horizontal axis of the screen, the y axis is the vertical axis of the screen, and the z axis is coming out of the screen. We can think of the sphere's center as simply sitting on the screen. Given the (x, y) window coordinates of the point where the user has clicked, we can easily find the z coordinate on the sphere using the sphere equation $(x - c_x)^2 + (y - c_y)^2 + (z - 0)^2 - r^2 = 0$, where $[c_x, c_y, 0]^t$ are the window coordinates of the center of the sphere.

Using this approach, we still need to compute the center of the sphere in window coordinates, as well as its projected radius on the screen. This will require an understanding of camera matrices, a topic we will cover in chapter 10. For completeness, we give code for this procedure on the book's website.

Exercise

8.1 Implement the arcball and trackball interfaces. This can be done either using a quaternion or matrix implementation. Our web page provides a function that returns the approximate center and radius on the screen of the projected sphere.

9 Smooth Interpolation

Let us consider a technique known as keyframe animation. In this setting, an animator describes snapshots of a 3D computer graphics animation at a set of discrete times. Each snapshot is defined by some set of modeling parameters. These parameters may include the locations and orientations of various objects as well as the camera. Other parameters may include things like the joint angles of a model that has movable limbs. To create a smooth animation from these *keyframes*, the computer's job is to smoothly "fill in" the parameter values over a continuous range of times. If one of these animated parameters is called, say, c, and each of our discrete snapshots is called c_i where i is some range of integers, then our job is to go from the discrete snapshots of this parameter to a continuous function of time, $c(t)$. We will typically want the function $c(t)$ to be sufficiently smooth so that the animation does not appear too jerky.

In this chapter, we will discuss simple ways to smoothly interpolate such a set of discrete values over a part of the real line using *splines*. For example, in figure 9.1 we show a function $c(t)$, with $t \in [0 \ldots 8]$, that interpolates the discrete values associated with the integers c_i, with $i \in -1 \ldots 9$, shown as blue dots (the need for the extra noninterpolated values at -1 and 9 will be made clear later). Our splines will be functions that are made up of individual pieces, where each piece is some low order polynomial function. These polynomial pieces will be selected so that they "stitch up" smoothly. Splines are often used in computer graphics because they are easy to represent, evaluate, and control. In particular, their behavior is much easier to predict than, say, a function described by a single high-order polynomial function.

We will also show how such representations can be used to describe curves in the plane and curves in space. Such curves have many uses beyond animation. For example, they can be used to describe the outlines of character shapes in a font.

9.1 Cubic Bezier Functions

We start by just looking at how to represent a cubic polynomial function $c(t)$ with $t \in [0 \ldots 1]$ (see figure 9.2). There are many possible ways to do this; here we describe

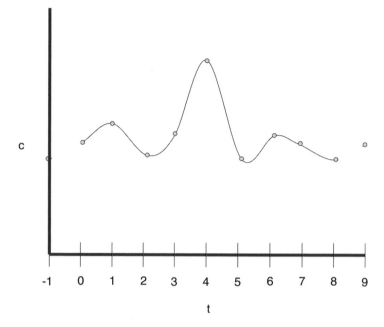

c

-1   0   1   2   3   4   5   6   7   8   9

t

Figure 9.1
A spline function is used to interpolate smoothly a set of control values shown as dots.

the *Bezier* representation. This is a convenient representation where the parameters have a geometric interpretation and where evaluation reduces to repeated linear interpolation.

In the cubic Bezier representation, a cubic function is described by four values c_0, d_0, e_0, and c_1 called *control values*. In figure 9.2, we have visualized these data as points in the 2D (t, c) plane with coordinates $[0, c_0]^t$, $[1/3, d_0]^t$, $[2/3, e_0]^t$, and $[1, c_1]^t$. We have also drawn in light blue a poly-line connecting these points; this is called the *control polygon*.

To evaluate the function $c(t)$ at any value of t, we perform the following sequence of linear interpolations

$$f = (1-t)c_0 + td_0 \qquad\qquad (9.1)$$

$$g = (1-t)d_0 + te_0$$

$$h = (1-t)e_0 + tc_1$$

$$m = (1-t)f + tg$$

$$n = (1-t)g + th$$

$$c(t) = (1-t)m + tn.$$

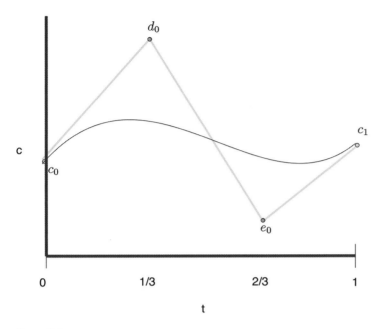

Figure 9.2
A Bezier cubic function is defined by four control values.

In figure 9.3, we have visualized the steps of this computation for $t = 0.3$ as linear interpolation in 2D.

9.1.1   Properties
It is easy to verify the following properties of the function $c(t)$.

By unwrapping the evaluation steps above, we can verify that $c(t)$ has the form

$$c(t) = c_0(1-t)^3 + 3d_0 t(1-t)^2 + 3e_0 t^2(1-t) + c_1 t^3.$$

Clearly, it is a cubic function. Moreover, the c_i are interpolated: $c(0) = c_0$ and $c(1) = c_1$. Taking derivatives, we see that $c'(0) = 3(d_0 - c_0)$ and $c'(1) = 3(c_1 - e_0)$. In figure 9.2, we see indeed that the slope of $c(t)$ matches the slope of the control polygon at 0 and 1. We can also see that if we set $c_0 = d_0 = e_0 = c_1 = 1$, then $c(t) = 1$ for all t. This property is called *partition of unity* and means that adding a constant value to all control values results in simply adding this constant to $c(t)$.

9.1.2   Translation
If we want a cubic function to interpolate values c_i and c_{i+1} at $t = i$ and $t = i + 1$, respectively, and calling our two other control points d_i and e_i, we just have to "translate" the evaluation algorithm of equation (9.1) to get

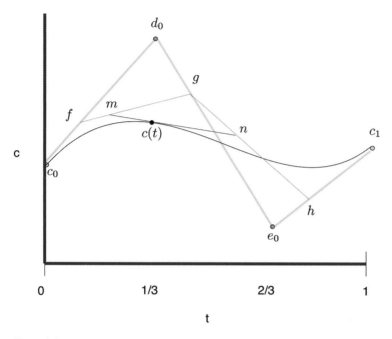

Figure 9.3
For any value of t, the Bezier function can be evaluated by a sequence of linear interpolation steps visualized here.

$$f = (1 - t + i)c_i + (t - i)d_i$$

$$g = (1 - t + i)d_i + (t - i)e_i$$

$$h = (1 - t + i)e_i + (t - i)c_{i+1}$$

$$m = (1 - t + i)f + (t - i)g$$

$$n = (1 - t + i)g + (t - i)h$$

$$c(t) = (1 - t + i)m + (t - i)n.$$

9.2   Catmull–Rom Splines

Let us return now to our original problem of interpolating a set of values c_i for $i \in -1 \ldots n+1$. An easy way to do this is using *Catmull–Rom splines*. This method defines a function $c(t)$ for values of $t \in [0 \ldots n]$. The function is defined by n cubic functions, each supported over a unit interval $t \in [i \ldots i+1]$. The pieces are chosen to interpolate the c_i values and to agree on their first derivatives.

Each function is described in its Bezier representation using four control values: c_i, d_i, e_i, and c_{i+1}. From our input data, we already have the c_i values. To set the d_i and e_i values, we impose the constraint $c'(i) = \frac{1}{2}(c_{i+1} - c_{i-1})$. In other words, we look forward and backward one sample to determine its slope at $t = i$; this is why we need the extra extreme values c_{-1} and c_{n+1}. Meanwhile, for the Bezier function defined over the unit inverval $t \in [i \dots i+1]$, we have $c'(i) = 3(d_i - c_i)$ and $c'(i+1) = 3(c_{i+1} - e_i)$. This tells us that we need to set

$$d_i = \frac{1}{6}(c_{i+1} - c_{i-1}) + c_i$$

$$e_i = \frac{-1}{6}(c_{i+2} - c_i) + c_{i+1}.$$

This process is visualized in figure 9.4. Here we show the c, d, and e values (in red) that are needed for one cubic segment. We show the control polygon of one cubic piece in light blue. The d and e are determined using the chords shown in dark blue.

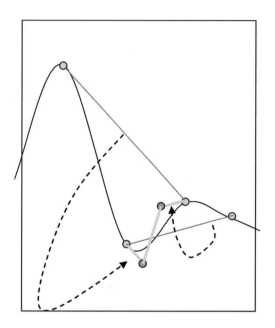

Figure 9.4
A Catmull–Rom spline function is made up of individual cubic pieces. Each piece can be described in Bezier form. Here we show how one of the Bezier forms is determined from the input control values. The arrows point to segments that have the same slope.

9.3 Quaternion Splining

The Bezier and Catmull–Rom representations can be used to interpolate any real-valued animation parameter. For example, if we have a time-varying translation, each of its three defining parameters t_x, t_y, and t_z can be interpolated independently.

If we want to interpolate a set of orientations, the theory does not directly apply. There is ongoing research on the best theoretical approach to use in this case. One efficient hack is to simply substitute appropriate quaternion operations for the scalar operations in the algorithms given earlier. With these substitutions, scalar addition becomes quaternion multiplication, scalar negation becomes quaternion inversion, and scalar multiplication becomes quaternion power. Doing so, Bezier evaluation steps of the form

$$r = (1-t)p + tq$$

become

$$r = \texttt{slerp(p,q,t)},$$

and the d_i and e_i quaternion values are defined as

$$d_i = \left[(c_{i+1} c_{i-1}^{-1})^{\frac{1}{6}} \right] c_i$$

$$e_i = \left[(c_{i+2} c_i^{-1})^{\frac{-1}{6}} \right] c_{i+1}.$$

As in section 7.4, in order to interpolate "the short way," we negate the quaternion $c_{i+1} c_{i-1}^{-1}$ before applying the power operator if its first coordinate is negative.

Other slerp-based quaternions spline methods are described in [68] and [66]. Another more natural but more expensive method based on n-way spherical blends is described in [10].

Another alternative, often used in practice, is simply to treat the quaternions as points in $\mathbb{R}^4$, do standard splining on these four coordinates, and then normalize the result to get a unit norm quaternion. In this context, the conditions needed for continuity between segments are described in [22].

9.4 Other Splines

There are a variety of other types of spline functions whose names we will mention (as you may run across these) but will not go into in detail. These splines are studied heavily in the field of *computer-aided geometric design*. The interested reader may wish to read [21] and [59].

A *natural cubic spline* is a function that interpolates its control values and minimizes the integral of second derivative. Such a spline is in some sense "the smoothest" interpolant. It turns out that a natural spline will be made up of cubic pieces that meet up with agreement in both first and second derivative. A linear system needs to be solved to determine such a natural cubic spline. The behavior of this spline is global: moving one control value will affect the function over its entire range.

A *uniform (cubic) B-spline* represents a function using a set of cubic polynomials that are stitched together so that they match in second derivative as well. Unlike the natural cubic spline, this function changes only locally with changes in a control value. A B-spline, however, does not interpolate any of its control values but merely approximates them.

A *nonuniform B-spline* is a generalization of the uniform B-spline that allows for non-uniform spacing of the control values over the t line while maintaining two degrees of continuity.

Finally, a *nonuniform rational B-spline* (or NURB) is a generalization of the non-uniform B-spline where each "piece" of the function is a rational expression (a ratio) of two polynomial functions. The rational form allows one to model many classical algebraic shapes.

9.5 Curves in Space

For the purpose of animation, we have looked at univariate scalar functions (where we think of the free variable as time). One can also use a spline representation to describe curves in space. In this case, the spline curve is controlled by a set of *control points* $\tilde{c}_i$ in 2D or 3D. Applying the spline construction independently to the x, y, and z coordinates, one gets a point-valued spline function $\tilde{c}(t)$: You can think of this as a point flying through space over time, tracing out the spline curve, γ.

Using the Bezier construction with four control points, we obtain a *Bezier curve* (see figure 9.5), and using the Catmull–Rom construction on a set of control points, we obtain a *Catmull–Rom curve* (see figure 9.6).

In the context of curves, the partition of unity property implies that if one translates all of the control points by some fixed amount, then this just translates the curve γ by that amount.

Additionally, for Bezier (and also B-spline) curves, for each t, the value $\tilde{c}(t)$ is obtained by some mixture of the positions of the control points, where the mixing amounts are always between 0 and 1. As a result, the curve must lie in the "convex hull" of the control polygon defined by connecting the control points in space. This implies that the curve will not wander too far away from its control polygon.

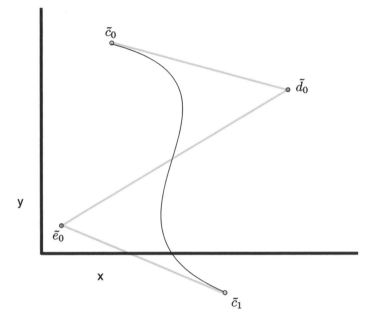

Figure 9.5
A Bezier curve in 2D.

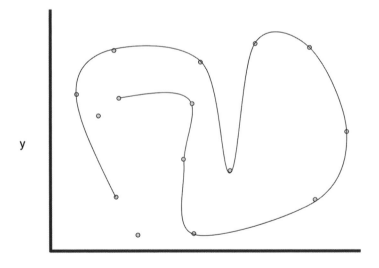

Figure 9.6
A Catmull–Rom curve in 2D.

Exercises

9.1 In this exercise, your task is to implement a keyframing infrastructure. You should begin with your robot code from Exercise 7.1.

Your system will maintain a linked list of key frames. Each keyframe will store the state of the world, including all of the joint angles and the positions and orientations of the robots and eye. At any given time, you will be in a "current frame." At any given time, you also have a "current state," which stores the joint angles, positions, and orientations of the robots and eye that are being displayed on the screen. When the user manipulates the scene, the current state is updated. You should implement the following hot keys:

- space: Copy the current keyframe to the current state.
- u: Copy the current state to the current keyframe.
- >: Advance to the next keyframe (if the current frame is not the last one). Then copy the current keyframe to the current state.
- <: Retreat to the previous keyframe (if the current frame is not the first one). Then copy the current keyframe to the current state.
- d: Delete the current keyframe (unless it is keyframe 0). Copy the previous frame to the current state. Make the previous frame the current frame.
- n: Create a new keyframe immediately after the current keyframe. Copy the current state to the new keyframe. Advance to the new keyframe.
- i: Read keyframes from input file. You are free to choose your own file format to store the keyframe data.
- w: Write the keyframes to an output file. Make sure the file format is consistent with the input format.

9.2 Your next task is to implement simple linear interpolation to create an animation from the keyframes. You will have to interpolate each joint angle, as well as the positions and orientations (represented as quaternions) of the robots and eye. In between any two keyframes, you will interpolate the above quantities using simple linear interpolation.

During the animation, you will create intermediate states by evaluating the linear interpolator at each intermediate time and then use these intermediate states to display each frame of the animation. For the orientations, you will need to use quaternion linear interpolation.

Hot keys:

- y: Play the animation.
- +: Make the animation go faster.
- −: Make the animation go slower.

You can think of the sequence of keyframes as being numbered from -1 to $n + 1$.

You will only show the animation between frames 0 and n. This will be useful when doing Catmull–Rom interpolation in the next exercise. Because the animation only runs between keyframes 0 and n, you will need at least four keyframes to display an animation. If the user tries to play the animation and there are less than four keyframes, you can ignore the command and print a warning to the console. After playing the animation, you should make the current state be keyframe n, and display this frame.

For playing back the animation, you can use the GLUT timer function `glutTimerFunc(int ms, timerCallback, int value)`. This function asks GLUT to invoke `timerCallback` with argument `value` after `ms` milliseconds have passed. Inside `timerCallback` you can call `glutTimerFunc` again to schedule another invocation of the `timerCallback`, effectively making each frame schedule the drawing of the following frame.

A possible way of implementing the animation playback is listed below. Calling `animateTimerCallback(0)` triggers the playing of the animation sequence.

```
   // Controls speed of playback.
static int millisec_between_keyframes = 2000;
   // Draw about 60 frames in each second
static int millisec_per_frame = 1000/60;

// Given t in the range [0, n], perform interpolation
// and draw the scene for the particular t.
// Returns true if we are at the end of the animation
// sequence,  false otherwise.
bool interpolateAndDisplay(float t) {...}

// Interpret "value" as milliseconds into the animation
static void animateTimerCallback(int value) {
    float t = value/(float)millisec_between_keyframes;

    bool endReached = interpolateAndDisplay(t);
    if (!endReached)
        glutTimerFunc(millisec_per_frame,
            animateTimerCallback, value + millisec_per_frame);
    else { ... }
}
```

9.3 Starting from the previous exercise, you will substitute the linear interpolation used in the first part with Catmull–Rom interpolation.

You will have one spline for each joint angle, for the positions of the robots and eye, and for the orientations of the robots and the eye.

During the animation, you will create intermediate states by evaluating the Bezier curves at intermediate times and then use these intermediate states to display an intermediate frame. For the orientations, you will need to use quaternion splines.

III CAMERAS AND RASTERIZATION

10   Projection

Until now, we have described our objects and eye in three dimensions. Our next step is to understand how to turn this into a 2D image as would be seen from the eye. To do this, we will need to model a simple camera. Throughout, we will assume that the camera is placed at the origin of the eye frame $\vec{\mathbf{e}}^t$ and that it is looking down the eye's negative z axis. We will use the notation $[x_e, y_e, z_e, 1]^t$ to refer to the eye coordinates of a point.

10.1   Pinhole Camera

The simplest possible camera is a pinhole camera (see figure 10.1). As light travels toward the film plane, most is blocked by an opaque surface placed at the $z_e = 0$ plane. But we place a very small hole in the center of the surface, at the point with eye coordinates $[0, 0, 0, 1]^t$. Only rays of light that pass through this point reach the film plane and have their intensity recorded on film. The image is recorded at a film plane placed at, say, $z_e = 1$.

In the physical world, any real camera needs a finite-sized aperture so that a measurable amount of light can pass to the film plane. And once the aperture is finite sized, a lens is needed to better "organize" and focus the incoming light. But these issues need not concern us now, as we are not building physical cameras. See chapter 21 for more on this.

In our pinhole camera, the data on the film plane need to be flipped later to obtain the desired photo. Mathematically, we can avoid this step if we instead model the pinhole camera with the film plane *in front* of the pinhole, say at the $z_e = -1$ plane (see figure 10.2). This would not make any sense in the physical world, but it works just fine as a mathematical model of a pinhole camera.

Once the picture has been created, if we hold up the photograph at the $z_e = -1$ plane and observe it with our own eye placed at the origin (see figure 10.3), it will look to us just like the original scene would have. We are exactly reproducing the data that would have reached our eye if we had stood there and looked at the scene. If we move the picture around in space, say closer to or farther from our eye, we will no longer be exactly reproducing the original scene-stimulus, but it will still appear like a reasonably valid visual representation of the original scene.

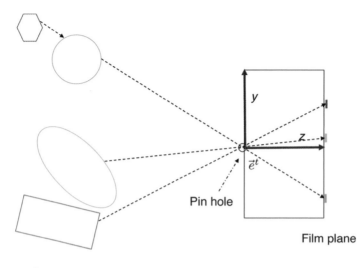

Scene geometry

Figure 10.1
A 2D pinhole camera. Light rays coming off the surfaces of the scene geometry travel (along dotted lines) through the pinhole and have their colors recorded on the film plane at $z_e = 1$. Some of these colored pixels are shown. The blue hexagon is occluded and does not appear in the image.

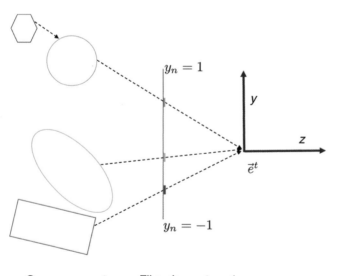

Scene geometry   Film plane at z=-1

Figure 10.2
The basic pinhole camera can be modeled with the film plane *in front of* the origin, at $z_e = -1$. The uppermost point on the image plane has a y_n normalized device coordinate of 1, and the lowermost has a y_n coordinate of -1. Any point along a dotted line would map to the same pixel in the image.

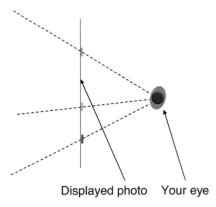

Displayed photo   Your eye

Figure 10.3
If the film plane is replaced by the photograph, and your eye is placed at the origin, then the data reaching the image will be indistinguishable from the original scene.

10.2 Basic Mathematical Model

This pinhole camera is easy to model mathematically. Let us use coordinates $[x_n, y_n]^t$ to specify points on our film plane. For the present, we choose a 2D coordinate system on our film plane such that these coordinates happen to match the eye coordinates (i.e., $x_n = x_e$ and $y_n = y_e$), but soon we shall relax this specification.

Given a point $\tilde{p}$ in the scene with eye coordinates $[x_e, y_e, z_e, 1]^t$, it is easy enough to see (say using a similar-triangles argument) that the ray from $\tilde{p}$ to the origin hits the film plane at

$$x_n = -\frac{x_e}{z_e} \tag{10.1}$$

$$y_n = -\frac{y_e}{z_e} \tag{10.2}$$

We can model this expression as a matrix operation as follows:

$$\begin{bmatrix} 1 & 0 & 0 & 0 \\ 0 & 1 & 0 & 0 \\ - & - & - & - \\ 0 & 0 & -1 & 0 \end{bmatrix} \begin{bmatrix} x_e \\ y_e \\ z_e \\ 1 \end{bmatrix} = \begin{bmatrix} x_c \\ y_c \\ - \\ w_c \end{bmatrix} = \begin{bmatrix} x_n w_n \\ y_n w_n \\ - \\ w_n \end{bmatrix}, \tag{10.3}$$

where a dash ($-$) means "don't care (yet)." We call this matrix the *projection matrix*. The raw output of the matrix multiplication, $[x_c, y_c, -, w_c]^t$, is called the *clip coordinates* of $\tilde{p}$. (They are so named because this raw data is then used in the clipping phase, described in section 12.1.) $w_n = w_c$ is a new variable called the w-coordinate. In such clip coordinates, the fourth entry of the coordinate 4-vector is not necessarily a zero or a one.

We say that $x_n w_n = x_c$ and $y_n w_n = y_c$. If we want to extract x_n alone, we must perform the division $x_n = \frac{x_n w_n}{w_n}$ (and likewise for y_n). When we do this, we exactly recover the computation of equation 10.1, our simple camera model.

Our output coordinates, with subscripts n, are called *normalized device coordinates* because they address points on the image in abstract units without specific reference to numbers of pixels. In computer graphics, we keep all of the image data in the *canonical square* $-1 \leq x_n \leq +1$, $-1 \leq y_n \leq +1$, and ultimately map this onto a window on the screen. Data outside of this square are not recorded or displayed. This is exactly the model we used to describe 2D OpenGL drawing in appendix A.

10.3 Variations

By changing the entries in the projection matrix, we can slightly alter the geometry of the camera transformation.

10.3.1 Scales

If we were to move the film plane to $z_e = n$, where n is some negative number (see figure 10.4), we could model this camera as

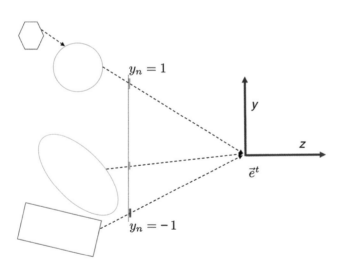

Scene geometry   Zoomed film plane

Figure 10.4
In this camera model, we have moved the film plane out to the $z_e = n$ plane. We still keep the portion of the film plane with $-1 < y_n = y_e < 1$. This simulates a telephoto setting.

$$x_n = \frac{x_e n}{z_e}$$

$$y_n = \frac{y_e n}{z_e}.$$

This corresponds to changing the zoom on a lens. In matrix form, this becomes

$$\begin{bmatrix} x_n w_n \\ y_n w_n \\ - \\ w_n \end{bmatrix} = \begin{bmatrix} -n & 0 & 0 & 0 \\ 0 & -n & 0 & 0 \\ - & - & - & - \\ 0 & 0 & -1 & 0 \end{bmatrix} \begin{bmatrix} x_e \\ y_e \\ z_e \\ 1 \end{bmatrix}.$$

This is in fact the same as starting with our original camera with the film plane at $z_e = -1$, then scaling the recorded image by a factor of $-n$, and finally keeping only the part that is inside of the canonical square (see figure 10.5). As such, it is best to no longer think of the normalized device coordinates as agreeing with any eye coordinates on the film plane but simply as some intrinsic coordinates in the image plane.

One useful way of controlling the scale factor is to determine $-n$ by specifying instead the vertical angular *field of view* of the desired camera. In particular, suppose we want our camera to have a field of view of θ degrees. Then we can set $-n = \frac{1}{\tan(\frac{\theta}{2})}$ (see figure 10.6), giving us the projection matrix

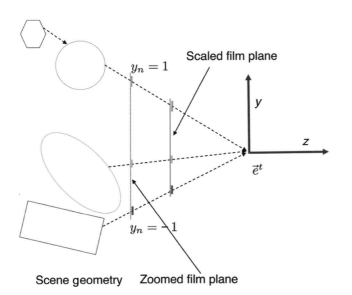

Figure 10.5
The zoomed camera is identical to a camera with a film plane at $z_e = -1$ but with scaled image coordinates $y_n = -n y_e$.

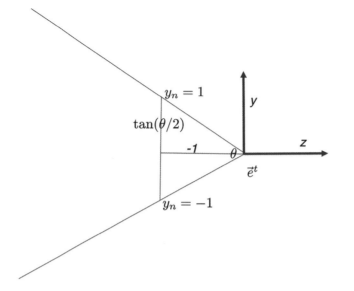

Figure 10.6
The scale of a camera can be conveniently expressed by choosing its vertical field of view: θ. In this case, we can think of the film plane at $z_e = -1$ and with bounds $-\tan(\theta/2) < y_e < \tan(\theta/2)$, mapping normalized device coordinates to $-1 < y_n < 1$.

$$
\begin{bmatrix}
\frac{1}{\tan(\frac{\theta}{2})} & 0 & 0 & 0 \\
0 & \frac{1}{\tan(\frac{\theta}{2})} & 0 & 0 \\
- & - & - & - \\
0 & 0 & -1 & 0
\end{bmatrix}.
\tag{10.4}
$$

We can directly verify that any point whose ray from the origin forms a vertical angle of $\frac{\theta}{2}$ with the negative z axis maps to the boundary of the canonical square in the image plane, and therefore that the camera's field of view is θ. For example, the point with eye coordinates $[0, \tan(\frac{\theta}{2}), -1, 1]^t$ maps to normalized device coordinates $[0, 1]^t$.

More generally, we can scale our original image by differing horizontal and vertical factors of s_x and s_y, respectively, to obtain the following camera model:

$$
\begin{bmatrix}
x_n w_n \\
y_n w_n \\
- \\
w_n
\end{bmatrix}
=
\begin{bmatrix}
s_x & 0 & 0 & 0 \\
0 & s_y & 0 & 0 \\
0 & 0 & 1 & 0 \\
0 & 0 & 0 & 1
\end{bmatrix}
\begin{bmatrix}
1 & 0 & 0 & 0 \\
0 & 1 & 0 & 0 \\
- & - & - & - \\
0 & 0 & -1 & 0
\end{bmatrix}
\begin{bmatrix}
x_e \\
y_e \\
z_e \\
1
\end{bmatrix}
$$

$$
=
\begin{bmatrix}
s_x & 0 & 0 & 0 \\
0 & s_y & 0 & 0 \\
- & - & - & - \\
0 & 0 & -1 & 0
\end{bmatrix}
\begin{bmatrix}
x_e \\
y_e \\
z_e \\
1
\end{bmatrix}.
$$

In computer graphics, this nonuniformity is useful when dealing with nonsquare windows on the screen. Suppose the window is wider than it is high. In our camera transform, we need to squish things horizontally so a wider horizontal field of view fits into our retained canonical square. When the data is later mapped to the window, it will be stretched out correspondingly and will not appear distorted.

Define a, the *aspect ratio* of a window, to be its width divided by its height (measured, say, in pixels). We can then set our projection matrix to be

$$\begin{bmatrix} \frac{1}{a\tan(\frac{\theta}{2})} & 0 & 0 & 0 \\ 0 & \frac{1}{\tan(\frac{\theta}{2})} & 0 & 0 \\ - & - & - & - \\ 0 & 0 & -1 & 0 \end{bmatrix}. \tag{10.5}$$

The vertical behavior of this camera is unchanged from that of equation (10.4), but an appropriately wider horizontal field is used to generate the image.

When the window is taller than it is wide, and thus $a < 1$, we can still use the matrix of equation (10.5), but we may not be happy with the resulting narrow horizontal field of view. If we want θ to be the minimal vertical/horizontal field of view, then, whenever $a < 1$, we need to use the following projection matrix:

$$\begin{bmatrix} \frac{1}{\tan(\frac{\theta}{2})} & 0 & 0 & 0 \\ 0 & \frac{a}{\tan(\frac{\theta}{2})} & 0 & 0 \\ - & - & - & - \\ 0 & 0 & -1 & 0 \end{bmatrix}.$$

These are exactly the matrices that are produced by our procedure `makeProjection` that we called in section (6.2).

There is often a trade-off when choosing a field of view to use in computer graphics. On the one hand, a wider field of view, in say a game environment, lets the viewer see more of what is around them. On the other hand, in a typical viewing environment (unless one has his or her head right up against the screen), the screen occupies only a small angular extent of the viewer's surroundings. In this case, the viewing geometry will not match the imaging environment (as it did in figure 10.3), and the image will have a distorted appearance (e.g., spheres may not appear as circles).

10.3.2 Shifts

Less commonly, we may wish to translate the 2D normalized device coordinates by $[c_x, c_y]^t$. This can be modeled in the projection matrix as

$$
\begin{bmatrix} x_n w_n \\ y_n w_n \\ - \\ w_n \end{bmatrix} = \begin{bmatrix} 1 & 0 & 0 & c_x \\ 0 & 1 & 0 & c_y \\ 0 & 0 & 1 & 0 \\ 0 & 0 & 0 & 1 \end{bmatrix} \begin{bmatrix} 1 & 0 & 0 & 0 \\ 0 & 1 & 0 & 0 \\ - & - & - & - \\ 0 & 0 & -1 & 0 \end{bmatrix} \begin{bmatrix} x_e \\ y_e \\ z_e \\ 1 \end{bmatrix}
$$

$$
= \begin{bmatrix} 1 & 0 & -c_x & 0 \\ 0 & 1 & -c_y & 0 \\ - & - & - & - \\ 0 & 0 & -1 & 0 \end{bmatrix} \begin{bmatrix} x_e \\ y_e \\ z_e \\ 1 \end{bmatrix}.
$$

This corresponds to a camera with a *shifted film plane* (see figure 10.7). This may seem uncommon, but in fact due to manufacturing as well as optical issues, most real cameras do have some small shifts in them.

In computer graphics, the main use for shifted cameras is for tiled displays (see figure 10.8) where we place multiple displays next to each other to create a larger one. In this case, each of these subimages is correctly modeled as an appropriately shifted camera. Another application is for creating pairs of images for stereo viewing on a single screen.

Often in computer graphics, shifted (and scaled) cameras are specified by first specifying a near plane $z_e = n$. On this plane, a rectangle is specified with the eye coordinates of an axis aligned rectangle. (For nondistorted output, the aspect ratio of this rectangle should

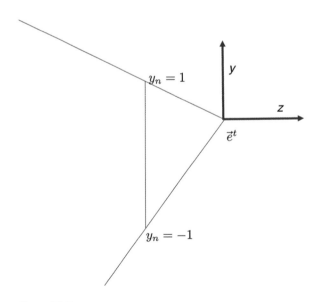

Figure 10.7
In a shifted camera, we translate the normalized device coordinates and keep the $[-1 \ldots 1]$ region in these shifted coordinates.

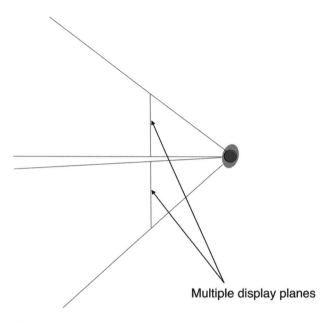

Multiple display planes

Figure 10.8
In this setting, the viewer is presented with two display planes creating the full image. Each image should be modeled as a shifted camera.

match that of the final window.) The values l, r specify the left and right sides of this rectangle in x_e coordinates, and the values t, b specify the top and bottom of this rectangle in y_e coordinates. In all, this specifies the shape of a 3D *frustum* in space. Rays through this rectangle and incident to the origin are then mapped to the canonical image square using the projection matrix

$$
\begin{bmatrix}
-\frac{2n}{r-l} & 0 & \frac{r+l}{r-l} & 0 \\
0 & -\frac{2n}{t-b} & \frac{t+b}{t-b} & 0 \\
- & - & - & - \\
0 & 0 & -1 & 0
\end{bmatrix}
\tag{10.6}
$$

(see figure 10.9).

10.3.3 And the Rest

The remaining two zeros in the upper left 2 by 2 block of the matrix in equation (10.6) are typically not touched in our camera models. Together, they represent the rotation and shearing of the pixel grid. Shearing does not typically arise in real cameras nor is it often useful in computer graphics. Of course we can rotate the entire camera about its optical

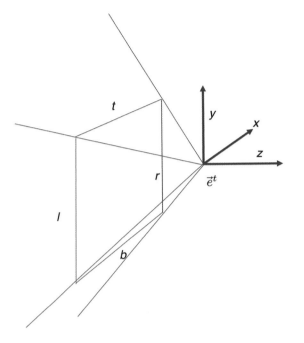

Figure 10.9
The 3D frustum is defined by specifying an image rectangle on the near plane.

axis, but this can be done as an appropriate camera rotation in the original definition of the $\vec{e}^l$ frame!

10.4   Context

The projection operation we have described is a mapping that can be applied to any point given in eye coordinates to obtain its normalized device coordinates. In OpenGL, though, this mapping is only applied to the vertices of a triangle. Once the normalized device coordinates of the three vertices of a triangle are obtained, the interior points are simply filled in by computing all of the pixels that fall in the interior of the triangle on the image plane.

Exercises

10.1 Suppose we take a picture of an ice cube. Let us draw the projection of the front face with a solid outline and the rear face with a dotted outline. Suppose three images are taken using fields of view of 40, 30, and 20 degrees, respectively. All other camera parameters remain fixed. Which of the following three sequences is plausible:

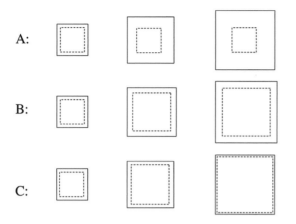

A:

B:

C:

10.2 (Tricky) Look at the following two photographs (from [26], copyright Phillip Green-spun):

Can you figure out how these were taken? What is the difference in the eye coordinates systems and projection matrices used? (Hint: Remember that we can build a camera with a shifted film plane.)

10.3 (Tricky) Let $\vec{\mathbf{e}}^t = \vec{\mathbf{w}}^t E$ and let P be a camera matrix that is just some arbitrary 4 by 4 matrix with "dashes" in its third row. Given the world coordinates of six points in space as well as their normalized device coordinates, how would one compute the 12 unknown entries in the matrix $P E^{-1}$? (Note: This can only be solved up to an unknown scale factor.) (Hint: Set up an appropriate homogeneous linear system with a right-hand side of zero.)

11 Depth

11.1 Visibility

In the physical world, if object A is in front of object B, then the light from object B will be blocked by object A before reaching the camera, and it will not appear in the image (e.g., the blue hexagon of figure 10.2). In computer graphics, we need to model this computationally.

There is a variety of approaches that can be used to ensure that only surfaces that are visible to the camera appear in the image. One idea is to sort the triangles by their depths and then draw them in back-to-front order. The idea is that the front-most triangles will redraw over the occluded triangles and produce the correct image. There are a number of difficulties with this so-called painter's approach. For example, a scene may include interpenetrating triangles. It may also include visibility cycles of noninterpenetrating triangles such as shown in figure 11.1.

Another very general approach, which we will discuss in chapter 20, is ray casting. In this approach, for each pixel, we explicitly calculate every scene point observed along the pixel's line of sight. The closest intersected point is then used to color the pixel.

In a rasterization-based renderer such as OpenGL, we use something called a *z-buffer* to perform our visibility calculations. In this approach, the triangles can be drawn in any order. At each pixel of our framebuffer, we store not only a color value but also a "current depth" value. This represents the depth of the geometry that was used to set the current value of the pixel. When a new triangle tries to set the color of a pixel, we first compare its depth to the value stored in the z-buffer. Only if the observed point in this triangle is closer do we overwrite the color and depth values of this pixel. Because this is done on a per-pixel basis, it can properly handle interpenetrating triangles.

11.1.1 Other Uses of Visibility Calculations

Visibility calculations can also be important when calculating the color of an observed point. In particular, it may be important to determine if the observed point can directly see some "light source" or whether it is in shadow. In OpenGL, this can be done using an algorithm

Figure 11.1
Three triangles forming a visibility cycle. There is no way to order them back-to-front.

called shadow mapping (described in section 15.5.2). In the context of ray tracing, we can simply use our ray intersection code to see what geometry is intersected by the ray going from the observed point toward the light.

Visibility computation can also be used to speed up the rendering process. If we know that some object is occluded from the camera, then we don't have to render the object in the first place. This might be used for example in an indoor scene where we can typically not see too far past the surrounding room. In this context, we can use a *conservative visibility* test; such a test quickly tells us whether some object **may be** or is **definitely not** visible. If the object may be visible, then we continue and render the object with our z-buffer. But if the object is definitely not visible, then we can skip its drawing entirely.

11.2 Basic Mathematical Model

In OpenGL, we use a z-buffer to compute visibility. To use a z-buffer, in addition to the $[x_n, y_n]$ coordinates of a point, we also need a depth value. To accomplish this, for every point described in eye coordinates, we define its $[x_n, y_n, z_n]^t$ coordinates using the following matrix expression:

$$
\begin{bmatrix} x_n w_n \\ y_n w_n \\ z_n w_n \\ w_n \end{bmatrix} = \begin{bmatrix} x_c \\ y_c \\ z_c \\ w_c \end{bmatrix} = \begin{bmatrix} s_x & 0 & -c_x & 0 \\ 0 & s_y & -c_y & 0 \\ 0 & 0 & 0 & 1 \\ 0 & 0 & -1 & 0 \end{bmatrix} \begin{bmatrix} x_e \\ y_e \\ z_e \\ 1 \end{bmatrix}.
\tag{11.1}
$$

Again, the raw output is called the clip coordinates, and, as before, to obtain the values of x_n and y_n, we need to divide by the w_n value. But now we also have the value $z_n = \frac{-1}{z_e}$. Our plan is to use this z_n value to do depth comparisons in our z-buffer.

First, let us verify that the z_n values resulting from equation (11.1) can indeed be used for depth comparison. Given two points $\tilde{p}^1$ and $\tilde{p}^2$ with eye coordinates $[x_e^1, y_e^1, z_e^1, 1]^t$ and $[x_e^2, y_e^2, z_e^2, 1]^t$. Suppose that they both are in front of the eye (i.e., $z_e^1 < 0$ and $z_e^2 < 0$). And suppose that $\tilde{p}^1$ is closer to the eye than $\tilde{p}^2$, that is, $z_e^2 < z_e^1$. Then $-\frac{1}{z_e^2} < -\frac{1}{z_e^1}$, meaning $z_n^2 < z_n^1$.

All together, we can now think of the process of that transforms eye coordinates to normalized device coordinates as an honest-to-goodness 3D geometric transformation. This kind of transformation is generally neither linear nor affine, but is something called a 3D *projective transformation*.

Projective transformations are a bit funny; for example, in the above case, any point with $z_e = 0$ will cause a "divide by zero." At this juncture, the most important thing we need to know about projective transformations (the argument is given later) is that they preserve co-linearity and co-planarity of points (see figures 11.2 and 11.3). Co-linearity means that, if three or more points are on a single line, the transformed points will also be on some single line.

As a result of this preservation of co-planarity, we know that for points on a fixed triangle, we will have $z_n = ax_n + by_n + c$, for some fixed a, b, and c. Thus, the correct z_n value for

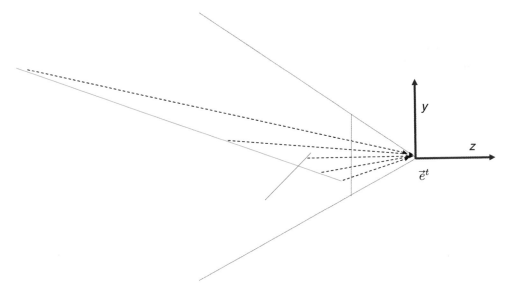

Figure 11.2
Here our scene geometry is two lines. Evenly spaced pixels on the film plane map unevenly onto the geometry.

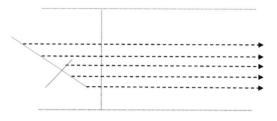

Figure 11.3
The scene from figure 11.2 in normalized device coordinates. Through the projective transformation, each point with coordinates $[y_e, z_e]^t$ is mapped to normalized device coordinates $[y_n, z_n]^t$. The y_n coordinate gives its image location on the film plane, and the z_n value is used for depth comparisons. Rays that passed through the origin in eye coordinates are mapped to parallel rays in normalized device coordinates. Co-linearity and co-planarity is preserved by the map.

a point can be computed using linear interpolation over the 2D image domain as long as we know its value at the three vertices of the triangle (see appendix B for more on linear interpolation).

Note, though, that **distances are not preserved by a projective transform**. Looking again at figures 11.2 and 11.3, we see that evenly spaced pixels on the film do not correspond to evenly spaced points on the geometry in eye space. Meanwhile, such evenly spaced pixels do correspond with evenly spaced points in normalized device coordinates.

As a result of this distance distortion, linear interpolation of z_e values over the screen would give the wrong answer. Consider the 2D drawing of figure 11.4, with interpenetrating segments, one orange and one blue. The z_e values of the vertices are shown. The two segments cross right at the midpoint of the image plane, so in the correct image, the top half should be blue and the bottom half should be orange. Suppose we linearly interpolated the z_e values in each segment in image space. All of the blue pixels would have interpolated z_e values of -1. On the orange triangle, going from bottom (with $z_e = -0.1$) to top (with $z_e = -1000000$ or so), the interpolated z_e value would become less than -1 almost immediately. Thus, in the z-buffered image, almost the entire image would be blue! In chapter 13, we will see how we can properly interpolate the z_e value over a triangle on the screen.

11.2.1 Lines Are Preserved by Projective Transforms (Optional)

Here, we sketch the steps needed to establish that lines are preserved by projective transforms.

First, let us define a projective transform acting on a 3D affine space. Fixing our frame, each point is represented by $\mathbf{c}$, a 4-coordinate vector with 1 as its last entry. We then multiply this by a chosen 4 by 4 matrix P to obtain $\mathbf{d} = P\mathbf{c}$. There are no restrictions on the fourth row of P, but we will assume that the matrix is invertible. Finally, we divide each of the four entries in $\mathbf{d}$ by the fourth entry of $\mathbf{d}$. This gives us our result $\mathbf{e}$, which we interpret as the coordinates of another point in our affine space. (Let us ignore the case where the fourth entry happens to be 0.) Such a transformation $\mathbf{c} \Rightarrow \mathbf{e}$. is called a projective transformation.

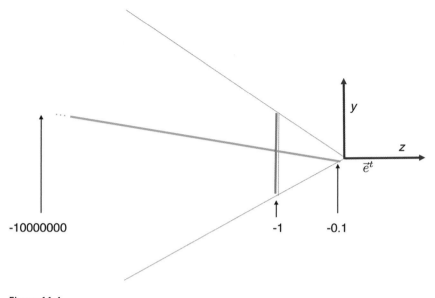

Figure 11.4
Linear interpolation of the z_e value over the screen gives the wrong answer.

To see that this kind of transformation preserves co-linearity, let us think of **c** as a coordinate vector in the four-dimensional (4D) linear space $\mathbb{R}^4$. If we started with points that all lie on some line in our 3D affine space, then all the associated **c** coordinates must also represent vectors in $\mathbb{R}^4$ that lie on some corresponding 2D vector subspace of $\mathbb{R}^4$. Let us now think of the multiplication by P as simply a linear transform acting on vectors in $\mathbb{R}^4$. This, as any linear transform, must map 2D subspaces to 2D subspaces. So all of the resulting **d** coordinates must lie on some fixed 2D subspace in $\mathbb{R}^4$. Finally, when we divide by the fourth coordinate, we are simply scaling each of the resulting vectors so that they also lie on the 3D hyperplane in $\mathbb{R}^4$ with a last coordinate of 1. Any such **e** must lie in a one-dimensional (1D) line within the 3D hyperplane. This hyperplane is isomorphic to our 3D affine space, and thus the resulting points of the projective transform must be co-linear.

11.3 Near and Far

When using the projection matrix of equation (11.1), there can be numerical difficulties when computing z_n. As z_e goes toward zero, the z_n value diverges off toward infinity. Conversely, points very far from the eye have z_n values very close to zero. The z_n of two such faraway points may be indistinguishable in a finite precision representation, and thus the z-buffer will be ineffective in distinguishing which is closer to the eye.

In computer graphics, this issue is typically dealt with by replacing the third row of the matrix in equation (11.1) with the more general row $[0, 0, \alpha, \beta]$. Once again, it is easy to verify that if the values α and β are both positive, then the z-ordering of points (assuming they all have negative z_e values) is preserved under the projective transform.

To set α and β, we first select depth values n and f called the *near* and *far* values (both negative), such that our main region of interest in the scene is sandwiched between $z_e = n$ and $z_e = f$. Given these selections, we set $\alpha = \frac{f+n}{f-n}$ and $\beta = -\frac{2fn}{f-n}$. We can verify now that any point with $z_e = f$ maps to a point with $z_n = -1$ and that a point with $z_e = n$ maps to a point with $z_n = 1$ (see figures 11.5 and 11.6). Any geometry not in this [near ... far] range is clipped away by OpenGL and ignored (clipping is covered in section 12.1).

Putting this together with the projection matrix of equation (10.5), we obtain the matrix

$$\begin{bmatrix} \frac{1}{a \tan(\frac{\theta}{2})} & 0 & 0 & 0 \\ 0 & \frac{1}{\tan(\frac{\theta}{2})} & 0 & 0 \\ 0 & 0 & \frac{f+n}{f-n} & -\frac{2fn}{f-n} \\ 0 & 0 & -1 & 0 \end{bmatrix}.$$

Alternatively, putting this together with the projection matrix of equation (10.6), and using the near plane to define our bounding rectangle using the scalars l, r, b, t, we obtain the frustum projection matrix

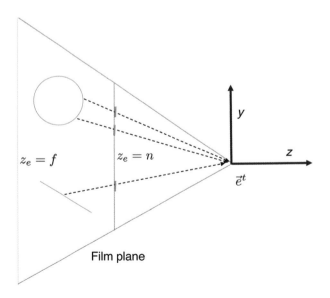

$z_e = f$ $z_e = n$

y

z

$\vec{e}^t$

Film plane

Figure 11.5
In this camera model, we have specified both a near and (green) far plane. We can think of the film plane as living on the near plane.

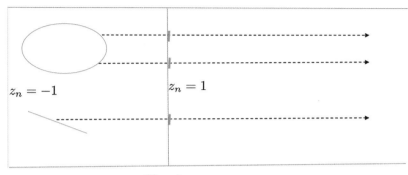

Film plane

Figure 11.6
Here, we show the geometry of figure 11.5 after undergoing the projective transform of equation (11.2). The near plane maps to $z_n = 1$ and the far plane to $z_n = -1$.

$$\begin{bmatrix} -\frac{2n}{r-l} & 0 & \frac{r+l}{r-l} & 0 \\ 0 & -\frac{2n}{t-b} & \frac{t+b}{t-b} & 0 \\ 0 & 0 & \frac{f+n}{f-n} & -\frac{2fn}{f-n} \\ 0 & 0 & -1 & 0 \end{bmatrix}. \tag{11.2}$$

The effect of this projection matrix is to map the frustum to the canonical cube with corners $[-1, -1, -1]^t$, $[1, 1, 1]^t$.

For various historical reasons, there are a few variants of this matrix that appear in the literature and in OpenGL documentation. For example, some conventions assume that n is given as the *distance* to the near plane and is thus a positive number. As another example, some conventions flip the signs of the entries in the third row of the matrix. In the resulting (left-handed) normalized device coordinates, nearer means smaller z_n. Because we do not do this flipping, we must explicitly tell OpenGL which sign to use for depth comparison; we do this with the call to glDepthFunc(GL_GREATER).

11.4 Code

In OpenGL, use of the z-buffer is turned on with a call to glEnable(GL_DEPTH_TEST). We also need a call to glDepthFunc(GL_GREATER), as we are using a right-handed coordinate system where "more-negative" is "farther from the eye."

Putting this all together, all we really need to do is to write procedures

```
Matrix4 makeProjection(double minfov, double aspectratio,
double zNear, double zFar)
```

and

```
Matrix4 makeProjection(double top, double bottom, double
left, double right, double zNear, double ZFar)
```

that return the appropriate projection matrices. We also need the procedure

```
sendProjectionMatrix(projmat)
```

to send the projection matrix to the appropriately named matrix variable in the vertex shader. The code for these procedures is found on the book's website. The actual multiplication with the projection matrix is done in the vertex shader as we did in section 6.3.

Exercises

11.1 Suppose we have two triangles such that the closest-in-z vertex of one triangle is farther than the farthest-in-z vertex of the other triangle? If we linearly interpolated the z_e value over the interior of a triangle, would z-buffering produce a picture with the correct occlusion?

11.2 Starting from the projection matrix P of equation (11.2), suppose we replace P with PQ where

$$Q = \begin{bmatrix} 3 & 0 & 0 & 0 \\ 0 & 3 & 0 & 0 \\ 0 & 0 & 3 & 0 \\ 0 & 0 & 0 & 1 \end{bmatrix}.$$

What will be the effect in our resulting image?

11.3 Suppose we replace P with PS where

$$S = \begin{bmatrix} 3 & 0 & 0 & 0 \\ 0 & 3 & 0 & 0 \\ 0 & 0 & 3 & 0 \\ 0 & 0 & 0 & 3 \end{bmatrix}.$$

What will be the effect in our resulting image?

11.4 Suppose we replace P with QP. What will be the effect in our resulting image?

12 From Vertex to Pixel

Once the user has specified the three vertices of a triangle, and these vertices have all passed through the vertex shader, these data now go through a fixed set of processing steps that are done by OpenGL. This processing determines where on the screen the triangle should be placed, which pixels are inside of the triangle, and what are the appropriately interpolated values of the varying variable data for each pixel. These data are then passed on to the user's fragment shader for more processing to determine the final color. In this chapter, we explore some of the details of the triangle's journey from vertices to pixels. We will not dwell on all of the details but try to point out the most interesting ones. In figure 12.1, we show how the steps described in this chapter fit in to the rendering pipeline. In this chapter and the next, we will rely on some basic facts about *affine functions*. We describe this material in appendix B.

12.1 Clipping

The job of the clipping stage is to deal with triangles that lie fully or partially outside of the viewing frustum. Some of this processing is done for the obvious reason that we wish to discard unviewed geometry in order to minimize computation. But, more importantly, unless clipping is done, we can have problems arising from triangles that cross the $z_e = 0$ plane (i.e., extend both in front of and behind the eye).

Consider the geometry of figure 12.2 (where we suppress the x direction to simplify the drawing). In this scene, we have a single geometric segment (this would be a triangle in 3D) with one vertex in front of the eye and one vertex behind it. Suppose we apply the projective camera transform of chapter 10. The front vertex will project to an image point near the bottom of the image, and the back vertex will project to an image point near the top of the image.

If, on the screen, we just draw the pixels that lie *between* these projected vertices, we will be drawing in completely the wrong area. The correct rendering should draw the pixels starting from the bottom projected vertex and proceeding down until the bottom of the image is reached as in figure 12.3.

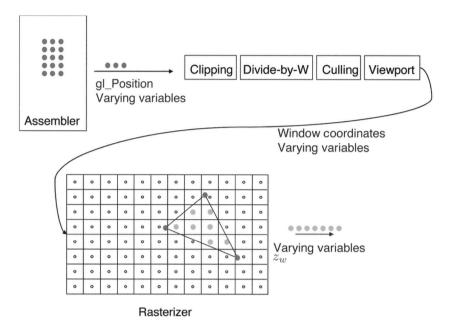

Figure 12.1
Here we flesh out some of steps of the rendering pipeline described in this chapter (compare with figure 1.3).

In computer graphics, the easiest way to solve this problem is first to alter the scene geometry, replacing such eye-spanning triangles with smaller triangles that do not extend behind the eye (see figre 12.4). This step is called *clipping*. In particular, we clip each triangle to all six faces of the frustum implied by the near plane, far plane, and the "left, right, top, and bottom" image boundaries.

There are other approaches to this problem that avoid doing any geometric clipping at all. The interested reader can read more about this in [52].

12.1.1   Which Coordinates To Use

We could do clipping in eye coordinates, but this processing would also need to know about the parameters of the camera projection, which is inconvenient.

Conversely, testing in normalized device coordinates would be quite canonical: Ultimately, we would be happy if our triangles never left the canonical cube

$$-1 < x_n < 1. \tag{12.1}$$

$$-1 < y_n < 1 \tag{12.2}$$

$$-1 < z_n < 1 \tag{12.3}$$

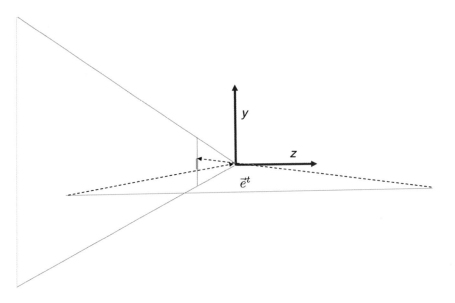

Figure 12.2
In this scene, the orange floor segment extends both in front of and behind the eye. Its vertices project to the image plane as shown by the dotted lines. If pixels between the projected vertices are filled in, we will get the wrong image.

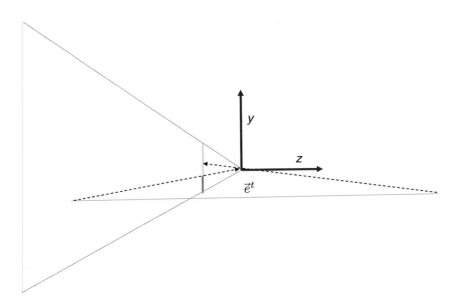

Figure 12.3
The correct image would draw the pixels from the projection of the front vertex of the floor until the bottom of the image.

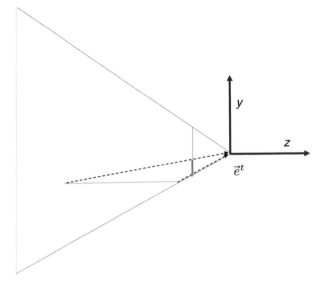

Figure 12.4
The correct drawing is accomplished by clipping the floor geometry, replacing it with a smaller segment that does not leave the viewing frustum.

Unfortunately, by the time we get to normalized device coordinates, the trouble-causing flip has already occurred.

The usual solution in computer graphics is to do clipping in the so-called clip co-ordinates, described earlier. In these coordinates, the canonical conditions of equation (12.1) translate to

$$-w_c < x_c < w_c$$

$$-w_c < y_c < w_c$$

$$-w_c < z_c < w_c.$$

Because we have not done any divisions yet, no flip can have happened yet. Our triangles in 3D eye space have simply mapped to triangles in 4D clip space.

12.1.2   Updating the Variables

The actual coding of the clipping step is beyond the scope of our interest here. The interested reader may consult [5]. But this process typically creates "new" vertices where some triangle edge passes out of the frustum. Here, we comment on the variables associated with these new vertices.

The new vertex is computed in clip coordinates, and thus has its own four new associated clip coordinates $[x_c, y_c, z_c, w_c]^t$. Each new vertex, like the original ones, has associated with it a set of values for each varying variable.

All of the varying variables represent functions that are affine in the object coordinates (x_o, y_o, z_o); thus, using the reasoning of section B.5 of appendix B, these are also affine in (x_c, y_c, z_c, w_c). Therefore, if the new vertex is some fraction, α, of the way between two triangle vertices, we simply interpolate the varying variables "α of the way" and use these new values to set the varying variables at this vertex.

12.2 Backface Culling

Suppose we are using triangles to draw a closed solid object, such as a cube. Let us label the two sides of each triangle as "front" or "back." No matter how we turn the cube, we will never see the back side of any triangle as it must be occluded by some triangle whose front side we are observing (see figure 12.5). As such, we may as well *cull* these backfacing polygons as soon as possible and not draw them at all. For a "non-watertight" geometric model, we may wish to see both sides of a triangle; in this case, backface culling would be inappropriate.

In OpenGL, backface culling is turned on by calling glEnable(GL_CULL_FACE). For each face, we somehow need to tell OpenGL which side is the front and which is the back. To do

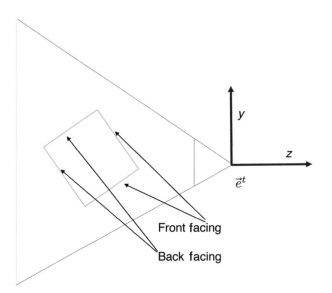

Figure 12.5
When drawing a closed object, the back sides of faces can never be observed.

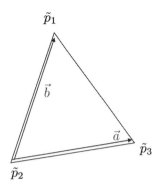

Figure 12.6
The vertices are given in counterclockwise order as seen from this side. The cross product $\vec{a} \times \vec{b}$ points out of the page.

this, we use the convention of ordering the three vertices so that they are counterclockwise when looking at its front side. When drawing each triangle, we use this vertex ordering in the vertex buffer object.

Using the normalized device coordinates of the vertices, OpenGL can now easily determine which side of a triangle we are observing in the current image. Here's how (see figure 12.6). Let $\tilde{p}_1$, $\tilde{p}_2$, and $\tilde{p}_3$ be the three vertices of the triangle projected down to the $(x_n, y_n, 0)$ plane. Define the vectors $\vec{a} = \tilde{p}_3 - \tilde{p}_2$ and $\vec{b} = \tilde{p}_1 - \tilde{p}_2$. Next, compute the cross product $\vec{c} = \vec{a} \times \vec{b}$. If the three vertices are counterclockwise in the plane, then $\vec{c}$ will be in the $-z_n$ direction. Otherwise, it will be in the positive z_n direction. In summary, all we need to do is compute the z coordinate of the cross product in normalized device coordinates. When all the dust settles, this coordinate is

$$(x_n^3 - x_n^2)(y_n^1 - y_n^2) - (y_n^3 - y_n^2)(x_n^1 - x_n^2). \tag{12.4}$$

To test if three vertices are counterclockwise, we simply compute the value of equation (12.4). If it is positive, then the vertices are counterclockwise as viewed from the camera.

12.3   Viewport

At this point, we wish to position our triangle on the image screen and decide which pixels are inside of the triangle. Thus, we wish to move from the abstract normalized device coordinates to the so-called *window coordinates*, where each pixel center has an integer coordinate. This will make subsequent pixel computations more natural.

Recall that in normalized device coordinates, the extent of our image is the canonical square with lower left corner at $[-1, -1]^t$ and upper right corner at $[1, 1]^t$. Let us now suppose that our window is W pixels wide and H pixels high. We want the lower left pixel center to have 2D window coordinates of $[0, 0]^t$ and the upper right pixel center to have coordinates $[W - 1, H - 1]^t$. We think of each pixel as owning the real estate that extends 0.5 pixel units in the positive and negative, horizontal and vertical directions from the pixel center. Thus, in this model, we think of each pixel as being a 1 pixel unit by 1 pixel unit square, with its center at integer coordinates. Thus, the extent of 2D window rectangle covered by the union of all our pixels is the rectangle in window coordinates with lower left corner $[-0.5, -0.5]^t$ and upper right corner $[W - 0.5, H - 0.5]^t$ (see figure 12.7).

All that we need now is a transformation that performs the appropriate vertical and horizontal scales and shifts, such that it maps the canonical square to the window's rectangle. We can verify that the following matrix provides the (unique) solution:

$$
\begin{bmatrix} x_w \\ y_w \\ z_w \\ 1 \end{bmatrix} = \begin{bmatrix} W/2 & 0 & 0 & (W-1)/2 \\ 0 & H/2 & 0 & (H-1)/2 \\ 0 & 0 & 1/2 & 1/2 \\ 0 & 0 & 0 & 1 \end{bmatrix} \begin{bmatrix} x_n \\ y_n \\ z_n \\ 1 \end{bmatrix}.
\tag{12.5}
$$

This matrix is called the *viewport matrix*, and it implements the viewport transformation. In OpenGL, we set up this viewport matrix with the call `glViewport(0,0,W,H)`.

(A functionally equivalent model, which we will not use, but is often used in OpenGL documentation, defines the window x, y coordinates as ranging from $[0, 0]^t$ to $[W, H]^t$,

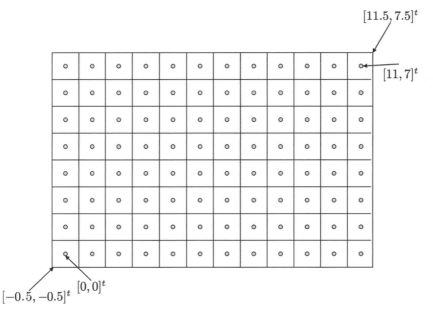

Figure 12.7
The geometry of window coordinates of an image that is 12 pixels wide and 8 pixels high.

while thinking of each pixel center as having half-integer coordinates. In this model, we use a different matrix and we also use different coordinates to address the pixels.)

The third row of this matrix is used to map the $[-1 \ldots 1]$ range of z_n values to the more convenient $[0 \ldots 1]$ range. And thus in our conventions, $z_w = 0$ is far and $z_w = 1$ is near. Thus, we must also tell OpenGL that when we clear the z-buffer, we should set it to 0; we do this with the call `glClearDepth(0.0)`.

12.3.1 Texture Viewport

For some (probably not very good) reason, the abstract domain for textures is not the canonical square but instead is the *unit square* in $[x_t, y_t]^t$ texture coordinates. Its lower left corner is $[0, 0]^t$ and upper right corner is $[1, 1]^t$. Again assuming that the texture image is W pixels wide by H pixels high, in this case the coordinate transformation matrix is

$$\begin{bmatrix} x_w \\ y_w \\ - \\ 1 \end{bmatrix} = \begin{bmatrix} W & 0 & 0 & -1/2 \\ 0 & H & 0 & -1/2 \\ - & - & - & - \\ 0 & 0 & 0 & 1 \end{bmatrix} \begin{bmatrix} x_t \\ y_t \\ - \\ 1 \end{bmatrix}. \tag{12.6}$$

These details with the $1/2$s and all may seem a bit picky, but understanding them is essential if you want to know exactly where the pixels are in your images and textures.

12.4 Rasterization

Rasterization is the process of taking the vertices of a triangle and filling in the pixels. Starting from the window coordinates for the three vertices, the rasterizer needs to figure out which pixel centers are inside of the triangle. (Later in section 16.3, we will explore the possibility of using numerous spatial samples within a pixel's square to determine its color.)

There are many ways that rasterization can be done in either hardware or software. Here, for example, is a simple brute force approach (see figure 12.8). Each triangle on the screen can be defined as the intersection of three half-spaces. Each such half-space is defined by a line that coincides with one of the edges of the triangle and can be tested using an "edge function" of the form

$$\text{edge} = ax_w + by_w + c,$$

where the (a, b, c) are constants that depend on the geometry of the edge. A positive value of this function at a pixel with coordinates $[x_w, y_w]^t$ means that the pixel is inside the specified half-space. If all three tests pass, then the pixel is inside the triangle.

This brute force approach can be sped up in many ways. For example, we can use the minimum and maximum x_w and y_w values of the three vertices to determine a bounding box of the triangle. Only pixels within this bounding box need to be tested. In addition, to reduce the number of "pixel-in-triangle" tests, there are ways to design a simple conservative test

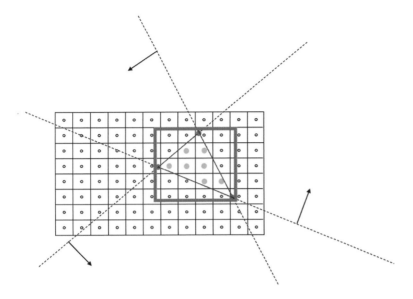

Figure 12.8
We can think of one triangle as the intersection of three half-spaces (dotted), each defined by a linear function. We can test each pixel against these three functions. We only need to test the pixels with the triangle's axis aligned bounding box (cyan).

that determines if an entire block of pixels is entirely inside or outside a triangle. Individual pixels only need to be tested when this test is inconclusive. As another optimization, we note that once we have evaluated such a linear function at, say, one pixel, we can then evaluate it at a neighboring pixel *incrementally*. For example, as we step one pixel horizontally, we just need to increment the evaluated edge function by the value a.

As input to rasterization, each vertex also has some auxiliary data associated with it. These data include a z_w value, as well as other data that are related but not identical to the varying variables (see chapter 13). It is also the job of the rasterizer to linearly interpolate these data over the triangle.

Each such value v to be linearly interpolated can be represented as an affine function over screen space with the form

$$v = ax_w + by_w + c. \tag{12.7}$$

The (a, b, c) constants can be determined using equation (B.2) in appendix B. An affine function can be easily evaluated at each pixel by the rasterizer. Indeed, this is no different from evaluating the edge test functions just described.

During rasterization, it is important to carefully treat the boundary cases. In particular, suppose two triangles in a mesh abut along one edge whose projection lands exactly on a pixel. If the pixel is not drawn, then a gap will appear in the projected mesh. If the pixel is drawn twice, this can cause problems if we are modeling transparency using alpha blending (see section 16.4). Boundary rules must be implemented carefully to ensure that such a pixel is only drawn once by this pair of triangles.

A related topic to triangle rasterization is line/curve rasterization. In this case, we are not looking for pixels "inside" of a 2D shape such as a triangle, but instead pixels "near" a 1D shape. Thus, even defining the problem is a bit trickier, and it is one that we will not delve into here. The interested reader can consult [5].

Exercises

12.1 Assume that in the vertex shader of section 6.3 we added the following line at the end: `gl_Position = gl_Position/gl_Position.w;`. What impact would this have on clipping?

12.2 What is the formula for finding the $[x_t, y_t]^t$ abstract texture coordinates (in the unit square) of a texture pixel with integer texture-pixel index of (i, j).

12.3 Starting from the viewport matrix V from equation (12.5), suppose we replace V with QV where

$$Q = \begin{bmatrix} 3 & 0 & 0 & 0 \\ 0 & 3 & 0 & 0 \\ 0 & 0 & 1 & 0 \\ 0 & 0 & 0 & 1 \end{bmatrix}.$$

What will be the effect in our resulting image?

12.4 How can one use equation (B.2) in appendix B to obtain the coefficients of an edge function for use in rasterization?

13 Varying Variables (Tricky)

To represent functions that vary across a triangle, we need to interpolate the varying variable data from the three vertices of a triangle to each pixel inside of the triangle. In this chapter, we explore how this is properly done. Surprisingly, this innocuous looking step is actually a bit complicated. Before reading this chapter, you should be familiar with the material in appendix B.

13.1 Motivating the Problem

We already saw earlier in figure 11.4 that we cannot determine the correct z_e value at a point using linear interpolation. Here is another motivating example. Let us look at the simple case of mapping an image of a checkerboard pattern onto the $+z$ face of a cube (see figure 13.1). This face is made up of two triangles. We wish to glue to each triangle the appropriate triangular half of the checkerboard image. We do this by associating $[x_t, y_t]^t$ texture coordinates for each vertex. In the interior of a triangle, we wish $[x_t, y_t]^t$ to be determined as the unique interpolant functions over the triangle that are affine in (x_o, y_o, z_o). These interpolated texture coordinates can then be used to fetch color data from that point in the texture image. Texture mapping and its variants are discussed more fully in chapter 15.

If we view the cube face perpendicularly, then the appropriate part of our window should look just like the original checkerboard image. If the face is angled away from us, as in figure 13.1, then we expect to see some "foreshortening"; farther squares on the board should appear smaller, and parallel lines in object space should appear to converge at a vanishing point in the image.

How does OpenGL obtain this correct image? Suppose we attempt to determine $[x_t, y_t]^t$ at the pixels by simply linearly interpolating them over the screen. Then, as we move by some fixed 2D vector displacement on the screen, the texture coordinates will be updated by some fixed 2D vector displacement in texture coordinates. In this case, all of the squares of the texture will map to equal-sized parallelograms. This will clearly give us the wrong image (see figure 13.2). Moreover, because incorrect things happen on each of the two

Figure 13.1
The correct image of a checkerboard image mapped to a face of the cube.

Figure 13.2
When texture coordinates are linearly interpolated in window coordinates, an incorrect image results.

triangles of our face, the two halves of the texture will meet up in an unexpected way over the face's diagonal.

13.2 Rational Linear Interpolation

The problems just described arise because our desired functions (texture coordinates in this case) are simply not affine functions over the screen variables (x_w, y_w). If we use linear interpolation to blend the values on the screen, we are treating them as if they were, and we get the wrong answer.

To figure out the correct way to interpolate these data, let us reason as follows:

Recall that given our modelview matrix M, and our projection matrix P, for each point on our triangle, the normalized device coordinates are related to object coordinates through the relation

$$
\begin{bmatrix} x_n w_n \\ y_n w_n \\ z_n w_n \\ w_n \end{bmatrix} = PM \begin{bmatrix} x_o \\ y_o \\ z_o \\ 1 \end{bmatrix}.
$$

Inverting our matrices, this implies that at each point on the triangle, we have the relation:

$$
\begin{bmatrix} x_o \\ y_o \\ z_o \\ 1 \end{bmatrix} = M^{-1}P^{-1} \begin{bmatrix} x_n w_n \\ y_n w_n \\ z_n w_n \\ w_n \end{bmatrix}.
$$

Now suppose that v is an affine function of (x_o, y_o, z_o) (such as the x_t texture coordinate). We also make use of the obvious fact that the constant function 1 is also affine in (x_o, y_o, z_o). Thus, for some (a, b, c, d), we have

$$
\begin{bmatrix} v \\ 1 \end{bmatrix} = \begin{bmatrix} a & b & c & d \\ 0 & 0 & 0 & 1 \end{bmatrix} \begin{bmatrix} x_o \\ y_o \\ z_o \\ 1 \end{bmatrix},
$$

and therefore

$$
\begin{bmatrix} v \\ 1 \end{bmatrix} = \begin{bmatrix} a & b & c & d \\ 0 & 0 & 0 & 1 \end{bmatrix} M^{-1}P^{-1} \begin{bmatrix} x_n w_n \\ y_n w_n \\ z_n w_n \\ w_n \end{bmatrix}
$$

$$= \begin{bmatrix} e & f & g & h \\ i & j & k & l \end{bmatrix} \begin{bmatrix} x_n w_n \\ y_n w_n \\ z_n w_n \\ w_n \end{bmatrix}$$

for some appropriate values $e \ldots l$.

Now divide both sides by w_n and we get

$$\begin{bmatrix} \frac{v}{w_n} \\ \frac{1}{w_n} \end{bmatrix} = \begin{bmatrix} e & f & g & h \\ i & j & k & l \end{bmatrix} \begin{bmatrix} x_n \\ y_n \\ z_n \\ 1 \end{bmatrix}.$$

This tell us that $\frac{v}{w_n}$ and $\frac{1}{w_n}$ are affine functions of normalized device coordinates.

Using the fact that normalized device coordinates are related to window coordinates by a matrix multiplication (and no divisions), we can use the reasoning of section B.5 of appendix B to deduce that $\frac{v}{w_n}$ and $\frac{1}{w_n}$ are affine functions of window coordinates (x_w, y_w, z_w).

Finally, because we started with a triangle, which is planar in object coordinates, we are also dealing with a planar object in window coordinates. Thus, assuming that the triangle has non-zero area in the window, we can apply the reasoning of section B.4 of appendix B to remove the dependence on z_w.

Doing this, we can conclude: $\frac{v}{w_n}$ **and** $\frac{1}{w_n}$ **are both affine functions of** (x_w, y_w). This is great news. It means that we can calculate their values at each pixel, just given their values at the vertices. In fact, to compute them we do not even need to figure out the specific constant values of our derivation above. All we need are the values of v and w_n at each vertex.

Now we can see how OpenGL can perform the correct interpolation to calculate v at each pixel. This process is called *rational linear interpolation*.

• The vertex shader is run on each vertex, calculating clip coordinates and varying variables for each vertex.

• Clipping is run on each triangle; this may create new vertices. Linear interpolation in clip coordinate space is run to determine the clip coordinates and varying variable values for each such new vertex.

• For each vertex, and for each varying variable v, OpenGL creates an internal variable $\frac{v}{w_n}$. Additionally, for each vertex, OpenGL creates one internal variable $\frac{1}{w_n}$.

• For each vertex, division is done to obtain the normalized device coordinates. $x_n = \frac{x_c}{w_c}$, $y_n = \frac{y_c}{w_c}$, $z_n = \frac{z_c}{w_c}$.

• For each vertex, the normalized device coordinates are transformed to window coordinates.

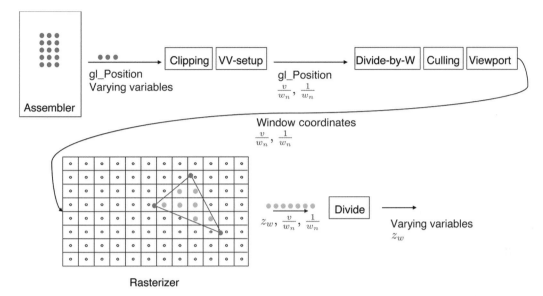

Figure 13.3
Here we show how the treatment of varying variables fits into the rendering pipeline.

- The $[x_w, y_w]^t$ coordinates are used to position the triangle on the screen.
- For every interior pixel of the triangle, linear interpolation is used to obtain the interpolated values of z_w, $\frac{v}{w_n}$ (for all v) and $\frac{1}{w_n}$.
- At each pixel, the interpolated z_w value is used for z-buffering.
- At each pixel, and for all varying variables, division is done on the interpolated internal variables to obtain the correct answer $v = (\frac{v}{w_n})/(\frac{1}{w_n})$.
- The varying variable v is passed into the fragment shader.

   In figure 13.3, we show how these steps fit into the rendering pipeline.

Exercises

13.1 Assume that in our vertex shader we add the following line at the end: gl_Position = gl_Position/gl_Position.w;. And let us assume that all triangles are strictly in front of the eye. What extra varying variables and code do you need to add to your vertex and fragment shaders so that you produce the correct image? (You can code this if you wish.)

13.2 Suppose some triangle is fronto-planar; that is, its eye coordinates are of the form

$$
\begin{bmatrix} a \\ b \\ c \\ 1 \end{bmatrix}, \begin{bmatrix} d \\ e \\ c \\ 1 \end{bmatrix}, \begin{bmatrix} f \\ g \\ c \\ 1 \end{bmatrix}
$$

with the same $z_e = c$. Is there a difference between doing rational linear interpolation on the varying variables versus doing linear interpolation?

13.3 Starting from the projection matrix P from equation (11.2), suppose we replace P with PQ for all of the vertices where

$$
Q = \begin{bmatrix} 3 & 0 & 0 & 0 \\ 0 & 3 & 0 & 0 \\ 0 & 0 & 3 & 0 \\ 0 & 0 & 0 & 3 \end{bmatrix}.
$$

What will be the effect on the interpolated varying variables?

13.4 Suppose we replace P with PQ *at only one vertex* of a triangle. What will be the effect on the interpolated varying variables?

13.5 In this chapter, we have seen that over a triangle, the quantity $\frac{v}{w_n}$ is affine in the quantities (x_n, y_n), and we can say that

$$
\frac{v}{w_n} = \begin{bmatrix} a & b & c \end{bmatrix} \begin{bmatrix} x_n \\ y_n \\ 1 \end{bmatrix}
$$

for some (a, b, c). What is the relationship between the quantity v and the quantities (x_c, y_c, w_c)?

IV PIXELS AND SUCH

14 Materials

The job of the fragment shader is to determine the color of the point on a triangle corresponding to a single pixel in the image. The fragment shader has access to the interpolated varying variables and to data passed to it from the user's program in the form of uniform variables. Uniform variables are often used to describe things like the positions of some light sources in the scene, which do not change from pixel to pixel. Varying variables are often used to describe the coordinate vector of the point (with respect to, say, the eye frame), a normal for the point, and parameters describing the material properties at the point (such as its underlying material color). The fragment shader then typically takes these data and simulates how light would bounce off of this material, producing a color in the image. In this chapter, we will cover the most common of such shading calculations used in material simulation. In the following chapter, we will explore the other main computation typically done in the fragment shader: texture mapping.

Fragment shading is a very rich topic and is at the core of making computer-generated images look as detailed and realistic as they do. It is a core topic in OpenGL rendering, and you should plan to learn more about it than we can cover in this book. One good reference is *The CG Tutorial* [19]; it uses the *CG shading language* instead of our choice, GLSL, but the translation between the two is mostly straightforward. Another good reference is the book *Real-Time Rendering* [2]. More detailed descriptions of materials can be found in the book *Digital Modeling of Material Appearance* [17].

14.1 Basic Assumptions

When light hits a physical material, it is scattered in various outgoing directions. Different kinds of materials scatter light in different patterns, and this results in different appearances when observed by the eye or a camera. Some materials may appear glossy and others matte. By simulating this scattering process, we can give a realistic physical appearance to a 3D rendered object.

Figure 14.1 visualizes, for example, how light reflects off of a single point on a piece of PVC plastic. The light is coming in from the direction pointed to by the vector $\vec{l}$. The blob shows how bright this point would appear when observed from the various directions above

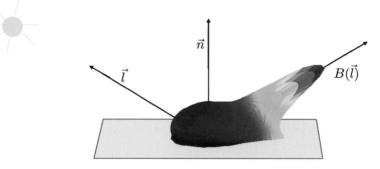

Figure 14.1
The blob shows how light bounces off from a piece of PVC plastic. (From [51], copyright Eurographics and Blackwell Publishing Ltd.)

the plastic. Brighter directions are colored red, and the shape of the blob extends out further in such bright directions. The dimmer directions are colored blue. Note that this figure just describes the result of light that comes in from the specific shown direction $\vec{l}$. For other incoming directions, we would need a different blob to visualize the resulting scattering.

From this figure, we see that the plastic will appear brightest when observed in the directions clustered about the "bounce" direction of the light: $B(\vec{l})$. In particular, most of the light bounces off in the direction "opposite" of where it came in from (think of how light bounces off of a mirror or how a billiard ball bounces off a billiard table's wall). Given any vector $\vec{w}$ (not necessarily of unit norm) and a unit normal vector $\vec{n}$, we can compute the bounce vector of $\vec{w}$ as

$$B(\vec{w}) = 2(\vec{w} \cdot \vec{n})\vec{n} - \vec{w}. \tag{14.1}$$

See figure 14.2 for a visual derivation of this equation.

In OpenGL, we can simulate this scattering process at the vertex resolution in our vertex shader and then just interpolate the resulting color values over each triangle using varying variables. For a higher-quality appearance, we can, at greater cost, simulate this Process at each pixel in our fragment shader. In this chapter, we will take this pixel-based approach.

To understand properly and simulate light scattering, we really need to understand the proper units used to measure light, the actual physics of light scattering, and the proper equations used to model scattering. We cover this in more detail in chapter 21. Moreover, in a true physical setting, light can be coming toward a surface from all directions, and light bounces around our scene multiple times before it is finally all absorbed. These issues, too, will be covered in chapter 21. In this chapter, we will take the more pragmatic approach of computing a reasonable looking appearance using concepts that are physically motivated but not physically accurate.

At this point, we will restrict ourselves to the simple setting of figure 14.3, where we assume that all light comes from a single *point light source* that is pointed to by the *light*

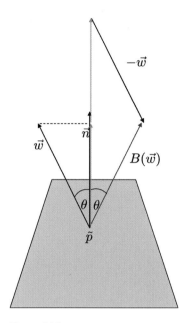

Figure 14.2
Computation of the bounce direction.

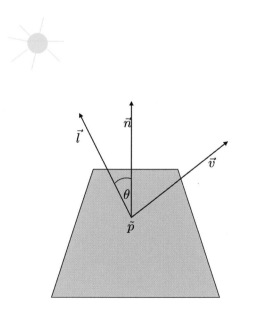

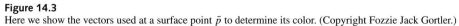

Figure 14.3
Here we show the vectors used at a surface point $\tilde{p}$ to determine its color. (Copyright Fozzie Jack Gortler.)

vector, $\vec{l}$. The light hits the point $\tilde{p}$ on some triangle with normal $\vec{n}$. The angle between the surface normal and the vector pointing toward the light is denoted as θ. In this setting, we want to compute the amount of light reflected toward the eye along the *view vector*, $\vec{v}$. To handle color, we just compute three reflected quantities for red, green, and blue (RGB). Note that this use of RGB is not physically accurate (see section 19.5 later in the text). These quantities are then directly used as the RGB values for the pixel. We will assume here that all coordinates of points and vectors are written with respect to the eye frame.

As we mentioned long ago (see figure 6.1), the normal does not have to be the "true normal" of the flat triangular geometry. Instead, it is defined by the user at each vertex and interpolated as a varying variable. In this way, we can get the effect, during material simulation, of a smooth surface with smoothly varying normals.

14.2 Diffuse

Diffuse materials, like rough wood, appear equally bright when observed from all directions $\vec{v}$. Thus, when calculating the color of a point on a diffuse surface, we do not need to use the $\vec{v}$ vector at all. Diffuse materials appear brighter when light hits them "from above" and appear dimmer when light hits them from a grazing angle. This is because (see chapter 21) the amount of incoming photons hitting a small, fixed-sized patch of material is proportional to $\cos(\theta) = \vec{n} \cdot \vec{l}$. Given these assumptions, we can calculate the color of a diffuse material in the following fragment shader (which we also used earlier in section 6.4).

```
#version 330

uniform vec3 uLight;

in vec3 vColor;
in vec3 vNormal;
in vec4 vPosition;

out fragColor;

void main(){
  vec3 toLight = normalize(uLight - vec3(vPosition));
  vec3 normal = normalize(vNormal);
  float diffuse = max(0.0, dot(normal, toLight));
  vec3 intensity = vColor * diffuse;
  fragColor = vec4(intensity.x, intensity.y, intensity.z, 1.0);
}
```

The normalize call is used to make sure the interpolated vectors have unit norm. The max call is used so that we do not try to produce negative colors at points that face away from the light. The calculated value of `diffuse` is used to modulate the intrinsic surface color passed in as `vColor`.

We have used this shader to draw our simple cube figures such as figure 5.1 and the ovoid shape in figure 14.4.

This shader can be easily extended in a number of ways:

• In this shader, the light itself has not been given a color of its own. This, too, can be easily modeled with the addition of another uniform variable.

• Multiple lights can also be easily added to this code.

• In the real world, light bounces multiple times around a scene, and thus there is always some light hitting each surface from every direction. This can be very crudely modeled in our computation by simply adding some constant *ambient* color value to `intensity`.

• Sometimes, it may be more convenient to model the light as coming from a direction, described by a vector, instead of from a point. In this case, when modeling such a *directional light*, the vector `toLight` would be passed in as a uniform variable.

14.3 Shiny

Many materials, such as plastics, are not diffuse; for a fixed incoming light distribution, they appear brighter when observed from some directions and dimmer when observed from others. Round objects made up of such materials have bright highlights wherever the

Figure 14.4
A diffusely shaded ovoid.

surface-normal points "just right." The exact form of this kind of reflection can be measured for a particular material with some kind of device. It can also at times be predicted using "micro-facet" theory [14]. In this theory, one thinks of a material as being made up of lots of microscopic true mirrors interacting in some statistical manner.

A simple, somewhat plausible computation that is often used in practice is to simply calculate the light's bounce vector $B(\vec{l})$, and then compute its angle with $\vec{v}$. When the bounce and view vectors are well aligned, we draw a very bright pixel. When they are not well aligned, we draw a dimmer pixel.

An even simpler way to get the same effect is first to compute the *halfway vector*

$$\vec{h} = \text{normalize}(\vec{v} + \vec{l})$$

and then measure its angle ϕ with $\vec{n}$ (see figure 14.5). The vectors $\vec{h}$ and $\vec{n}$ are well aligned only when $\vec{v}$ and $B(\vec{l})$ are. We compute the cosine of ϕ using a dot product, giving us a value in $[0 \ldots 1]$ that falls off as $\vec{h}$ and $\vec{n}$ diverge. To model shiny materials, we want the brightness to fall off very quickly in angle, so we then raise $\cos(\phi)$ to a positive power (64 in the code that follows).

Putting these ideas all together, we get the following shader:

```
#version 330

uniform vec3 uLight;
in vec3 vColor;
```

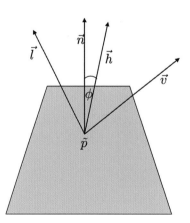

Figure 14.5
Here we show the vectors used to shade a shiny material.

```
in vec3 vNormal;
in vec4 vPosition;

out fragColor;

void main(){
  vec3 toLight = uLight - vec3(vPosition);
  vec3 toV= -normalize(vec3(vPosition));
  toLight = normalize(toLight);
  vec3 h = normalize(toV + toLight);
  vec3 normal = normalize(vNormal);

  float specular = pow(max(0.0, dot(h, normal)), 64.0);
  float diffuse = max(0.0, dot(normal, toLight));
  vec3 intensity = vec3(0.1,0.1,0.1) + vColor * diffuse
       + vec3(0.6,0.6,0.6) * specular;

  fragColor = vec4(intensity.x, intensity.y, intensity.z, 1.0);
}
```

The coordinates of the vector $\vec{v}$ (stored here in a variable named toV) are particularly easy to compute, as, in eye coordinates, the eye's position coincides with the origin. Also notice that, in this code, the specular component is white and is unrelated to any material color. This is quite typical for plastic materials, where the highlights match the color of the incoming light, regardless of the material color.

We have used this shader to draw our ovoid shapes, such as in figure 6.1 and here in figure 14.6.

14.4 Anisotropy

The two previous material models, as well as many others, have the property of *isotropy*. This means that there is no preferred "grain" to the surface. All that matters is the relative geometry of the light, view, and normal vectors. In contrast, some materials, like brushed metal, behave in an *anisotropic* manner. If one takes a flat sample of such a material and spins it around its normal, the material's appearance changes. When modeling such a material, we will assume that a preferred tangent vector, $\vec{t}$, is somehow included in the model and given to the shader (see figure 14.7). In the code that follows we show a shader described in [42] based on equations derived by Kajiya and Kay [33] to simulate light bouncing off of an anisotropic furry surface. These equations were derived based on the assumption that the surface is made up of tiny cylinders; the details of this derivation are beyond the scope of this book.

Figure 14.6
A shiny ovoid.

```
#version 330

uniform vec3 uLight;

in vec3 vColor;
in vec3 vNormal;
in vec4 vPosition;
in vec4 vTangent;

out fragColor;

void main(void){
  vec3 toLight = normalize(uLight - vec3(vPosition));
  vec3 toV = -normalize(vec3(vPosition));
  toLight = normalize(toLight);
  vec3 h = normalize(toV + toLight);
  vec3 normal = normalize(vNormal);

  vec3 vTangent3 = vec3(pTangent);

  vTangent3=normalize(cross(vNormal,vTangent3));

  float nl = dot(normal, toLight);
  float dif = max(0,.75*nl+.25);
```

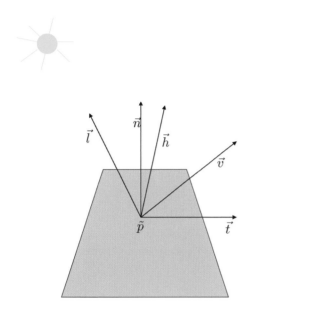

Figure 14.7
To model an anisotropic material, we also need to include a preferred tangent direction.

Figure 14.8
An anisotropically shaded ovoid.

```
float v = dot(vTangent3, h);
v = pow(1.0 - v*v, 16.0);

float r =  pColor.r * dif + 0.3 * v;
float g =  pColor.g * dif + 0.3 * v;
float b =  pColor.b * dif + 0.3 * v;

fragColor = vec4(r, g, b, 1);
}
```

We have used this shader to render an ovoid shape in figure 14.8.

Exercise

14.1 This chapter is just a jumping-off point for numerous reading and coding projects. We invite the reader to learn more about material simulation used in computer graphics starting from the references given.

15 Texture Mapping

In chapter 14, we saw how a simple model of interaction between light and materials can be used to compute a pixel's color. The second main tool typically used by a fragment shader to compute a pixel's color is to fetch data from an auxiliary image called a *texture*. In this chapter, we will explore basic *texture mapping* as well as a number of variants. Such techniques are one of the main tools used to make our renderings look detailed and rich.

Figure 15.1 shows a simple example of texture mapping. On the left, we see a simple model made up of a few dozen triangles. One triangle is highlighted in red. We associate x_t, y_t *texture coordinates* with each vertex of each triangle (top). These coordinates "map" each vertex to some location in the texture. The texture coordinates are then interpolated over the triangle (bottom), giving us texture coordinates for each pixel. The fragment shader then grabs the texture color that is pointed to by its texture coordinates and sends it to the framebuffer. The resulting rendered image is shown on the right.

15.1 Basic Texturing

In basic texturing, we simply "glue" part of an image onto a triangle by specifying texture coordinates at the three vertices. In this model, we assume that each of the variables x_t and y_t are functions over a triangle that are affine in object coordinates. This allows us to translate and rotate (or even scale and shear) the texture image in this gluing process.

The code for loading a texture is described in section A.4 of appendix A. As described there, a uniform variable is used to point to the desired texture unit, which is the same for all pixels processed in this draw-call. Varying variables are used to store texture coordinates at vertices, which point into some specific 2D location in the texture.

Here, we describe the relevant shaders needed for basic texture mapping. In this basic texturing example, the vertex shader simply passes the texture coordinates out to the fragment shader as varying variables.

```
#version 330

uniform mat4 uProjMatrix;
uniform mat4 uModelViewMatrix;
```

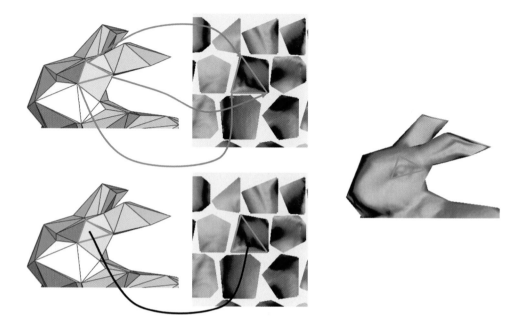

Figure 15.1
Top: Each vertex of a triangle is given x, y texture coordinates. These point into the texture image. Bottom: These coordinates are interpolated as varying variables at the pixel resolution. In the fragment shader, we can grab the color pointed to by the texture coordinates and use it in our rendering (right). (From [65], copyright ACM.)

```
in vec2 aTexCoord;
in vec4 aVertex;

out vec2  vTexCoord;

void main(){
  vTexCoord = aTexCoord;
  gl_Position = uProjMatrix * uModelViewMatrix * aVertex;
}
```

The following fragment shader then uses these interpolated texture coordinates to lookup the desired color data from the texture and set the color in the framebuffer.

```
#version 330

uniform sampler2D uTexUnit0;

in vec2  vTexCoord;
out fragColor
```

```
void main(){
  vec4 texColor0 = texture2D(uTexUnit0, vTexCoord);
  fragColor = texColor0;
}
```

The data type `sampler2D` is a special GLSL data type that refers to an OpenGL texture unit. The call to `texture2D` fetches a value from the texture unit.

In this simplest incarnation, we just fetch r,g,b values from the texture and send them directly to the framebuffer. Alternatively, the texture data could be interpreted as, say, the diffuse material color of the surface point, which would then be followed by the diffuse material computation described in section 14.2.

15.2 Normal Mapping

The data from a texture can also be interpreted in more interesting ways. In *normal mapping*, the r,g,b values from a texture are interpreted as the three coordinates of the normal at the point. These normal data can then be used as part of some material simulation, as described in chapter 14. See figure 15.2 for such an example.

Normal data have three coordinate values, each in the range $[-1 \dots 1]$, while RGB textures store three values, each in the range $[0 \dots 1]$. Thus, the normal data need to be transformed into this format before being stored in the texture, as in `r = normal_x/2. +.5;`. Conversely, your fragment shader needs to undo this transformation, as in `normal_x = 2r-1;`.

Figure 15.2
On the left we show a rendering of a teapot model. The teapot is shaded with smoothly interpolated normals, and the triangle edges are shown. (Copyright Hugues Hoppe.) On the right, we show the same surface, but now it is rendered using a normal field fetched from a high-resolution texture. These normals are used in the lighting calculations and give the effect of highly resolved geometric detail. (From [54], copyright ACM).

15.3 Environment Cube Maps

Textures can also be used to model the *environment* in the distance around the object being rendered. In this case, we typically use six square textures representing the faces of a large cube surrounding the scene. Each texture pixel represents the color as seen along one direction in the environment. This is called a *cube map*. GLSL provides a cube-texture data type, samplerCube, specifically for this purpose. During the shading of a point, we can treat the material at that point as a perfect mirror and fetch the environment data from the appropriate incoming direction. An example is shown in figure 15.3.

To implement this idea, we use equation (14.1) to calculate the bounced view vector, $B(\vec{v})$. This bounced vector will point toward the environment direction that would be observed in a mirrored surface. By looking up the cube map using this direction, we give the surface the appearance of a mirror.

```
#version 330
uniform samplerCube texUnit0;

in vec3 vNormal;
in vec4 vPosition;

out fragColor;

vec3 reflect(vec3 w, vec3 n){
  return - w + n * (dot(w, n)*2.0);
}
```

Figure 15.3
On the left, the environment is stored as a cube texture. This is used to render a mirrored lizard. (From [25], copyright IEEE.)

```
void main(void){
  vec3 normal = normalize(vNormal);
  vec3 reflected = reflect(normalize(vec3(-vPosition)), normal);
  vec4 texColor0 = textureCube(texUnit0,reflected);

  fragColor = vec4(texColor0.r, texColor0.g, texColor0.b, 1.0);
}
```

In eye coordinates, the eye's position coincides with the origin, and thus -vPosition represents the view vector $\vec{v}$. textureCube is a special GLSL function that takes a direction vector and returns the color stored at this direction in the cube texture map. In this code, all of our vectors are expressed in eye coordinates, and so we are also assuming that our cube texture represents the environment data in eye coordinates. If our cube texture were representing directions using, say, world coordinates, then appropriate coordinates for the rendered point would need to be passed to the fragment shader.

This same idea, but modeling refraction instead of mirror reflection, has been used to generate the fountain image of figure 22.4.

15.4 Projector Texture Mapping

There are times when we wish to glue our texture onto our triangles using a *projector* model instead of the affine gluing model assumed in section 15.1. For example, we may wish to simulate a slide projector illuminating some triangles in space (see figure 15.4). This is not as unusual as it may first appear. For example, suppose we have taken a photograph of the

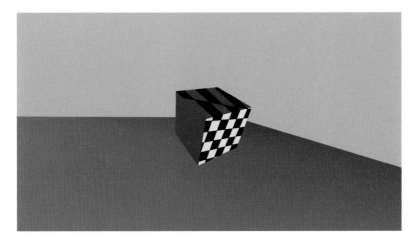

Figure 15.4
The checkerboard image is slide projected on to the front and top faces of the cube.

façade of a building with a camera and then wish to paste it appropriately on a digital 3D model of the building. To do this pasting, we should invert the geometry of the photography process by replacing the camera with a virtual slide projector in the same position relative to the building (see figure 15.5).

In *projector texture mapping*, the slide projector is modeled using 4 by 4 modelview and projection matrices, M_s and P_s. These define the relation

$$
\begin{bmatrix} x_t w_t \\ y_t w_t \\ - \\ w_t \end{bmatrix} = P_s M_s \begin{bmatrix} x_o \\ y_o \\ z_o \\ 1 \end{bmatrix}
\tag{15.1}
$$

with the texture coordinates defined as $x_t = \frac{x_t w_t}{w_t}$ and $y_t = \frac{y_t w_t}{w_t}$. To color a point on a triangle with object coordinates $[x_o, y_o, z_o, 1]^t$, we fetch the texture data stored at location $[x_t, y_t]^t$ (see Figure 15.6).

Because of the division by w_t, the values x_t and y_t are not affine functions of (x_o, y_o, z_o) and thus would not be appropriately interpolated if directly implemented using varying

Figure 15.5
Left: Actual photograph. Middle: Rendered geometric model. Right: Rendered with projector texture mapping. (From [15], copyright ACM.)

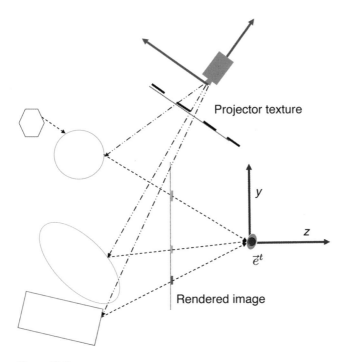

Projector texture

Rendered image

Figure 15.6
In projector texture mapping, to determine the color of a point observed in the eye's camera, we map this to a point in the "projectors image." The color from this texture is used to color the point.

variables. But, from section B.5 of appendix B, we see that, indeed, the three quantities $x_t w_t$, $y_t w_t$, and w_t are all affine functions of (x_o, y_o, z_o). Thus, these quantities will be properly interpolated over a triangle when implemented as varying variables. In the fragment shader, we need to divide by w_t to obtain the actual texture coordinates.

When doing projector texture mapping, we do not need to pass any texture coordinates as attribute variables to our vertex shader. We simply use the object coordinates already available to us. We do need to pass in, using uniform variables, the necessary projector matrices. Here is the relevant part of our vertex shader:

```
#version 330
uniform mat4 uModelViewMatrix;
uniform mat4 uProjMatrix;

uniform mat4 uSProjMatrix;
uniform mat4 uSModelViewMatrix;

in vec4 aVertex;
out  vec4  aTexCoord;
```

```
void main(){
  vTexCoord= uSProjMatrix * uSModelViewMatrix * aVertex;
  gl_Position = uProjMatrix * uModelViewMatrix * aVertex;
}
```

And our fragment shader is

```
#version 330

uniform sampler2D vTexUnit0;

in vec4 vTexCoord;
out fragColor

void main(void){
  vec2 tex2;
  tex2.x = vTexCoord.x/vTexCoord.w;
  tex2.y = vTexCoord.y/vTexCoord.w;
  vec4 texColor0 = texture2D(vTexUnit0, tex2);
  fragColor=  texColor0;
}
```

Full disclosure: To produce the image of figure 15.4, in our vertex shader we also computed the normal at each vertex in the "eye" coordinates of the projector. A diffuse lighting equation was then added to our fragment shader to modulate the texture color. As a result, the top face in the image is a bit dimmer than the rightmost face.

Conveniently, OpenGL even gives us a special call, texture2DProj(vTexUnit0, pTexCoord), which actually does the divide for us. Inconveniently, when designing our slide projector matrix uSProjMatrix, we have to deal with the fact that (as described in section 12.3.1) the canonical texture image domain in OpenGL is the *unit square* whose lower left and upper right corners have coordinates $[0, 0]^t$ and $[1, 1]^t$, respectively, instead of the *canonical square* from $[-1, -1]^t$ to $[1, 1]^t$ used for the display window. Thus, the appropriate projection matrix passed to the vertex shader would be of the form makeTranslation(Cvec3(0.5,0.5,0.5)) * makeScale(Cvec3(0.5,0.5,1)) * makeProjection(...).

15.5 Multipass

More interesting rendering effects can be obtained using multiple rendering passes over the geometry in the scene. In this approach, the results of all but the final pass are stored offline and not drawn to the screen. To do this, the data are rendered into something called a *frameBufferObject*, or FBO. After rendering, the FBO data is then loaded as a texture and thus can be used as input data in the next rendering pass. For coding details on FBOs, you might start with [53].

15.5.1 Dynamic Reflection Mapping

Dynamic reflection mapping is a simple example of multipass rendering. In this case, we want one of the rendered objects to be mirrored and reflect the rest of the scene. To accomplish this, we first render the rest of the scene as seen from, say, the center of the mirrored object. Because the scene is 360 degrees, we need to render six images from the chosen viewpoint, looking right, left, back, forth, up, and down. Each of these six images has a 90-degree vertical and horizontal field of view.

These data are then transferred over to a cube map. The mirrored object can now be rendered using the cube map shaders from section 15.3 (see figures 15.7 and 15.8 for an example). This calculation is not completely correct, as the environment map stores the view of the scene as seen *from one point only*. Meanwhile, true reflection needs to look at the appropriate bounced ray from each point of the object (see figure 15.9). Nonetheless, for casual use, reflection mapping can be quite effective.

15.5.2 Shadow Mapping

In our simple material calculations of chapter 14, the color computation at a point does not depend on any of the rest of the geometry in the scene. Of course, in the real world, if some occluding object is situated between a surface point and the light, the point will be in shadow and thus be darker. This effect can be simulated using a multipass technique called

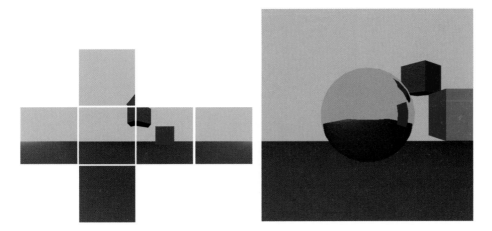

Figure 15.7
In dynamic reflection mapping, the scene (floor and cubes) is first rendered into a cube map. This is used as environment map to render the mirrored sphere.

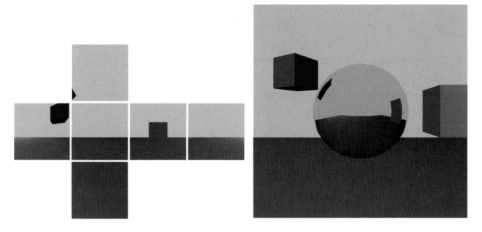

Figure 15.8
The blue cube is moved. The cube map is re-created and the image redrawn.

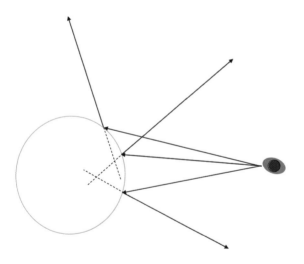

Figure 15.9
To render a mirrored sphere correctly, we need to follow a set of bounce rays that do not all intersect in a single point.

shadow mapping. The idea is first to create and store a z-buffered image from the point of view of the light, and then compare what we see in our view to what the light saw in its view (see figure 15.10). If a point observed by the eye is not observed by the light, then there must be some occluding object in between, and we should draw that point as if it were in shadow.

In a first pass, we render into an FBO the scene as observed from some camera whose origin coincides with the position of the point light source. Let us model this camera transform as

$$
\begin{bmatrix} x_t w_t \\ y_t w_t \\ z_t w_t \\ w_t \end{bmatrix} = P_s M_s \begin{bmatrix} x_o \\ y_o \\ z_o \\ 1 \end{bmatrix}
$$

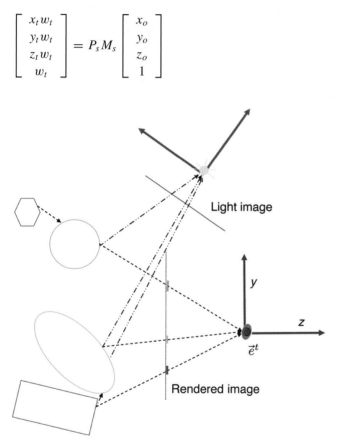

Figure 15.10
In shadow mapping, we first render an (FBO) image from the point of view of the light. Only depth values are stored in this image. In a second pass, we render the scene from the point of view of our eye. Using the same mathematics from projector texturing, for every point observed by the eye, we can compare its light depth to that stored in the light's image. If these agree (orange and green points), the point was seen by the light, and we color it appropriately. If these disagree (purple), then the point was occluded from the eye and is in shadow, and we color it differently.

Figure 15.11
In shadow mapping, the scene is first rendered from the point of view of the light (visualized on the left). The depth values are stored in a texture. In the second pass, the light texture data are used to determine if the surface point is directly observed by the light. This gives us the final rendered image on the right. (Copyright Hamilton Chong.)

for appropriate matrices, P_s and M_s. During this first pass, we render the scene to an FBO using M_s as the modelview matrix and P_s as the projection matrix. In the FBO, we store not the color of the point but rather its z_t value. Because of z-buffering, the data stored at a pixel in the FBO represent the z_t value of the *geometry closest to the light* along the relevant line of sight. This FBO is then transferred to a texture.

During the second rendering pass, we render our desired image from the eye's point of view, but for each pixel, we check and see if the point we are observing was also observed by the light or if it was blocked by something closer in the light's view. To do this, we use the same computation that was done with projector texture mapping in section 15.4. Doing so, in the fragment shader, we can obtain the varying variables x_t, y_t, and z_t associated with the point $[x_o, y_o, z_o, 1]^t$. We then compare this z_t value with the z_t value stored at $[x_t, y_t]^t$ in the texture. If these values agree (to within a small precision tolerance), then we are looking at a point that was also seen by the light; such a point is not in shadow and should be shaded accordingly. Conversely, if these values disagree, then the point we are looking at was occluded in the light's image, is in shadow, and should be shaded as such. See figure 15.11 for an example.

Exercise

15.1 This chapter is just a jumping-off point for numerous reading and coding projects. For example, you can implement normal, environment, reflection, or shadow mapping.

16 Sampling

It is now time for us to focus a bit more on how we treat images. There are really two notions of images that we have implicitly been using so far, discrete (also called digital) and continuous. In the following chapters, we will investigate this dichotomy more closely and discuss the appropriate ways to move back and forth between the discrete and continuous model.

In this chapter, we will focus on the variety of visual artifacts that can arise when creating a digital image in computer graphics. These artifacts include distracting jagged patterns at triangle boundaries and go by the name *aliasing* artifacts. Aliasing artifacts can occur when, in some sense, there is too much visual complexity to fit in a single pixel. In this case, when we try to determine the pixel's color value by looking at only a single point location in the image domain, we can get a less than optimal result. As we will see, these artifacts can be mitigated by averaging together the colors over many sample locations within the pixel's square. This process is known as *anti-aliasing*.

16.1 Two Models

A *continuous image*, $I(x_w, y_w)$, is a bivariate function. As discussed in section 12.3, the domain, $\Omega = [-0.5 \ldots W - 0.5] \times [-0.5 \ldots H - 0.5]$, of the function is the real-valued 2D window coordinates $[x_w, y_w]^t$. (In the rest of this chapter and the next, we drop the w subscript unless needed.) The range of the function is a color space, for which we use an RGB (linear) color space.

A *discrete image* I[i][j] is a 2D array of color values. Each such array entry is called a pixel. The array's size is W in width by H in height, thus i is an integer in $[0 \ldots W - 1]$, and j is an integer in $[0 \ldots H - 1]$. We associate each pair of integers i, j, with the continuous image coordinates $x_w = i$ and $y_w = j$ (i.e., real coordinates that happen to have integer values). Each color value is a triplet of scalars representing a color in a color space. Again, we use an RGB (linear) color space. Finally, each of the R, G, and B coordinates is represented in some numerical format.

In OpenGL, we describe a scene using shaded triangles in 3D. Under projection, these map to colored triangles in the continuous 2D image domain and thus define a continuous image. Ultimately, we wish to display this image on a monitor or save it in an image file. As such, we need to know how to transform the continuous image into a discrete one.

16.2 The Problem

The simplest and most obvious method to go from a continuous to a discrete image is by *point sampling*; that is, to obtain the value of a pixel i,j, we sample the continuous image function at a single integer valued domain location:

I[i][j] ← $I(i, j)$.

It turns out that there are many situations where point sampling results in unwanted artifacts. For example, consider a scene composed of some black and white triangles. When point sampling the image, near the boundary between a white and black triangle, the image will display some sort of staircase pattern; this artifact is referred to as "the jaggies" (see figure 16.1). During animation, some pixel values will change suddenly from white to black, and the jagged edge pattern will appear to crawl. This is called "the crawling jaggies."

We can get other bad artifacts when dealing with very small triangles. Suppose we are rendering a picture of a herd of zebras (or small black-and-white squares on a faraway checkerboard). Suppose one of the zebras is far away in the background, so far away that it covers just a single pixel. What will the color of that pixel be? If the point sample happens to land on a black triangle, then the pixel will be black, whereas if it happens to land on a white triangle, the pixel will be white (see figure 16.2). If we are unlucky, the resulting pixel colors will form some distracting *moire* pattern as in figure 16.1. During animation, if the zebra moves, these pixels will then take on changing patterns of black and white. This artifact is referred to as "flickering." Such artifacts can also occur during texture mapping if a highly detailed texture is mapped to a small region on the screen (see figure 18.2).

These types of errors occur when the continuous image has lots of detail in a small region. In the zebra example, the continuous image has a whole lot of zebra in the space of a few pixels. With the jagged triangle example, the continuous image has an exact sharp edge with an immediate transition, not a gradual one. For technical reasons, these kinds of problems are known as *aliasing*.

16.3 The Solution

When there is a lot of detail in a small region, it is unlikely that we can maintain all of the information in our discrete representation. But by taking only a single sample to determine the pixel's color, we are making matters even worse for ourselves, possibly just picking a meaningless value. It seems sensible that we would be better off setting the pixel value using

Figure 16.1
Top row: A checkerboard drawn as a bunch of little black-and-white squares. (No texture mapping is used here.) The image has been blown up on the right to show the pixel values more clearly. On the edges of squares, jaggies are seen. In distant regions, moire patterns are seen. Middle row: The image created using multisampling in OpenGL. This improves the image significantly. Bottom row: The image created offline using a very high rate of super sampling. This is, ideally, what we would like our rendering to look like.

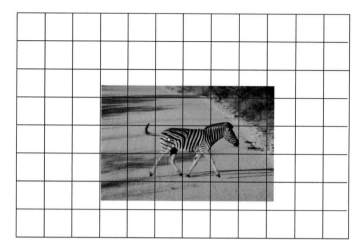

Figure 16.2
When the continuous image has lots of high-resolution detail (a zebra) and a single sample (light blue) is used to determine the pixel value, we obtain a useless value. (Copyright Stuart Maxwell.)

some kind of average value over some appropriate region. In the zebra example, perhaps we would be better off just setting the pixel to gray.

There is a variety of ways mathematically to model this problem and look for an optimal solution. For example, using "Fourier analysis," one could look at which "frequencies" are representable with a certain number of pixels and how to best deal with the unrepresentable frequencies. For such a discussion, see [6]. From an optimization point of view, one could try to minimize the difference between the original continuous image with the light pattern that is ultimately displayed on the screen. (On the screen, each pixel is drawn with a finite extent and thus we can think of the light pattern on the screen as a synthesized continuous image.)

From these various points of view, which we will not pursue here in detail, it turns out that it is best to set the pixel value using an expression of the form:

$$\mathtt{I[i][j]} \leftarrow \int\int_{\Omega} dx\, dy\, I(x, y) F_{i,j}(x, y), \tag{16.1}$$

where $F_{i,j}(x, y)$ is some function that tells us how strongly the continuous image value at $[x, y]^t$ should influence the pixel value $\mathtt{i,j}$. In this setting, the function $F_{i,j}(x, y)$ is called a *filter*.

In other words, the best pixel value is determined by performing some continuous weighted averaging near the pixel's location. Effectively, this is like blurring the continuous image before point sampling it to obtain a discrete image. The use of equation (16.1) to create a discrete image is referred to as *anti-aliasing*.

The optimal choice for $F_{i,j}$ turns out to depend on the particular mathematical approach used to model the problem. In theory, such an optimal $F_{i,j}$ might have a wide support, and even take on negative values. In practice, we do not require complete optimality, and we often choose the filters $F_{i,j}(x, y)$ to be something that can more easily be used in computation. The simplest such choice is a *box filter*, where $F_{i,j}(x, y)$ is zero everywhere except over the 1 by 1 square centered at $x = i$, $y = j$. Calling this square $\Omega_{i,j}$, we arrive at

$$\texttt{I[i][j]} \leftarrow \int\int_{\Omega_{i,j}} dx\, dy\, I(x, y). \tag{16.2}$$

In this case, the desired pixel value is simply the average of the continuous image over the pixel's square domain (see figure 16.3).

In computer graphics, even the integral of equation (16.2) is too difficult to exactly compute. Instead, it is approximated by some sum of the form:

$$\texttt{I[i][j]} \leftarrow \frac{1}{n} \sum_{k=1}^{n} I(x_k, y_k), \tag{16.3}$$

where k indexes some set of locations (x_k, y_k) called the *sample locations*. We call this *oversampling* (see figure 16.4).

To do oversampling, the renderer first produces a "high-resolution" color and z-buffer "image," where we will use the term *sample* to refer to each of these high-resolution pixels.

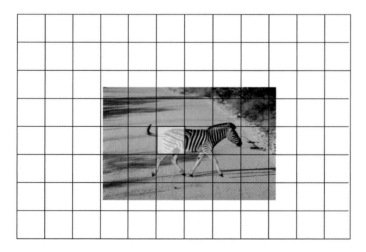

Figure 16.3
We obtain a better answer if we replace the point sample with an integral over the pixel's square domain. (Copyright Stuart Maxwell.)

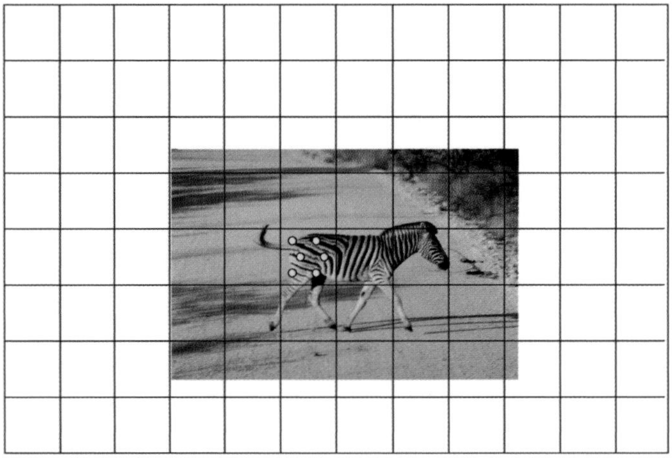

Figure 16.4
We can approximate the true integral with a set of discrete samples (six in this example). (Copyright Stuart Maxwell.)

Then, once rasterization is complete, groups of these samples are averaged together, using equation (16.3), to create the final, lower-resolution image.

If the sample locations for the high-resolution image form a regular, high-resolution grid, then this is called *super sampling*. See figure 16.1 (bottom) to see the effect of super sampling using a very high oversampling rate. We can also choose other sampling patterns for the high-resolution "image," as visualized in figure 16.4. Such less regular patterns can help us avoid systematic errors that can arise when using equation (16.3) to approximate equation (16.2). For a more detailed discussion of some of the benefits of such nonregular patterns, see [12, 49].

In OpenGL, the details of the sampling patterns are hardware dependent. They can be changed by API calls or, more easily, by changing settings for the hardware driver in an interactive control panel.

In OpenGL, we can also choose to do *multisampling*. In this case, OpenGL draws to a "high-resolution" color and z-buffer, as in oversampling. During the rasterization of each triangle, "coverage" and z-values are computed at this sample level. But for efficiency, the fragment shader is called **only once per final resolution pixel**. These color data are shared among all of the samples hit by the triangle in a single (final-resolution) pixel. As above, once rasterization is complete, groups of these high-resolution samples are averaged together, using equation (16.3) to create the final lower-resolution, image. Multisampling can be an effective anti-aliasing method, as, without texture mapping, colors tend to vary quite slowly over each triangle, and thus they do not need to be computed at high spatial resolution. See figure 16.1 (middle) to see the effect of using multisampling when rendering a scene without texture mapping.

To deal with aliasing that occurs during texture mapping, we have the advantage of possessing the texture image in hand at the outset of the rendering process. This leads to specialized techniques such as *mip mapping* described in section 18.3. We defer our discussion of texture anti-aliasing and mip mapping until after we have covered the topic of image reconstruction in chapter 17.

16.3.1 In the Wild

In digital cameras, anti-aliasing is accomplished by a combination of the spatial integration that happens over the extent of each pixel sensor, as well as by the optical blurring that happens due to the lens. Some cameras also include additional optical elements specifically to blur the continuous image data before it is sampled at the sensors. Aliasing can sometimes be seen in digital images of scenes containing certain regular patterns, such as those in tweed jackets.

In human vision, aliasing artifacts are not typically encountered. Most of the anti-aliasing, at least in the foveal (central) region of vision, is due to the optical blurring of light, which happens well before it hits the receptor cells [78]. The irregular spatial layout of the sensor cells in the retina also helps by effectively providing spatial jitter (randomness), which turns noticeable aliasing into less conspicuous noise.

16.3.2 Anti-aliased Lines

Lines are ideally 1D, and the notion of what it means to draw a properly filtered line is a more complicated question. Smooth line drawing is available in OpenGL, but this is beyond our scope. The interested reader may see [48] and references therein.

16.4 Alpha

Suppose we have two discrete images, a foreground, I^f, and a background, I^b, that we want to combine into one image, I^c. For example, we may want to superimpose the foreground picture of a weatherman over the background image of a weather map. The most obvious solution is to cut out the weatherman pixels from his image. In the composite image, we could simply replace those weather-map pixels with weatherman pixels.

Unfortunately, this will give us a jagged boundary in the weatherman/weather map transition region (see figure 16.5, left). In a real photograph or an image rendered using equation (16.2), the pixel color on the man/map boundary would be set using some average of man and map colors. The problem is that in our discrete image layers, we have only saved one color value per pixel, and this can no longer calculate the correct composite pixel colors.

A reasonable solution to this can be obtained using a technique called *alpha blending*. The basic idea is to associate with each pixel in each image layer a value, $\alpha[i][j]$, that describes the overall *opacity* or *coverage* of the image layer at that pixel. An alpha value of 1 represents a fully opaque/occupied pixel, and a value of 0 represents a fully transparent/empty one.

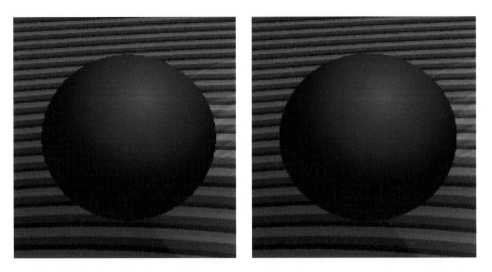

Figure 16.5
An image of a ball is composited over a textured background. Look carefully at the boundary of the ball. On the left, the all/nothing compositing is done. On the right, alpha values are used for the blending. (Copyright Hamilton Chong.)

A fractional value represents a partially transparent (partially occupied) pixel. For example, in the weatherman image, we would expect every pixel fully covered by the man to have an alpha value of 1 and those in his silhouette to have a fractional value, as those pixels are only partially occupied by the weatherman.

Then, to composite two image layers, at each pixel we use these alpha values to determine how to combine the foreground and background colors.

More specifically, let $I(x, y)$ be a continuous image, and let $C(x, y)$ be a binary valued *coverage function* over the continuous (x, y) domain, with a value of 1 at any point where the image is "occupied" and 0 where it is not. Let us store in our discrete image the values

$$\texttt{I[i][j]} \leftarrow \int\int_{\Omega_{i,j}} dx\, dy\, I(x, y)C(x, y)$$

$$\alpha\texttt{[i][j]} \leftarrow \int\int_{\Omega_{i,j}} dx\, dy\, C(x, y).$$

The colors in this format are often called *premultiplied* (see section 16.4.2 for the non-premultiplied version).

Given these values, when we want to compose $\texttt{I}^f\texttt{[i][j]}$ *over* $\texttt{I}^b\texttt{[i][j]}$, we compute the composite image colors, $\texttt{I}^c\texttt{[i][j]}$, using

$$\texttt{I}^c\texttt{[i][j]} \leftarrow \texttt{I}^f\texttt{[i][j]} + \texttt{I}^b\texttt{[i][j]}(1 - \alpha^f\texttt{[i][j]}). \tag{16.4}$$

That is, the amount of observed background color at a pixel is proportional to the transparency of the foreground layer at that pixel.

Likewise, alpha for the composite image can be computed as

$$\alpha^c[\texttt{i}][\texttt{j}] \leftarrow \alpha^f[\texttt{i}][\texttt{j}] + \alpha^b[\texttt{i}][\texttt{j}](1 - \alpha^f[\texttt{i}][\texttt{j}]). \tag{16.5}$$

Often, the background layer is completely opaque at all pixels, in which case, so is the composite image. But this formula is general enough to model the composition of two partially opaque images, which can produce a composite image with fractional alpha values; this can be used as an intermediate result when dealing with more than two layers.

Figure 16.5 shows the result of compositing a foreground image of a ball over an image of a textured background. In the foreground image, the pixels at the boundary of the ball (right) have fractional alpha values. In the resulting composite image, the boundary of the ball shows a blend of foreground and background colors.

The operation of equations (16.4) and (16.5) is called the discrete binary *over* operation. One can easily verify that the over operation is associative but not commutative. That is,

$$\texttt{I}^a \text{ over } (\texttt{I}^b \text{ over } \texttt{I}^c) = (\texttt{I}^a \text{ over } \texttt{I}^b) \text{ over } \texttt{I}^c,$$

but

$$\texttt{I}^a \text{ over } \texttt{I}^b. \neq \texttt{I}^b \text{ over } \texttt{I}^a.$$

16.4.1 Comparison with Continuous Composition (Optional)

Alpha blending is based on the notion of treating our pixels as semitransparent objects. Let us see how the result of discrete alpha blending compares with a correctly anti-aliased, continuously composited image.

Let C^f be the binary valued coverage function of the foreground continuous image I^f. And let C^b be the binary valued coverage function of the background continuous image I^b. (For generality, we allow the background image to be unoccupied at some points.) We assume that, at any point (x, y), if $C^f(x, y)$ is 1, we observe the foreground color, and, if $C^f(x, y)$ is 0, we observe the background color. Then, the box-filtered anti-aliased discrete image at pixel i, j should be

$$\texttt{I}^c[\texttt{i}][\texttt{j}] \leftarrow \iint_{\Omega_{i,j}} dx\, dy\, I^f(x,y)C^f(x,y) + I^b(x,y)C^b(x,y) - I^b(x,y)C^b(x,y)C^f(x,y)$$

$$= \iint_{\Omega_{i,j}} dx\, dy\, I^f(x,y)C^f(x,y) + \iint_{\Omega_{i,j}} dx\, dy\, I^b(x,y)C^b(x,y)$$

$$- \iint_{\Omega_{i,j}} dx\, dy\, I^b(x,y)C^b(x,y)C^f(x,y).$$

Let us compare this with the alpha blended result:

$$\text{I}^c[\text{i}][\text{j}] \leftarrow \text{I}^f[\text{i}][\text{j}] + \text{I}^b[\text{i}][\text{j}](1 - \alpha^f[\text{i}][\text{j}])$$

$$= \int\int_{\Omega_{i,j}} dx\,dy\, I^f(x, y)C^f(x, y)$$

$$+ \left(\int\int_{\Omega_{i,j}} dx\,dy\, I^b(x, y)C^b(x, y)\right)\left(1 - \int\int_{\Omega_{i,j}} dx\,dy\, C^f(x, y)\right)$$

$$= \int\int_{\Omega_{i,j}} dx\,dy\, I^f(x, y)C^f(x, y) + \int\int_{\Omega_{i,j}} dx\,dy\, I^b(x, y)C^b(x, y)$$

$$- \int\int_{\Omega_{i,j}} dx\,dy\, I^b(x, y)C^b(x, y) \cdot \int\int_{\Omega_{i,j}} dx\,dy\, C^f(x, y).$$

The difference between two results is

$$\int\int_{\Omega_{i,j}} dx\,dy\, I^b(x, y)C^b(x, y)C^f(x, y) - \int\int_{\Omega_{i,j}} dx\,dy\, I^b(x, y)C^b(x, y)$$

$$\times \int\int_{\Omega_{i,j}} dx\,dy\, C^f(x, y).$$

This error is the difference between the integral of a product and a product of integrals. As such, we can think of this error as representing the amount of "correlation" between the distribution of foreground coverage in some pixel and the distribution of the background data within that pixel. If we assume that the foreground coverage is uniform and random, then we can safely ignore this error.

16.4.2 Non-premultiplied

In some uses of alpha, instead of storing I and α, we store $\text{I}' = \text{I}/\alpha$ together with α. This is called the "non-premultiplied" format. This improves data precision; when a pixel has a small coverage value, then I will be a small number and only utilize a few of the lower-order bits in a fixed point representation. In the non-premultiplied form, one can use all of the bits in the stored file format to describe the color independent of the coverage. In non-premultiplied form, the over operator becomes the more complicated:

$$\alpha^c[\text{i}][\text{j}] \leftarrow \alpha^f[\text{i}][\text{j}] + \alpha^b[\text{i}][\text{j}](1 - \alpha^f[\text{i}][\text{j}])$$

$$\text{I}'^c[\text{i}][\text{j}] \leftarrow \frac{1}{\alpha^c[\text{i}][\text{j}]}(\alpha^f[\text{i}][\text{j}]\text{I}'^f[\text{i}][\text{j}] + (\alpha^b[\text{i}][\text{j}]\text{I}'^b[\text{i}][\text{j}])(1 - \alpha^f[\text{i}][\text{j}])).$$

However, when all of the pixels in the background have alpha values of 1, this becomes

$$\alpha^c\texttt{[i][j]} \leftarrow 1$$

$$\texttt{I}'^c\texttt{[i][j]} \leftarrow \alpha^f\texttt{[i][j]}\texttt{I}'^f\texttt{[i][j]} + \texttt{I}'^b\texttt{[i][j]}(1 - \alpha^f\texttt{[i][j]}),$$

which is an expression you will sometimes run into.

One advantage of the premultiplied format is that if we want to shrink our image by a factor of two in each direction (which will be needed, e.g., for mip mapping, described in section 18.3), we simply have to average together the appropriate four I^f values. In the non-premultiplied format, this computation becomes uglier.

16.4.3 Pulling Mattes
Given real photographs, it is not easy to correctly pull out an image layer representing one observed object in the scene. Even if you have a weatherman standing in front of a blue screen, it may be easy to confuse a bluish opaque foreground pixel with a semitransparent gray one. This is an area of current research. For more on this, see [43] and references therein.

16.4.4 In Practice
In OpenGL, alpha is used not just for image compositing, but in a more general sense as a tool for modeling transparency and for blending color values. We can assign an alpha value as the fourth component of `fragColor` in a fragment shader, and this is used to combine `fragColor` with whatever is currently present in the framebuffer. For example, alpha can be used as a way of modeling (monochromatic) transparency. Blending is enabled with

Figure 16.6
A furry bunny is drawn as a series of larger and larger concentric bunnies. Each is partially transparent. Amazingly, this looks like fur.

the call glEnable(GL_BLEND), and the blending calculation to be used is specified by the arguments in a call to glBlendFuncSeparate.

For example, the furry bunny of figure 16.6 has been drawn in OpenGL using alpha blending. The bunny has been drawn as a series of "shells," each textured with an image representing a slice of fur. These textures include alpha values, so the spaces between the fur are semitransparent. This technique is described in [42].

The main difficulty in using alpha in graphics is that, for a noncommutative blending operation (such as the over operator), the object layers must be drawn in a specific order (say back to front). If we are given the layers out of order and must combine them as they are given to us, there is no way to get the desired answer. This makes transparency somewhat difficult to handle in a rasterization-based context. This is in contrast with the usual use of the z-buffer, where the opaque objects can be drawn in any order.

Exercise

16.1 Write a program that uses alpha blending to draw a furry sphere, as described in [42]. The basic idea is to draw a set of concentric spheres from inside out. Each sphere is to be textured with a dot pattern that is interpreted as the desired alpha values.

17 Reconstruction

Now let us look at the problem opposite that of chapter 16: Given a discrete image `I[i][j]`, how do we create a continuous image $I(x, y)$? As we will see, this problem is central to resizing images and to texture mapping. For example, in our fragment shader, we may wish to fetch a color from a texture using texture coordinates that fall *in between* the texture's pixels. In this case, we need to decide what texture colors to use. This process is called *reconstruction*.

17.1 Constant

Let us again assume that our pixels correspond to integer valued (x, y) locations and that we wish to determine a color at some fractional valued location. Perhaps the easiest image reconstruction approach is the *constant reconstruction* (or *nearest neighbor*) method. In this method, a real-valued image coordinate is assumed to have the color of the closest discrete pixel. This method can be described by the following pseudocode:

```
color constantReconstruction(float x, float y, color image[][]){
  int i = (int) (x + .5);
  int j = (int) (y + .5);
  return image[i][j]
}
```

The "`(int)`" typecast rounds a number p to the nearest integer not larger than p.

We can think of this method as defining a continuous image over the continuous (x, y) domain. We call this "constant reconstruction," as the resulting continuous image is made up of little squares of constant color. For example, the image has the constant value of `I[0][0]` in the square-shaped region: $-0.5 < x < 0.5$ and $-0.5 < y < 0.5$. Each pixel has an influence region of 1 by 1 (see figure 17.1, left).

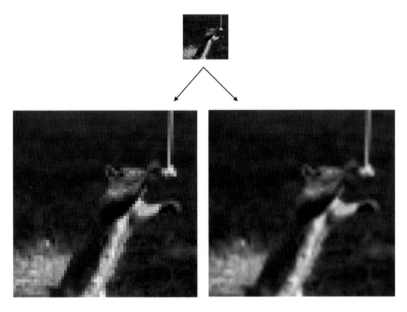

Figure 17.1
Top row: A 64 by 64 discrete image. Bottom left: Reconstructed using constant reconstruction. Bottom right:
Reconstructed using bilinear reconstruction. (Copyright Yasuhiro Endo.)

17.2 Bilinear

Constant reconstruction produces blocky looking images. We can create a smoother looking
reconstruction using *bilinear interpolation*. Bilinear interpolation is obtained by applying
linear interpolation in both the horizontal and vertical directions. It can be described by the
following code:

```
color bilinearReconstruction(float  x, float y, color image[][]){
  int intx = (int) x;
  int inty = (int) y;
  float fracx = x - intx;
  float fracy = y - inty;

  color  colorx1 = (1-fracx)* image[intx]  [inty] +
                   (fracx)  * image[intx+1][inty];
  color  colorx2 = (1-fracx)* image[intx]  [inty+1] +
                   (fracx)  * image[intx+1][ inty+1];

  color  colorxy  = (1-fracy)* colorx1 +
                    (fracy)  * colorx2;
  return(colorxy)
}
```

In this code, we first apply linear interpolation in x followed by linear interpolation of that result in y.

At integer coordinates, we have $I(i, j) = \texttt{I[i][j]}$; the reconstructed continuous image I agrees with the discrete image $\texttt{I}$. In between integer coordinates, the color values are blended continuously. Each pixel in the discrete image influences, to a varying degree, each point within a 2 by 2 square region of the continuous image. Figure 17.1 compares constant and bilinear reconstruction.

Let us look a bit more closely at the 1 by 1 square with coordinates $i < x < i+1$, $j < y < j+1$ for some fixed i and j. Over this square, we can express the reconstruction as

$$I(i + x_f, j + y_f) \leftarrow (1 - y_f)\left\{(1 - x_f)\texttt{I[i][j]} + (x_f)\texttt{I[i+1][j]}\right\} \tag{17.1}$$

$$+ (y_f)\left\{(1 - x_f)\texttt{I[i][j+1]} + (x_f)\texttt{I[i+1][j+1]}\right\},$$

where x_f and y_f are the $\texttt{fracx}$ and $\texttt{fracy}$ above. Rearranging the terms, we get

$$I(i + x_f, j + y_f) \leftarrow \texttt{I[i][j]}$$

$$+ (-\texttt{I[i][j]} + \texttt{I[i+1][j]})\, x_f$$

$$+ (-\texttt{I[i][j]} + \texttt{I[i][j+1]})\, y_f$$

$$+ (\texttt{I[i][j]} - \texttt{I[i][j+1]} - \texttt{I[i+1][j]} + \texttt{I[i+1][j+1]})\, x_f y_f.$$

Doing this, we see that the reconstructed function has terms that are constant, linear, and bilinear terms in the variables (x_f, y_f) and thus also in (x, y). This is where the name *bilinear* comes from. It is also clear that this reconstruction is symmetric with respect to the horizontal and vertical directions, and thus the horizontal-first ordering in the pseudocode is not critical.

17.3 Basis Functions

To get some more insight on the general form of our reconstruction methods, we can go back to equation (17.1) and rearrange it to obtain

$$I(i + x_f, j + y_f) \leftarrow (1 - x_f - y_f + x_f y_f)\texttt{I[i][j]}$$

$$+ (x_f - x_f y_f)\texttt{I[i+1][j]}$$

$$+ (y_f - x_f y_f)\texttt{I[i][j+1]}$$

$$+ (x_f y_f)\texttt{I[i+1][j+1]}.$$

In this form, we see that for a fixed position (x, y), the color of the continuous reconstruction is linear in the discrete pixel values of $\texttt{I}$. Because this is true at all (x, y), we see that our reconstruction in fact must be of the form

$$I(x, y) \leftarrow \sum_{i,j} B_{i,j}(x, y)\mathtt{I[i][j]} \tag{17.2}$$

for some appropriate choice of functions $B_{i,j}(x, y)$. These B are called *basis functions*; they describe how much pixel $\mathtt{i,j}$ influences the continuous image at $[x, y]^t$.

In the case of bilinear reconstruction, these B functions are called *tent functions*. They are defined as follows: Let $H_i(x)$ be a univariate *hat function* defined as

$$H_i(x) = x - i + 1 \qquad \text{for} \quad i - 1 < x < i$$

$$\qquad\qquad -x + i + 1 \quad \text{for} \quad i < x < i + 1$$

$$\qquad 0 \qquad\qquad\quad \text{else}$$

(see figure 17.2). (In 1D, the hat basis can be used to take a set of values on the integers and linearly interpolate them to obtain a continuous univariate function.) Then, let $T_{i,j}(x, y)$ be the bivariate function

$$T_{i,j}(x, y) = H_i(x)H_j(y).$$

This is called a tent function (see figure 17.3). It can be verified that plugging these tent functions into equation (17.2) gives us the result of the bilinear reconstruction algorithm.

Constant reconstruction can be modeled in this form as well, but in this case, the basis function, $B_{i,j}(x, y)$, is a *box function* that is zero everywhere except for the unit square surrounding the coordinates (i, j), where it has constant value 1.

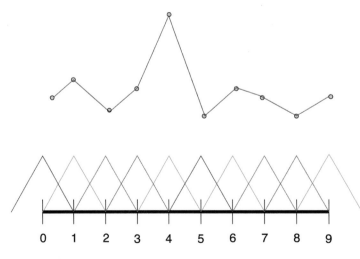

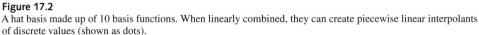

Figure 17.2
A hat basis made up of 10 basis functions. When linearly combined, they can create piecewise linear interpolants of discrete values (shown as dots).

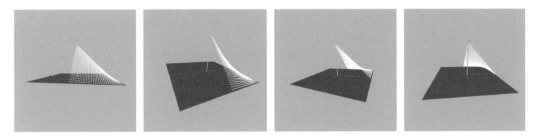

Figure 17.3
Four views of one quadrant of a single bilinear tent function. It has value 1 at its center and drops to 0 on the boundary of a 2 pixel by 2 pixel square.

More generally, we can choose basis functions with all kinds of sizes and shapes. In high-quality image editing tools, for example, reconstruction is done using some set of bicubic basis functions [50]. In this sense, a pixel is not really a little square. It is simply a discrete value that is used in conjunction with a set of basis functions to obtain a continuous function.

17.3.1 Edge Preservation

Linear methods, those that reconstruct an image using equation (17.2), naively fill in the space between the discrete pixels. When we look closely at the reconstructed continuous image, the edges appear to blur out. There are more advanced and nonlinear techniques that attempt to maintain sharp edges even in the reconstruction, but these are beyond our scope. For more on this, see [18] and references therein.

Exercises

17.1 Even though the graphics hardware can be set to do bilinear reconstruction, you can also simulate this process yourself in your fragment shader. For each desired texture lookup, your fragment shader should explicitly retrieve four texture pixels and then compute the correctly blended bilinear reconstruction using your own code in the fragment shader. To lookup the individual texture pixels exactly, you will also need carefully to understand the texture-viewport transform and its inverse (see section 12.3.1).

17.2 Suppose we plan to reconstruct a continuous image using linear combinations of basis functions in such a way that if we start with a discrete image where all the pixels share the exact same color value, then the reconstructed continuous image will be a "flat field" of that single color value. That is, if $I[i][j] = c$, for all i, j, and some color c, then we want the reconstructed continuous image to be $I(x, y) = c$ for all (x, y). Then what must be true of the following expression:

$$\forall x, y, \sum_{i,j} B_{i,j}(x, y).$$

18 Resampling

Now that we have discussed the basics of both image sampling and image reconstruction, we can revisit the process of texture mapping. We will see that, in this case, we start with a discrete image and end with a discrete image. As a result, the mapping technically involves both a reconstruction and sampling stage. In this context, we will explain the technique of mip mapping used for anti-aliased texture mapping.

18.1 Ideal Resampling

Suppose we start with a discrete image or texture `T[k][l]` and apply some 2D warp to this image to obtain an output image `I[i][j]`. How should we set each of the output pixels? In particular, during texture mapping, the triangle and camera geometry effectively warp a texture image onto some portion of the rendered image in the window.

Ideally, we should follow the following set of steps

- Reconstruct a continuous texture $T(x_t, y_t)$ using a set of basis functions $B_{k,l}(x_t, y_t)$, as in chapter 17.
- Apply the geometric warp to the continuous image.
- Integrate against a set of filters $F_{i,j}(x_w, y_w)$ to obtain the discrete output image, as in chapter 16.

Let the geometric transform be described by a mapping $M(x_w, y_w)$ that maps from continuous window to texture coordinates. Then, putting these three steps together, we obtain

$$\texttt{I[i][j]} \leftarrow \int\int_\Omega dx_w\, dy_w\; F_{i,j}(x_w, y_w) \sum_{k,l} B_{k,l}[M(x_w, y_w)]\texttt{T[k][l]}$$

$$= \sum_{k,l} \texttt{T[k][l]} \int\int_\Omega dx_w\, dy_w\; F_{i,j}(x_w, y_w) B_{k,l}[M(x_w, y_w)].$$

This expression tells us how each output pixel can be obtained as a linear combination of the input texture pixels.

Sometimes it is easier to visualize the integration over the texture domain instead of the window domain. Using the inverse mapping $N = M^{-1}$, this can be written as

$$\texttt{I[i][j]} \leftarrow \int\int_{M(\Omega)} dx_t\, dy_t\, |\det(\mathrm{D_N})|\ F_{i,j}[N(x_t, y_t)] \sum_{k,l} B_{k,l}(x_t, y_t)\texttt{T[k][l]}$$

$$= \int\int_{M(\Omega)} dx_t\, dy_t\, |\det(\mathrm{D_N})|\ F'_{i,j}(x_t, y_t) \sum_{k,l} B_{k,l}(x_t, y_t)\texttt{T[k][l]},$$

where D_N is the Jacobian of N, and $F' = F \circ N$. When F is a box filter, this becomes

$$\texttt{I[i][j]} \leftarrow \int\int_{M(\Omega_{i,j})} dx_t\, dy_t\, |\det(\mathrm{D_N})|\ \sum_{k,l} B_{k,l}(x_t, y_t)\texttt{T[k][l]}. \tag{18.1}$$

That is, we need to integrate over the region $M(\Omega_{i,j})$ on the texture domain and blend that data together.

When our transformation M effectively shrinks the texture, then $M(\Omega_{i,j})$ has a large footprint over $T(x_t, y_t)$ (see figure 18.1). If M is blowing up the texture, then $M(\Omega_{i,j})$

Figure 18.1
A checkerboard drawn as a single large geometric square texture mapped with a checkerboard image shown (dimmed) on the right. On the left, two (oversized) pixel squares $\Omega_{i,j}$ are visualized in orange and yellow. On the right, we visualize their footprints in the texture under the mapping $M(\Omega_{i,j})$. The orange footprint is very small, and filtering is not needed. The yellow footprint covers a large set of texture pixels, and filtering is needed to avoid artifacts.

has a very narrow footprint over $T(x_t, y_t)$. During texture mapping, M can also do funnier things, like shrink in one direction only.

18.2 Blow Up

Although equation (18.1) includes both a reconstruction ($\sum$) and a filtering ($\int$) component, in the case that we are blowing up the texture, the filtering component has minimal impact on the output. In particular, the footprint of $M(\Omega_{i,j})$ may be smaller than a pixel unit in texture space, and thus there is not much detail that needs blurring/averaging. As such, the integration step can be dropped, and the resampling can be implemented as

$$\mathtt{I[i][j]} \leftarrow \sum_{k,l} B_{k,l}(x_t, y_t)\mathtt{T[k][l]}, \tag{18.2}$$

where $(x_t, y_t) = M(i, j)$. In other words, we simply point sample the reconstructed and transformed texture. This, for example, is what we were proposing in chapter 17.

Bilinear reconstruction is most commonly used in this situation. We tell OpenGL to do this using the call

```
glTexParameteri(GL_TEXTURE_2D, GL_TEXTURE_MAG_FILTER, GL_LINEAR).
```

For a single texture lookup in a fragment shader, the hardware needs to fetch four texture pixels and blend them appropriately. This will work fine, say, for the pixel with the orange footprint of figure 18.1.

18.3 Mip Map

In the case that a texture is getting shrunk down, then, to avoid aliasing, the filtering component of equation (18.1) should not be ignored. Unfortunately, there may be numerous texture pixels under the footprint of $M(\Omega_{i,j})$, and we may not be able to do our texture lookup in constant time. (See, e.g., the yellow footprint in figure 18.1).

The standard solution in OpenGL is to use *mip mapping* (see figure 18.2). In mip mapping, one starts with an original texture $\mathtt{T}^0$ and then creates a series of lower and lower resolution (blurrier) textures $\mathtt{T}^i$. Each successive texture is twice as blurry. And because they have successively less detail, they can be represented with $1/2$ the number of pixels in both the horizontal and vertical directions. This collection, called a mip map, is built before any triangle rendering is done. Thus, the simplest way to construct a mip map is to average 2 by 2 pixel blocks to produce each pixel in a lower-resolution image; more sophisticated image shrinking techniques can be used as well.

Mip maps can be built by your own code and then passed to OpenGL using $\mathtt{glTexImage2D}$. Alternatively, they can be built and loaded automatically with a call to $\mathtt{gluBuild2DMipmaps}$

Figure 18.2
Top row: A checkerboard drawn as a single large geometric square texture mapped with a checkerboard image. This figure looks similar to figure 16.1, but in that figure, each square is drawn using its own small quad. Top row: No mip mapping used. Middle row: Mip mapping is used. This removes most of the aliasing but over-blurs the texture. Bottom row: Mip mapping with anisotropic sampling has been used. Notice that some jaggies remain on the back edge of the geometry. This is not dealt with by mip mapping.

(and no subsequent call to glTexImage2D). Because each of these different textures has different resolutions, each has its own viewport transform from canonical texture coordinates to pixel-based ones as in section 12.3.1 and exercise 12.2.

During texture mapping, for each texture coordinate (x_t, y_t), the hardware estimates how much shrinking is going on. This shrinking factor is then used to select from an appropriate resolution texture T^i from the mip map. Because we pick a suitably low-resolution texture, additional filtering is not needed, and again, we can just use equation (18.2), which can be done in constant time.

To avoid spatial or temporal discontinuities where/when the texture mip map switches between levels, we can use so-called trilinear interpolation. We use bilinear interpolation to reconstruct one color from T^i and another reconstruction from T^{i+1}. These two colors are then linearly interpolated. This third interpolation factor is based on how close we are to choosing level i or $i + 1$. Mip mapping with trilinear interpolation is specified with the call

```
glTexParameteri(GL_TEXTURE_2D, GL_TEXTURE_MIN_FILTER,
GL_LINEAR_MIPMAP_LINEAR).
```

Trilinear interpolation requires OpenGL to fetch eight texture pixels and blend them appropriately for every requested texture access.

It is easy to see that mip mapping does not do the exactly correct computation. First of all, each lower-resolution image in the mip map is obtained by isotropic shrinking, equally in every direction. But, during texture mapping, some region of texture space may get shrunk in only one direction (see figure 18.3). Second of all, even for isotropic shrinking, the data

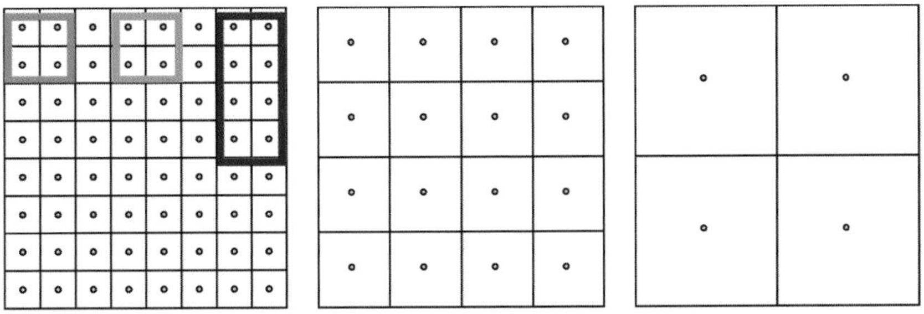

Figure 18.3
Three levels of resolution in a mip map. Each has half the horizontal and vertical texture resolution. Three potential footprints are shown in red, green, and blue. The integral over the red footprint is well represented in the middle texture image. The blue footprint arises from anisotropic shrinking and is not well represented in any of the mip map texture images. The green footprint arises from isotropic shrinking but is not well represented in any of the mip map texture images because of where it falls in the dyadic pattern.

in the low-resolution image only represent a very specific, dyadic pattern of pixel averages from the original image. These specific averages are then blended together when a texture pixel is fetched.

Equation (18.1) can be better approximated at the expense of more fetches from various levels of the mip map to approximately cover the area $M(\Omega_{i,j})$ on the texture. This approach is often called anisotropic filtering and can be enabled in an API or using the driver control panel (see figure 18.2).

V ADVANCED TOPICS

19 Color

In this section, we will explore the basic concept of color. We will talk about what color is and various ways to represent it. This is a rich topic of study, and many mysteries about human color perception remain unanswered. We will spend extra time on this subject because we find it very interesting and because of its importance not just to computer graphics but to digital imaging as well.

Color is, in fact, an overloaded term meaning many different things. When a light beam hits the retina, there is some initial neural response by the *cone cells* that occurs independently at each cell. We can refer to this as *retinal color*. Retinal color is then processed in an integrated fashion over the entire field of view resulting in the *perceived color* that we actually experience and base judgments upon. The perceived color is often associated with the object we are observing, which we might call the *object color*.

At all of these stages, the simplest thing we can say about two particular colors is simply whether they are the same or different. This is something that we can often record and quantify, and it is the main way we will deal with color in this chapter. At the perceptual color level, there is clearly a conscious experience of color that is much harder to deal with experimentally or formally.

Finally, there are further issues in how we typically organize our color perceptions into *named colors*, using words like red and green.

In this chapter, we will mostly focus on retinal color (and will drop the term retinal). Retinal color theory is relatively well understood and is the first step in understanding other notions of color. We will first describe retinal color from its now well-established biophysical basis. Then, we will re-derive the same model directly from perceptual experiments. We will then discuss some of the most common color representations in computer graphics.

19.1 Simple Biophysical Model

Visible light is electromagnetic radiation that falls roughly in the *wavelengths* $380 < \lambda < 770$, measured in nanometers. (You can just think of each wavelength as a different "physical flavor" of light.) We will talk about two kinds of beams of light. A *pure beam* l_λ has one "unit" of light (measured in units of irradiance) of a specific wavelength λ. A *mixed beam* $l(\lambda)$ has different amounts of various wavelengths. These amounts are determined by the function $l(\cdot) : R \rightarrow R_+$ and are in units of spectral irradiance. The value is always non-negative because there is no "negative light."

The human eye has various kinds of light-sensitive cells on the retina. The *cone* cells give us the sensation of color. Non–color blind humans have three different kinds of cones, which we will call short, medium, and long (after the wavelengths of light they are most sensitive to). Associated with these three types of cones are three sensitivity functions $k_s(\lambda)$, $k_m(\lambda)$, and $k_l(\lambda)$. A response function describes how strongly one type of cone "responds" to pure beams of light of different wavelengths. For example, $k_s(\lambda)$ tells us how much a short wavelength–sensitive cone will respond to the pure beam l_λ (see the upper left of figure 19.1).

Because each pure beam of light results in three response values on the retina, one for each type of cone, we can visualize this response as a single point in a 3D space. Let us define a 3D linear space, with coordinates labeled $[L, M, S]^t$. We will call this space the *LMS color space*. Then for a fixed λ, we can draw the retinal response as a single vector with coordinates $[k_l(\lambda), k_m(\lambda), k_s(\lambda)]^t$. As we let λ vary, such vectors will trace out a *lasso* curve in space (see the top row of figure 19.2). The lasso curve is parameterrized by λ.

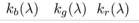

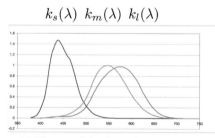

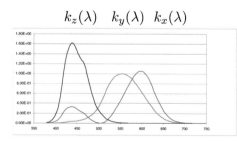

XYZ matching functions

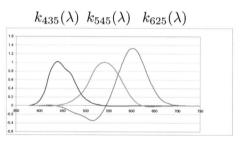

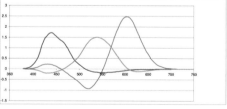

RGB matching functions

Figure 19.1
Sensitivity/matching functions.

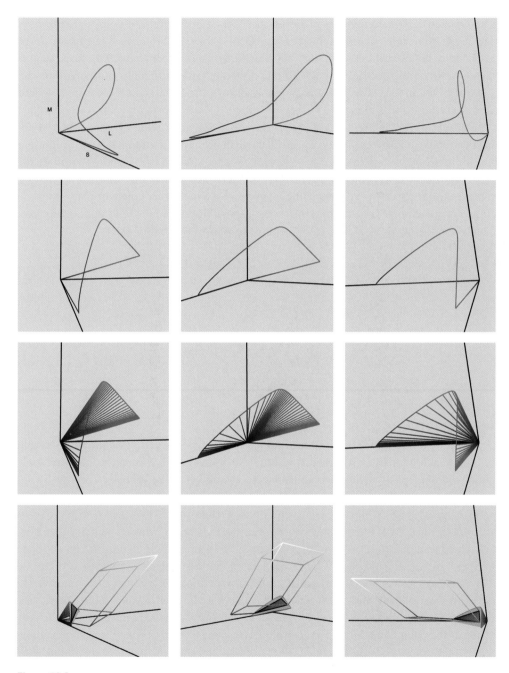

Figure 19.2
LMS color space: Each column shows a different view. First row: The lasso curve plotted in LMS coordinates. Second row: A "normalized" lasso curve is a horseshoe curve. Third row: Rays connecting the horseshoe curve to the origin. Fourth row: A slice of the convex cone over the lasso. The triangle shows actual colors in this slice. They are representable as positive sums of monitor colors R, G, and B. The rest of the RGB color cube is shown in wireframe.

The lasso curve lies completely in the positive octant because all responses are positive. The curve both starts and ends at the origin because these extreme wavelengths are at the boundaries of the visible region, beyond which the responses are zero. The curve spends a short time on the S axis (shown with blue-tinted points) and finally comes close to the L axis (shown in red). The curve never comes close to the M axis, as there is no light that stimulates these cones alone.

In this simple model, we think of the $[L, M, S]^t$ coordinates of the light beam as describing the (retinal) color sensation produced by the light beam. We use the symbol $\vec{c}$ to represent a color itself, which we equate, for now, with an actual retinal event. Soon we will define color more rigorously. Thus, in figure 19.2, we can think of each 3D vector as *potentially* representing some color. Vectors on the lasso curve are the *actual* colors of pure beams.

Within some ranges of intensity, the cones respond linearly to the light shining on them. Thus, for a mixed beam of light $l(\lambda)$, the three responses $[L, M, S]^t$ are

$$L = \int_\Omega d\lambda \; l(\lambda) \, k_l(\lambda) \qquad\qquad\qquad (19.1)$$

$$M = \int_\Omega d\lambda \; l(\lambda) \, k_m(\lambda) \qquad\qquad\qquad (19.2)$$

$$S = \int_\Omega d\lambda \; l(\lambda) \, k_s(\lambda), \qquad\qquad\qquad (19.3)$$

where $\Omega = [380 \ldots 770]$.

As we look at all possible mixed beams $l(\lambda)$, the resulting $[L, M, S]^t$ coordinates sweep out some set of vectors in 3D space. Because l can be any positive function, the swept set is composed of all positive linear combinations of vectors on the lasso curve. Thus, the swept set is the *convex cone* over the lasso curve, which we call the *color cone*. Vectors inside the cone represent actual achievable color sensations. Vectors outside the cone, such as the vertical axis, do not arise as the sensation from any actual light beam, whether pure or composite.

To help visualize the cone, we have broken down its drawing in figure 19.2 into a series of steps. In the second row, we have normalized the lasso curve, scaling each vector so $L + M + S = K$, for some constant K. Such a scaled lasso curve is called a *horseshoe curve*. We also add tails joining this horseshoe curve to the origin. In the third row, we add lines from the origin to the horseshoe curve. This is to try to give you a better feel for the shape of the color cone. Finally, in the fourth row, we place an opaque plane showing one slice of the color cone. On this plane, we also draw the actual colors that are on this slice and that are producible by linear combinations of R, G, and B: red, green, and blue monitor elements. (This RGB space will be discussed in detail later.) To draw the brightest colors, subject to these constraints, we have chosen the value of K in $L + M + S = K$ such that the slice includes the color with RGB coordinates $[1, 0, 0]^t$. In wireframe, we show the RGB-cube, the set of colors that can be achieved by combinations of red, green, and blue with coefficients in $[0 \ldots 1]$.

There are an infinite number of vectors making up the lasso curve, certainly more than three! Thus, for vectors strictly inside the color cone, there are many ways to generate some fixed $[L, M, S]^t$ coordinates using positive linear combinations of vectors on the lasso curve. Each of these is equivalent to some light beam that produces this fixed response. Thus, there must be many physically distinct beams of light, with different amounts of each wavelength, that generate the same color sensation. We call any two such beams *metamers*.

Here, we summarize the distinct data types we have just seen, as well as some that we will soon see later:

• A pure beam of light is denoted l_λ. A mixed beam of light is denoted $l(\lambda)$.

• A sensitivity function is denoted as $k(\lambda)$. We will later also call these *matching functions*.

• A retinal sensation of color is denoted by $\vec{c}$. Later, we will use three such colors to make a basis for color space.

• A color is represented by three coordinates, such as $[L, M, S]^t$. The coordinates of the observed color of a beam are calculated using the matching functions as in equation (19.1).

• Later, we will also see a reflection function $r(\lambda)$ that describes the fraction of each wavelength that is reflected by some physical material.

19.1.1 Map of Color Space

At this point, we already have enough information to roughly map out the color cone.

Scales of vectors in the cone correspond to brightness changes in our perceived color sensation and thus are not very interesting. (Though, when we dim an orange light, we actually perceive the color brown.) Thus, it is convenient to normalize our color diagram by scale, obtaining a 2D drawing (see figure 19.3). In this diagram, we have started with the slice of the cone from figure 19.2. All displayed colors have then been scaled so that one of R, G, or B is at full strength. We cannot display colors outside of the drawn triangle using positive combinations of the R, G, and B display elements of a monitor. We say that such colors lay outside of the *gamut* of our display.

Colors along the boundary of the cone are vivid and are perceived as "saturated." Starting from the L axis, and moving along the curved portion, we move along the rainbow colors from red to green to violet. These colors can only be achieved by pure beams. Additionally, the color cone's boundary has a planar wedge (a line segment in the 2D figure). The colors on this wedge are the pinks and purples. They do not appear in the rainbow and can only be achieved by appropriately combining beams of red and violet. As as we circle around the boundary, we move through the different "hues" of color.

As we move in from the boundary toward the central region of the cone, the colors, while maintaining their hue, desaturate, becoming pastel and eventually grayish or whitish.

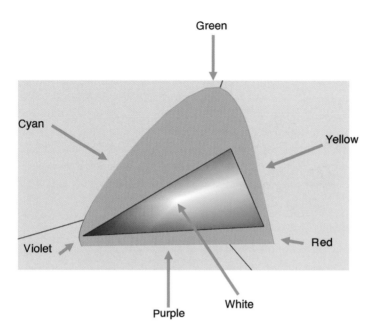

Figure 19.3
Two-dimensional color diagram. Colors outside of the triangle are beyond the gamut of a computer display.

(However, in our treatment we will not need to have a specific color formally selected as white.)

This general description can be numerically formulated in the so-called "hue saturation value" color system.

19.2   Mathematical Model

The model just described in section 19.1 was actually deduced in the 19th century using just a few perceptual experiments. They had no access to the technologies needed to study cells in an eye. This was an amazing feat. Here, we follow this original line of reasoning and explain how our color model can be deduced from the ground up with just the right kind of perceptual experiments. This will give us a more careful understanding of how to define color, and it will let us treat color space with all the tools of linear algebra, without reference to neural responses of any kind.

We start only with the basic knowledge from physics that light beams can be described as wavelength distributions $l(\lambda)$ and the rough observation that distinct light distributions can sometimes appear indistinguishable to a human observer. To carefully study such metamerism, and specifically to avoid any effects that may occur when a human observes a complicated scene, we design an experimental setup such as that shown in figure 19.4. This

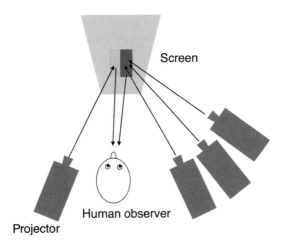

Figure 19.4
Basic color-matching experimental setup. Light projectors focus light beams with various wavelength distributions onto a large monochromatic screen in a way that forms two colored patches, each with a controlled wavelength distribution. Multiple projectors are placed on the right side so we can also test what happens when various light distributions are added together. A human observer is asked if the two patches can be distinguished by color or not.

allows us to present to an observer two light beams with known wavelength distributions. We can then ask the observer if these beams appear identical or different.

In our very first experiment, we test that the metameric relation is transitive (here we ignore the issue of just noticeable differences and thresholding effects). In particular we find that if $l_1(\lambda)$ is indistinguishable from $l_1'(\lambda)$ and $l_1'(\lambda)$ is indistinguishable from $l_1''(\lambda)$, then $l_1'(\lambda)$ will always be indistinguishable from $l_1''(\lambda)$.

Because of this transitivity, we actually *define* $\vec{c}\,[l_1(\lambda)]$, "the color of the beam $l_1(\lambda)$," as the collection of light beams that are indistinguishable from a human observer from $l_1(\lambda)$. So in our case, we would have $\vec{c}\,[l_1(\lambda)] = \vec{c}\,[l_1'(\lambda)] = \vec{c}\,[l_1''(\lambda)]$. Thus in our mathematical model, **a (retinal) color is an equivalence class of light beams**.

Ultimately, we would like to be able to treat the space of colors as a linear vector space. This, for example, would allow us to easily represent colors using coordinate vectors, and it would tell us how we could produce desired colors by mixing together various "primary" colors.

Our next step, then, is to figure out how to add two colors together. We know from physics that when two light beams, $l_1(\lambda)$ and $l_2(\lambda)$, are added together, they simply form a combined beam with light distribution $l_1(\lambda) + l_2(\lambda)$. Thus, we attempt to define the *addition* of two colors, as the color of the addition of two beams:

$$\vec{c}\,[l_1(\lambda)] + \vec{c}\,[l_2(\lambda)] := \vec{c}\,[l_1(\lambda) + l_2(\lambda)].$$

For this to be well defined, we must experimentally verify that it does not make a difference which beam we choose as representative for each color. In particular, if $\vec{c}\,[l_1(\lambda)] = \vec{c}\,[l'_1(\lambda)]$, then we must verify (again using our setup of figure 19.4) that, for all $l_2(\lambda)$, we have $\vec{c}\,[l_1(\lambda) + l_2(\lambda)] = \vec{c}\,[l'_1(\lambda) + l_2(\lambda)]$; that is, we must test that the beam $l_1(\lambda) + l_2(\lambda)$ is indistinguishable from $l'_1(\lambda) + l_2(\lambda)$. This property is indeed confirmed by experiment.

Our next step is to try to define what it means to multiply a color by a non-negative real number α. Again, because we can multiply a light beam by a positive scalar, we try the definition

$$\alpha\vec{c}\,[l_1(\lambda)] := \vec{c}\,[\alpha l_1(\lambda)]. \tag{19.4}$$

Again, we need to verify that the behavior of this operation does not depend on our choice of beam. Thus, when $\vec{c}\,[l_1(\lambda)] = \vec{c}\,[l'_1(\lambda)]$, we must verify that for all α we have $\vec{c}\,[\alpha l_1(\lambda)] = \vec{c}\,[\alpha l'_1(\lambda)]$; that is, we must test that the beam $\alpha l_1(\lambda)$ is indistinguishable from $\alpha l'_1(\lambda)$. This property is also confirmed by experiment.

19.2.1 One Technical Detail

In a real vector space, we are able to multiply a vector by a negative real number. If we try this on our color representation, we get $-\vec{c}(l_1) := \vec{c}(-l_1)$. This is undefined because there is no negative light.

Still, it would be nice to be able to treat colors as vectors and to apply the full power of linear algebra to them. In particular, as we will see later, because of the shape of the color horseshoe, we will not be able to represent all colors as positive combinations of just three colors. To do that, we will really need negative combinations as well.

Our mathematical solution is first to define a suitable notion of subtraction. The basic idea behind this subtraction operation can be summarized as follows: When we say $\vec{c}_1 - \vec{c}_2 = \vec{c}_3$, we will really mean $\vec{c}_1 = \vec{c}_3 + \vec{c}_2$. In other words, subtraction from one side of an equation will be just the same as adding that term to the other side. This addition is something real that we already understand! With this notion of subtraction, we can give meaning to "negative" colors. By adding together actual and negative colors, we can get a full linear space, which we can call *extended color space*.

More formally, let us refer to any of our original equivalence classes of light beams by the term *actual color*. Let us define an *extended color* as a formal expression of the form

$$\vec{c}_1 - \vec{c}_2,$$

where the $\vec{c}$ are actual colors. We define two extended colors $\vec{c}_1 - \vec{c}_2$ and $\vec{c}_3 - \vec{c}_4$, to be equivalent if $\vec{c}_1 + \vec{c}_4 = \vec{c}_3 + \vec{c}_2$, where the last expression is an equation about actual colors, and thus well defined. Any extended color that is not an actual color will be called an *imaginary color*.

We can now define all of our vector operations in the obvious way. Multiplication by -1 is $-(\vec{c}_1 - \vec{c}_2) := (\vec{c}_2 - \vec{c}_1)$ and addition is $(\vec{c}_1 - \vec{c}_2) + (\vec{c}_3 - \vec{c}_4) := (\vec{c}_1 + \vec{c}_3) - (\vec{c}_2 + \vec{c}_4)$. With these operations, we indeed have a linear space of extended colors!

Finally, to keep actual distinguishable colors from collapsing to the same extended color during this construction, we need to verify that our actual colors satisfy the *cancellation property*. This property states that if $\vec{c}\,[l_1(\lambda)] + \vec{c}\,[l_2(\lambda)] = \vec{c}\,[l_1'(\lambda)] + \vec{c}\,[l_2(\lambda)]$, then $\vec{c}\,[l_1(\lambda)] = \vec{c}\,[l_1'(\lambda)]$. Again we verify this by experiment.

As a result, we now have a real vector space of extended colors, as well as an embedding of the actual colors within this space. From now on, we will use the symbol $\vec{c}$ to refer to any extended color and will typically drop the term "extended." Additionally, we can interpret $\vec{c}\,[l(\lambda)]$ as a linear map from the space of light distributions to color space.

We do not yet know dimension of color space (but we will soon establish that it is three). We can now go back to figure 19.2 and think of it as a picture of extended color space. Vectors inside the cone are actual colors, whereas vectors outside the cone are imaginary colors. The vector, for example, represented with coordinates $[0, 1, 0]^t$ is an imaginary color.

19.3 Color Matching

The goal of the *color matching experiment* is to establish that the dimension of the space of colors is three. Additionally, it will give us [similar to equation (19.1)] a computational form for mapping a light beam $l(\lambda)$ to its color coordinates in a specific basis.

Using the setup of figure 19.4, the observer watches two screens. On the left side of the screen the observer is shown a pure *test beam* l_λ of some fixed wavelength λ. On the right side of the screen the observer sees a light that is made up of positive combinations of three pure *matching beams*, with wavelengths 435, 545, and 625 nanometers. The observer's goal is to adjust three knobs on the right side, controlling the intensities of the matching beams, so that the weighted combination of the three matching beams is indistinguishable from the test beam. For a fixed λ, and referring to the knob settings as $k_{435}(\lambda)$, $k_{545}(\lambda)$, and $k_{625}(\lambda)$, the goal is to set these knobs such that the beam $k_{435}(\lambda)l_{435} + k_{545}(\lambda)l_{545} + k_{625}(\lambda)l_{625}$ is a metamer with l_λ. If the user cannot succeed, then they are allowed to move one or more of the matching beams over to the left side and combine them with the test beam instead. In the mathematics of extended color space, this is the same as allowing some of the the the scalar values $k(\lambda)$ to go negative.

This process is repeated for all λ in the visual range. When the matching experiment is performed, we discover that the user can indeed succeed in obtaining a match for *all* visible wavelengths.

Moreover, the experiment gives us the three so-called matching functions $k_{435}(\lambda)$, $k_{545}(\lambda)$, and $k_{625}(\lambda)$, shown in the upper right of figure 19.1. Notice that at each of the wavelengths 435, 545, and 625, one of the matching functions is set to 1, whereas the other two are set to 0.

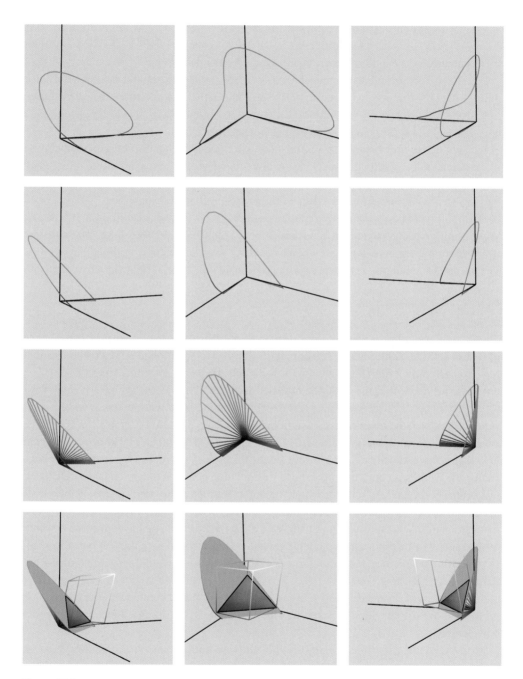

Figure 19.5
The color space arising from the matching experiment.

We can summarize the result of the experiment as

$$\vec{c}(l_\lambda) = [\vec{c}(l_{435})\ \vec{c}(l_{545})\ \vec{c}(l_{645})] \begin{bmatrix} k_{435}(\lambda) \\ k_{545}(\lambda) \\ k_{625}(\lambda) \end{bmatrix}.$$

Using some reasonable continuity assumptions about the linear map $\vec{c}$, we can upgrade this equation to apply to all mixed beans as well. Doing so, we obtain

$$\vec{c}[l(\lambda)] = [\vec{c}(l_{435})\ \vec{c}(l_{545})\ \vec{c}(l_{645})] \begin{bmatrix} \int_\Omega d\lambda\ l(\lambda)\, k_{435}(\lambda) \\ \int_\Omega d\lambda\ l(\lambda)\, k_{545}(\lambda) \\ \int_\Omega d\lambda\ l(\lambda)\, k_{625}(\lambda) \end{bmatrix}. \tag{19.5}$$

Informally, this equation corresponds to the idea that each mixed beam is really just an (uncountable) linear combination of pure beams.

From this we can conclude:

- Color space is 3D.

- $[\vec{c}(l_{435})\ \vec{c}(l_{545})\ \vec{c}(l_{645})]$ forms a basis for this space.

- The matching functions can be used to give us the coordinates of any light distribution with respect to this basis.

As we did with the LMS color space, we can visualize this color space in figure 19.5. Notice that, in this case, the lasso curve passes through each of the axes in turn, as our basis colors are monochromatic. Note however that, in this basis, the lasso curve does leave the first octant.

19.4 Bases

As any vector space, color space can be described using many different bases. Starting with equation (19.5), we can insert any (nonsingular) 3 by 3 matrix M and its inverse to obtain

$$\vec{c}(l(\lambda)) = \left([\vec{c}(l_{435})\ \vec{c}(l_{545})\ \vec{c}(l_{645})]M^{-1}\right) \left(M \begin{bmatrix} \int_\Omega d\lambda\ l(\lambda)\, k_{435}(\lambda) \\ \int_\Omega d\lambda\ l(\lambda)\, k_{545}(\lambda) \\ \int_\Omega d\lambda\ l(\lambda)\, k_{625}(\lambda) \end{bmatrix} \right)$$

$$= [\vec{c}_1\ \vec{c}_2\ \vec{c}_3] \begin{bmatrix} \int_\Omega d\lambda\ l(\lambda)\, k_1(\lambda) \\ \int_\Omega d\lambda\ l(\lambda)\, k_2(\lambda) \\ \int_\Omega d\lambda\ l(\lambda)\, k_3(\lambda) \end{bmatrix}, \tag{19.6}$$

where the $\vec{c}_i$ describe a new color basis defined as

$$[\vec{c}_1\ \vec{c}_2\ \vec{c}_3] = [\vec{c}(l_{435})\ \vec{c}(l_{545})\ \vec{c}(l_{645})]M^{-1}$$

and the $k(\lambda)$ functions form the new associated matching functions, defined by

$$
\begin{bmatrix} k_1(\lambda) \\ k_2(\lambda) \\ k_3(\lambda) \end{bmatrix} = M \begin{bmatrix} k_{435}(\lambda) \\ k_{545}(\lambda) \\ k_{625}(\lambda) \end{bmatrix}. \tag{19.7}
$$

Thus, there are three main conceptual ways to specify a basis for color space:

• Starting from any fixed basis for color space, such as $[\vec{c}(l_{435})\ \vec{c}(l_{545})\ \vec{c}(l_{645})]$, we can describe a new basis relative to the fixed basis by specifying an invertible 3 by 3 matrix M.

• We can directly specify three (non-coplanar) actual colors $\vec{c}_i$. Each such $\vec{c}_i$ can be specified by some light beam $l_i(\lambda)$ that generates it. {We can then plug each such $l_i(\lambda)$ into the right-hand side of equation (19.5) to obtain its coordinates with respect to $[\vec{c}(l_{435})\ \vec{c}(l_{545})\ \vec{c}(l_{645})]$. This fully determines the change of basis matrix M.}

• We can directly specify three new matching functions. To be valid matching functions, they must arise from a basis change like equation (19.6), and so each matching function must be some linear combination of $k_{435}(\lambda)$, $k_{545}(\lambda)$, and $k_{625}(\lambda)$ as in equation (19.7). If we attempt to use matching functions that are not of this form, they will not preserve metamerism; light beams that are indistinguishable to a human may map to different coordinate vectors, and vice versa. Ideally, the color sensors for a digital camera should be of this form, so that the camera can truly capture color (i.e., respect metamerism). (Additionally, the sensitivity functions of a manufactured camera must also be everywhere non-negative.)

Besides $[\vec{c}(l_{435})\ \vec{c}(l_{545})\ \vec{c}(l_{645})]$, we have already seen another basis for color space. In particular, the matching functions of equation (19.1) describe a basis for color space where the coordinates of a color are called $[L, M, S]^t$. The actual basis is made up of three colors we can call $[\vec{c}_l, \vec{c}_m, \vec{c}_s]$. The color $\vec{c}_m$ is in fact an imaginary color, as there is no real light beam with LMS color coordinates $[0, 1, 0]^t$.

19.4.1 Gamut

Suppose we want a basis where all actual colors have non-negative coordinates, and thus, where the lasso curve never leaves the first octant. Then we find that **at least one of the basis vectors defining this octant must lie outside of the cone of actual colors**. Such a basis vector must be an imaginary color. This is due simply to the shape of the lasso curve itself; we cannot find three vectors that both hit the lasso curve and contain the entire curve in their positive span.

Conversely, if all of our basis vectors are actual colors, and thus within the color cone, then there must be some actual colors that cannot be written with non-negative coordinates in this basis. We say that such colors lie outside the gamut of this color space.

19.4.2 Specific Bases

The central standard basis used for color space is the called the XYZ basis. It is specified by the three matching functions called $k_x(\lambda)$, $k_y(\lambda)$, and $k_z(\lambda)$, shown in the bottom left of figure 19.1. The coordinates for some color with respect to this basis is given by a coordinate vector that we call $[X, Y, Z]^t$. This 3D color basis is shown in figure 19.6. The bottom row shows the $X + Y + Z = K$ plane of the color cone. This is the typical 2D figure used to visualize color space.

These particular matching functions were chosen such that they are always positive and so that the Y-coordinate of a color represents its overall perceived "luminance." Thus, Y is often used as a black-and-white representation of the color. The associated basis $[\vec{c}_x, \vec{c}_y, \vec{c}_z]$ is made up of three imaginary colors; the axes in figure 19.6 are outside of the color cone.

Throughout this book, we have been using RGB coordinates to describe colors. In fact, there are a variety of different color spaces that use this name. The specific RGB color space currently in use is the *Rec. 709 RGB space* (see figure 19.7).

In this case, the basis $[\vec{c}_r, \vec{c}_g, \vec{c}_b]$ is made up of three actual colors intended to match the colors of the three phosphors of an ideal monitor/television display. Colors with non-negative RGB coordinates can be produced on a monitor and are said to lie inside the gamut of the color space. These colors are in the first octant of the figure. But similar to the case of $[\vec{c}(l_{435})\ \vec{c}(l_{545})\ \vec{c}(l_{645})]$, there exist actual colors with some negative RGB coordinates. **Such colors cannot be produced on a monitor.** Additionally, on a monitor, each phosphor maxes out at "1," which also limits the achievable outputs.

An image that has colors outside of the gamut must somehow be mapped into the gamut for display. The simplest solution for this is simply to clamp all negative values at 0. There are also more sophisticated methods for gamut mapping that will be beyond our scope.

In section 19.7.2, we will describe another commonly encountered color space called sRGB. As we will see, this is not a linear color space.

19.5 Reflection Modeling

When a beam of light $i(\lambda)$ from an illumination source hits a surface, some of that light is absorbed and some reflected. The fraction of reflected light depends on the physical properties of the surface's material. Let us specify how much of each wavelength is reflected using a reflectance function $r(\lambda)$. In this case, we can model the light beam reflecting off the surface using per-wavelength multiplication

$$l(\lambda) = i(\lambda)r(\lambda).$$

[Note: This does not model all types of interactions between a light and a surface, for example fluorescence. Additionally, in this discussion, we are not concerning ourselves with the dependence of $r(\lambda)$ on the angles of entering or exiting light, as will be done in

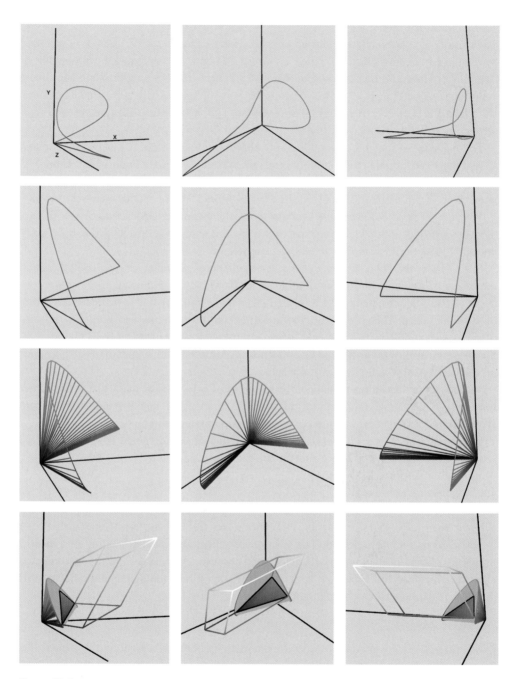

Figure 19.6
The XYZ color space.

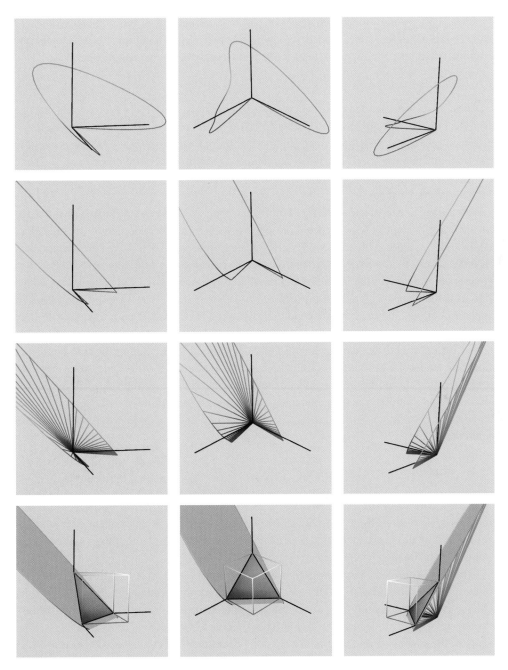

Figure 19.7
The RGB color space.

chapter 21.] This multiplication happens on a per-wavelength basis and cannot be simulated exactly in a 3D color space. Indeed, two materials may reflect metameric beams under one illuminant but may produce distinguishable beams under a second illuminant:

$$\vec{c}\,[i_1(\lambda)r_a(\lambda)] = \vec{c}\,[i_1(\lambda)r_b(\lambda)] \quad \nLeftrightarrow \quad \vec{c}\,[i_2(\lambda)r_a(\lambda)] = \vec{c}\,[i_2(\lambda)r_b(\lambda)].$$

As such, in some rendering situations, it is important to model this spectral dependence in reflection. More typically, we ignore this issue and model the illuminant by three, say RGB, color coordinates [throwing away the spectral information about $i(\lambda)$], and likewise use three reflectance "coefficients" to model the surface's reflectance property.

19.5.1 White Balance

Given a fixed scene, if we alter the illuminants, then the colors in an image will change as well. For example, if we switch from a fluorescent to an incandescent bulb, the colors observed by a camera will all move toward yellow. Often, we wish to adjust the image colors in order to approximate the image that would have been taken under a chosen "canonical illuminant" (say daylight). This process is called white balancing. It is not a basis change, but an actual transformation performed on all of the colors. The simplest such kind of transform allows the user to independently scale the R, G, and B coordinates with three gain factors.

As just described, we cannot hope to always succeed in producing the true picture of the scene under the canonical illuminant, as we have already lost the spectral information when creating the initial image. Indeed, some objects that should appear different under the canonical illuminant may be metameric under the current illuminant and have the exact same color coordinates in the current image. No amount of simple white balancing can undo this.

19.6 Adaptation

The color data from the retina undergo significant processing in the visual system, and humans by no means directly perceive the raw retinal color coordinates of an observed light beam. This processing results in a great deal of normalization; adapting to global and local trends across the field of view.

When the illuminant changes, say from sunlight to overcast sky, each of the directly observed color coordinates on the retina may undergo drastic changes. But these drastic changes are not ultimately perceived, and the colors for each object remain significantly "constant." For example, a scary tiger will be perceived as yellow under a surprisingly wide array of illuminants (impelling us to run). This phenomenon is called *color constancy*. As per our discussion of white balance, no such color constancy mechanism can be expected to be perfect, as too much spectral information has been thrown away by the process that

Figure 19.8
The squares marked A and B are in fact the same retinal shade of gray but are perceived differently because of our visual processing and local adaptation. (From [1], copyright Edward Adelson.)

converts incoming spectral beams into triplets of cone responses in the retina. But this process works to a great degree, which allows us to think about a material (tiger's fur) as actually possessing a color (scary orange).

Even when only a local region of the field of view undergoes an illumination change (say some part goes into shadow), our visual processing may adapt differently in this region, again keeping the end-perceived colors closely tied with the actual materials observed (see for e.g., figure 19.8). This process is not yet fully understood.

When we take a picture under some illuminant, but later view the picture under a different ambient illuminant, the viewer's adaptation state is affected by both the light coming from the image and the light from the surrounding room. Because of the effect of the room's light, the colors in the picture can ultimately "look wrong." This is, in part, why we need to do the white balancing described above.

19.7 Nonlinear Color

We have seen that retinal color can be modeled as a 3D linear space. In this section, we will see that there are also reasons to use a different set of retinal color representations that are not related linearly to our previous color coordinates.

19.7.1 Perceptual Distance

The Euclidean distance between two colors in any linear color space is not a good predictor as to how "different" they will appear to a human observer. For example, humans are much more sensitive to changes in dark colors than they are to bright ones. Various color representations have been designed that offer a better match to perceived color distances in humans. The mappings from a linear color space to such a color representation is nonlinear. Even so, we will still refer to such representations as "color coordinates."

For example, one such set of coordinates is called L^*ab coordinates. The L^* coordinate is called "lightness" and is computed (except for very small values) as

$$L^* = 116 \left(\frac{Y}{Y_n} \right)^{\frac{1}{3}} - 16, \tag{19.8}$$

where Y is the second coordinate in the XYZ basis, and Y_n is some normalizing factor. We will not go into the computation of the a and b coordinates in this representation.

There are many uses for such a space. In particular, if we are using a fixed point representation with 8 or fewer bits per coordinate, we are better off storing our data in a perceptually uniform space. When a continuum of Y values is bucketed into 256 evenly spaced bins, there will be significant visual gaps between dark colors. In L^* coordinates, tighter bins are used in the dark region, solving this problem. There will be correspondingly fewer bins for the brighter colors, but these gaps are not perceivable.

19.7.2 Gamma Correction

Gamma correction involves a transformation that looks similar to the power operator of equation (19.8). It was used originally to account for nonlinearities in cathode ray tube (CRT) devices but remains in use in part due to its better usage of fixed point representations.

Origins of Gamma   In days of yore, computer imagery was displayed on CRTs. Each pixel on such a display was driven by three voltages, say (R', G', B'). Letting the outgoing light from this pixel have a color with coordinates $[R, G, B]^t$, these outgoing coordinates were roughly

$$R = (R')^{\frac{1}{0.45}}$$

$$G = (G')^{\frac{1}{0.45}}$$

$$B = (B')^{\frac{1}{0.45}}.$$

Thus, if we wanted to obtain some specific $[R, G, B]^t$ output from a pixel, we needed to drive it with voltages:

$$R' = R^{0.45} \tag{19.9}$$

$$G' = G^{0.45} \tag{19.10}$$

$$B' = B^{0.45}. \tag{19.11}$$

Such $[R', G', B']^t$ values are called the *gamma corrected* RGB coordinates of a color. The prime (') notates that these are nonlinear color coordinates.

Figure 19.9
The data in the top image are a linear ramp of colors, thus displaying (on a monitor) equally spaced bins in $[R', G', B']^t$ coordinates. In the lower image, a linear ramp has been gamma corrected before being stored, thus displaying (on a monitor) equally spaced bins in $[R, G, B]^t$ coordinates. This should appear to move quickly out of the dark regime and spend more buckets on bright values.

Current Use of Gamma Similar to L^*ab color coordinates, gamma corrected colors have better perceptual uniformity than linear color coordinates and thus are very useful for digital color representation (see figure 19.9). In particular, popular image compression techniques, such as JPEG, start with colors represented in $[R', G', B']^t$, and then apply a linear transform to obtain yet a new kind of coordinates called $[Y', C'_B, C'_R]^t$. (Note that this Y' is not related to Y through a simple power equation.)

A related but slightly more involved nonlinear transform can be applied to $[R, G, B]^t$, instead of equation (19.9), to obtain sRGB coordinates, called $[R'_{srgb}, G'_{srgb}, B'_{srgb}]^t$. Modern LCD displays are programmed to assume input in these coordinates.

19.7.3 Quantization

The sRGB coordinates in the real range $[0 \ldots 1]$ must be represented numerically. This is often done (say in a framebuffer or file format) in a fixed point representation with values $[0 \ldots 255]$. In C, this is done using an unsigned char. We can specify the relationship between such quantized values and real color coordinates (for say the red coordinate) by

```
byteR = round(realR * 255);
```

```
realR = byteR/255.0;
```

Note that, for any setting of byteR, if we transform to the real representation and then back to the byte representation, we get back the value we started with. An alternative relationship satisfying this property can be imposed using the expressions:

```
byteR = round(f >= 1.0 ? 255 : (realR * 256)-.5);
```

```
realR = (byteR +.5)/ 256.0;
```

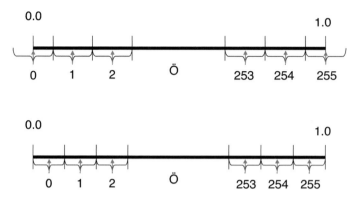

Figure 19.10
Two different mappings between real and byte values. Going from real to byte, we quantize each real range to the shown integer value. Going from byte to real, we use the small cyan arrows.

In this representation, and unlike the one above, the real bins quantized to byte values are all the same size. But the byte values of 0 and 255 do not map respectively to 0 and 1 (see figure 19.10).

19.7.4 Gamma and Graphics

On one hand, images are typically stored in gamma corrected coordinates, and the monitor screen is expecting colors in gamma corrected coordinates. On the other hand, computer graphics simulates processes that are linearly related to light beams. As such, most computer graphics computations should be done in a linear color representation, such as our $[R, G, B]^t$ space. For example, we can approximately model reflectance in $[R, G, B]^t$. Other rendering steps, such as modeling transparency, as well as blending of color values for anti-aliasing, also model processes that are linear in light beams, and thus should be done with linear color coordinates. In digital photography, white balance should ideally be performed in a linear color space. This discrepancy has been at the root of much confusion and hackery over the years.

The situation has improved recently. In current versions of OpenGL we can request an sRGB frame buffer using the call `glEnable(GL_FRAMEBUFFER_SRGB)`. Then we can pass linear $[R, G, B]^t$ values out from the fragment shader, and they will be gamma corrected into the sRGB format before being sent to the screen.

Additionally, for texture mapping, we can specify that the image being input to a texture is in sRGB format. This is done using the call

```
glTexImage2D(GL_TEXTURE_2D, 0, GL_SRGB, twidth, theight,
0, GL_RGB, GL_UNSIGNED_BYTE, pixdata)
```

Whenever this texture is accessed in a fragment shader, the data is first converted to linear $[R, G, B]^t$ coordinates before given to the shader.

Exercises

19.1 Given a computer screen with three kinds of color elements, can all (actual) colors be produced by the display?

19.2 Given a camera with three matching/sensitivity functions that are (linearly independent) linear combinations of the k_x, k_y, k_z matching functions, can all actual colors be captured by this camera?

19.3 Suppose that the human k_l, k_m, and k_s sensitivity functions were of a different form, such that there did in fact exist three light distributions with LMS color coordinates $[1, 0, 0]^t$, $[0, 1, 0]^t$, and $[0, 0, 1]^t$, respectively. What would this imply about the shape of the space of actual colors? Would this impact your answer to exercise 19.1?

19.4 Suppose that we are given the following matrix equation to change from $[A, B, C]^t$ color coordinates to $[D, E, F]^t$ coordinates:

$$\begin{bmatrix} D \\ E \\ F \end{bmatrix} = N \begin{bmatrix} A \\ B \\ C \end{bmatrix}.$$

Also, suppose we are given the following matrix equation relating the matching functions:

$$\begin{bmatrix} k_h(\lambda) \\ k_i(\lambda) \\ k_j(\lambda) \end{bmatrix} = Q \begin{bmatrix} k_a(\lambda) \\ k_b(\lambda) \\ k_c(\lambda) \end{bmatrix}.$$

What matrix equation can we write down to express the relation between $[D, E, F]^t$ coordinates and $[H, I, J]^t$ coordinates?

20 What Is Ray Tracing?

Ray tracing represents a different approach to rendering from the standard OpenGL pipeline. It is mostly beyond the scope of this book, but we will outline the basic ideas here. For more on this topic, see, for example, [23] or [56].

20.1 Loop Ordering

At its most basic, we can think of the OpenGL rasterization-based rendering as a form of the following algorithm:

```
initialize z-buffer
for all triangles
  for all pixels covered by the triangle
    compute color and z
    if z is closer than what is already in the z-buffer
      update the color and z of the pixel
```

This algorithm has the nice property that each triangle in the scene is touched only once and in a predictable order. It is for this reason, for example, that even the offline Renderman software from Pixar uses this basic algorithm. Another nice property is that during the processing of a triangle, setup computation is done only once and can be amortized over all of the pixels in it. As we have already seen, rasterization-based rendering can be enhanced with fancy shading computation and even with multipass algorithms. There are also advanced algorithms such as occlusion culling (see, e.g., [11] and references therein) that attempt to avoid rendering triangles that we know will be occluded by other objects in the scene.

In basic ray tracing, we reverse the loop orders to obtain

```
for all pixels on the screen
  for all objects seen in this pixel
    if this is the closest object seen at the pixel
      compute color and z
      set the color of the pixel
```

In the second line, we need to compute which objects are seen along the line of sight of a pixel (see figure 20.1). This step requires computing the intersection between a ray and the scene. Here are a few advantages of ray tracing:

• Using ray tracing, we never waste computation calculating the color of an occluded object.

• Because we have an ordered list of intersections along a ray, (nonrefractive) transparency is easy to model. The ordered intersection list allows us to apply the over operator from equation (16.4).

• Using ray intersections, we can directly render smooth objects without first having to dice them up into triangles.

• It is also easy to render solid objects described by volumetric set operations, such as the union or intersection of objects (see exercise 20.3).

• Most importantly, once ray intersection code is in place, we can use this infrastructure to do all kinds of assorted calculations that involve chasing geometric rays through the scene. For example, it is easy, using ray tracing, to model perfect mirror reflection, and to compute shadows.

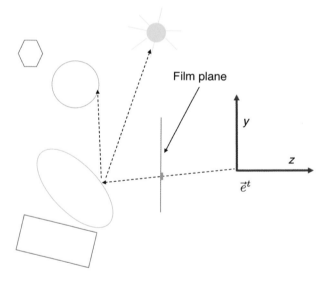

Scene geometry

Figure 20.1
To color a pixel on the film plane, a ray is sent out into the scene. We determine the first object intersected by this ray. Furthermore, at the intersection point, we can cast a shadow ray toward the light to see if we are in shadow. If the object is mirror-like, we can cast a bounce ray.

20.2 Intersection

The main computation needed in ray tracing is to compute the intersection of a geometric ray $(\tilde{p}, \vec{d})$ with an object in the scene. Here, $\tilde{p}$ is the start of the ray, which goes off in direction $\vec{d}$.

20.2.1 Plane

Suppose we wish to compute the intersection of $(\tilde{p}, \vec{d})$ with a plane described by the equation $Ax + By + Cz + D = 0$. We start by representing every point along the ray using a single parameter λ

$$\begin{bmatrix} x \\ y \\ z \end{bmatrix} = \begin{bmatrix} p_x \\ p_y \\ p_z \end{bmatrix} + \lambda \begin{bmatrix} d_x \\ d_y \\ d_z \end{bmatrix}. \tag{20.1}$$

Plugging this into the plane equation, we get

$$0 = A(p_x + \lambda d_x) + B(p_y + \lambda d_y) + C(p_z + \lambda d_z) + D$$

$$= \lambda(Ad_x + Bd_y + Cd_z) + Ap_x + Bp_y + Cp_z + D.$$

And we see that

$$\lambda = \frac{-Ap_x - Bp_y - Cp_z - D}{Ad_x + Bd_y + Cd_z}.$$

In the solution, λ tells us where along the ray the intersection point is (negative-valued λ are backwards along the ray). Comparisons between λ values can be used to determine which, among a set of planes, is the first one intersected along a ray.

20.2.2 Triangle

If we want to intersect a ray with a triangle, we can break it up into two steps. In the first step, we compute the A, B, C, D of the plane supporting the triangle and compute the ray–plane intersection as above. Next, we need a test to determine if the intersection point is inside or outside of the triangle. We can build such a test using the "counterclockwise" calculation of equation 12.4 as follows. Suppose we wish to test if a point $\tilde{q}$ is inside or outside of a triangle $\Delta(\tilde{p}_1 \tilde{p}_2 \tilde{p}_3)$ in 2D (see figures 20.2 and 20.3).

Consider the three "sub" triangles $\Delta(\tilde{p}_1 \tilde{p}_2 \tilde{q})$, $\Delta(\tilde{p}_1 \tilde{q} \tilde{p}_3)$, and $\Delta(\tilde{q} \tilde{p}_2 \tilde{p}_3)$. When $\tilde{q}$ is inside of $\Delta(\tilde{p}_1 \tilde{p}_2 \tilde{p}_3)$, then all three sub-triangles will agree on their clockwisedness. When $\tilde{q}$ is outside, then they will disagree.

20.2.3 Sphere

The ideas behind ray–plane intersection can be adapted to calculate the ray–sphere intersection. In this case, the sphere with radius R and center $\mathbf{c}$ is modeled as the set of points

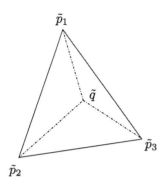

Figure 20.2
The point $\tilde{q}$ is inside the triangle. All three sub-triangles agree on their clockwisedness.

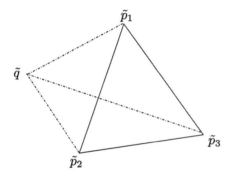

Figure 20.3
The point $\tilde{q}$ is outside of the triangle. The sub-triangle $\Delta(\tilde{p}_1\tilde{p}_2\tilde{q})$ disagrees in clockwisedness with the other two sub-triangles.

$[x, y, z]^t$ that satisfy the equation $(x - c_x)^2 + (y - c_y)^2 + (z - c_z)^2 - r^2 = 0$. Plugging this into equation (20.1), we get

$$
\begin{aligned}
0 &= (p_x + \lambda d_x - c_x)^2 + (p_y + \lambda d_y - c_y)^2 + (p_z + \lambda d_z - c_z)^2 - r^2 \\
&= (d_x^2 + d_y^2 + d_z^2)\lambda^2 + [2d_x(p_x - c_x) + 2d_y(p_y - c_y) + 2d_z(p_z - c_z)]\lambda \\
&\quad + (p_x - c_x)^2 + (p_y - c_y)^2 + (p_z - c_z)^2 - r^2.
\end{aligned}
$$

We can then use the *quadratic formula* to find the real roots λ of this equation. If there are two real roots, these represent two intersections, as the ray enters and exits the sphere. If there is one (doubled) real root, then the intersection is tangential. If there are no real roots, then the ray misses the sphere. As above, any of these intersections may be backwards along the ray.

At the intersection, the normal of the sphere at $[x, y, z]^t$ is in the direction $[x - c_x, y - c_y, z - c_z]^t$. This fact may be useful for shading calculations.

20.2.4 Early Rejection

When computing the intersection between a ray and the scene, instead of testing every scene object for intersection with the ray, we may use auxiliary data structures to quickly determine that some set of objects is entirely missed by the ray. For example, one can use a simple shape (say a large sphere or box) that encloses some set of objects. Given a ray, one first calculates if the ray intersects this volume. If it does not, then clearly this ray misses all of the objects in the bounded set, and no more ray intersection tests are needed. This idea can be further developed with hierarchies and spatial data structures (see, e.g., [73] and references therein).

20.3 Secondary Rays

Once we have a ray intersection infrastructure in place, it is easy to simulate many optical phenomenon. For example, we can compute shadows due to a point light source. To determine if a scene point is in shadow, one follows a "shadow ray" from the observed point toward the light to see if there is any occluding geometry (see figure 20.1).

Another easy calculation that can be done is mirror reflection (and similarly refraction). In this case, one calculates the bounce direction using equation (14.1) and sends a "bounce ray" off in that direction (see figure 20.1). The color of the point hit by this ray is then calculated and used to determine the color of the original point on the mirror. This idea can be applied recursively some number of times to simulate multiple mirror (or refractive) bounces (see figure 20.4).

20.3.1 Even More Rays

As described in more detail in chapter 21, more realistic optical simulation requires the computation of integrals, and these integrals can often be approximated by summing up contributions along a set of samples. Computing the values for these samples often involves tracing rays through the scene.

For example, we may want to simulate a scene that is illuminated by a large light with finite area. This, among other things, results in soft shadow boundaries (see figure 21.8 in chapter 21). Lighting due to such *area light sources* can be approximated by sending off a number of shadow rays toward the area light and determining how many of those rays hit the light source. Other similar effects such as focus effects of camera lenses and interreflection are discussed in chapter 21. These, too, can be calculated by tracing many rays through the scene.

Figure 20.4
One of the first published images rendered using recursive ray tracing. (From [77], copyright ACM.)

Exercises

20.1 Implement a basic ray tracer that shoots one ray out into the scene per pixel and shades the nearest surface point that is hit. You can test your ray tracer with a simple scene composed of planes, spheres, and triangles.

20.2 Add to your ray tracer shadow computation as well as (recursive) mirror reflection computation.

20.3 Add constructive solid geometry to your ray tracer:

Assume that your scene is built of solid "basic" objects, such as the solid interiors of spheres and ellipsoids (or even cylinders, and cubes). You can define new derived volumetric objects as the volumetric unions, differences, and intersections of these basic objects. This representation is called *constructive solid geometry* (CSG). You can continue recursively and define CSG objects applying set operations to other CSG objects. In full generality, a CSG object is defined by an expression tree with set operations in the interior nodes and basic objects at the leaves.

One can easily ray trace a CSG object, as long as one has code that computes ray intersections with the basic objects. When computing the intersection of a ray with a basic object, one stores not just the point of nearest intersection but instead computes and stores the entire interval of intersection. This interval starts where the ray enters the object and ends where the ray exits the object. To compute the ray intersection with, say, the intersection of two basic objects (each represented with its own interval), one simply computes the interval intersections of the two input intervals. This same idea can be applied to a general CSG expression tree. (Note that a general CSG object may be nonconvex, and thus the intersection between a ray and a general CSG object may be composed of several intersection intervals.)

21 Light (Technical)

In this chapter, we will describe in more detail how light and reflections are properly measured and represented. These concepts may not be necessary for doing casual computer graphics, but they can become important to do high-quality rendering. Such high-quality rendering is often done using stand-alone software and does not use the same rendering pipeline as OpenGL. We will cover some of this material, as it is perhaps the most developed part of advanced computer graphics. This chapter will be covering material at a more advanced level than that in the rest of this book. For an even more detailed treatment of this material, see Jim Arvo's Ph.D. thesis [3] and Eric Veach's Ph.D. thesis [71].

There are two steps needed to understand high-quality light simulation. First of all, one needs to understand the proper units needed to measure light and reflection. This understanding directly leads to equations that model how light behaves in a scene. Second, one needs algorithms that compute approximate solutions to these equations. These algorithms make heavy use of the ray tracing infrastructure described in chapter 20. In this chapter, we will focus on the more fundamental aspect of deriving the appropriate equations and only touch on the subsequent algorithmic issues. For more on such issues, the interested reader should see [71, 30].

Our basic mental model of light is that of "geometric optics." We think of light as a field of photons flying through space. In free space, each photon flies unmolested in a straight line, and each moves at the same speed. When photons hit a surface, they scatter in various directions from that point. We also assume that the field is in equilibrium.

21.1 Units

If we want to simulate realistic images carefully, we first need to understand the units used for measuring light. We will start this discussion with some simple photon measurements. These will lead us to a very useful unit called radiance.

21.1.1 Radiant Flux

We can think of light as a bunch of photons flying through space in various directions. Imagine a "sensor" (W, X) out in space, where X is a smooth imaginary reference surface, and W is a *wedge* of directions. In this sensor, we count the number of photons that come in from any direction within the wedge W and pass through the surface X. There may be a physical surface of our scene coincident with X or the imaginary sensor may be sitting in free space (see figure 21.1).

This sensor then counts the number of photons it receives each second. Each photon carries energy measured in units of *joules*. By dividing the energy by time (measured in seconds), we get a measurement called radiant flux, measured in *watts*. We use the symbol $\Phi(W, X)$ to represent such a measurement.

Next, we assume (or verify by experiment) that $\Phi(W, X)$ varies continuously as we continuously alter the geometry of the sensor (translate, rotate, or change its size). Given this assumption, we are now in the position to define a slew of useful radiometric measurements.

21.1.2 Irradiance

First, we want to define a measurement of light, say over a very small planar sensor X with normal $\vec{n}$, that does not depend on the actual size of the sensor X. We can get this by simply dividing our measured radiant flux by the area of the sensor (measured in square meters). Doing this, we get a measurement

$$E(W, X) := \frac{\Phi(W, X)}{|X|}.$$

We can measure $E(W, X)$ for smaller and smaller X around a single point $\tilde{x}$. Under reasonable continuity assumptions about Φ, this ratio converges (almost everywhere) to a value

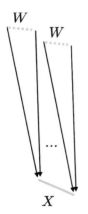

Figure 21.1
A sensor counts the photons that pass through X from incoming directions within the wedge W. This gives us $\Phi(W, X)$, a measurement called radiant flux.

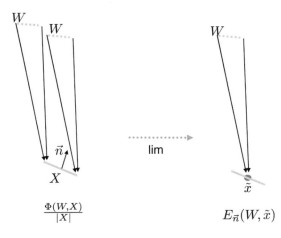

Figure 21.2
We can divide radiant flux by $|X|$. In the limit, this becomes the pointwise incoming irradiance measurement $E_{\vec{n}}(W, \tilde{x})$.

that we call an (incoming) *irradiance* measurement and write as $E_{\vec{n}}(W, \tilde{x})$ (see figure 21.2). We need to keep around the $\vec{n}$ parameter in order to specify the orientation of the smaller and smaller sensors used in this measurement sequence. If we had considered the same point $\tilde{x}$ in space on a different surface X' with a different normal $\vec{n}'$, we would obtain a different quantity $E_{\vec{n}'}(W, \tilde{x})$. [Moreover, because the wedge W is finite, there is no easy way to relate $E_{\vec{n}}(W, \tilde{x})$ to $E_{\vec{n}'}(W, \tilde{x})$. Later on, when we define a quantity called radiance, we will shrink W down to a single vector. In that case, a simple cosine factor will be able to relate measurements with different normals.]

Often in the literature, the first argument for E is dropped from the notation and is inferred somehow from conventions and context. For example, in some contexts, it may be clear that W is the entire upper hemisphere above the point. Similarly, the normal parameter is often dropped from the notation and inferred from context.

Suppose our finite sensor surface X is broken up into a bunch of smaller surfaces, X_i. Then we can compute flux over the entire sensor as the sum

$$\Phi(W, X) = \sum_i \Phi(W, X_i) = \sum_i |X_i| \, E(W, X_i).$$

Likewise, under reasonable continuity assumptions about Φ, we can compute flux from pointwise irradiance as

$$\Phi(W, X) = \int_X dA \, E_{\vec{n}(\tilde{x})}(W, \tilde{x}),$$

where $\int_X$ is an integral over the surface X, and dA is an area measure over the positions $\tilde{x}$.

21.1.3 Radiance

We next want to define a measurement that does not depend on the size of W, and so we want to divide out by $|W|$, the *solid angle* measure of W. The solid angle of a wedge of directions from the origin is simply defined as the area covered by the wedge on the unit sphere. These units are called *steradians*, where the wedge of *all* directions covers 4π steradians.

We now define a new radiometric measurement by dividing irradiance by steradians:

$$L_{\vec{n}}(W, \tilde{x}) = \frac{E_{\vec{n}}(W, \tilde{x})}{|W|}.$$

We can measure this using smaller and smaller wedges around a vector $\vec{w}$ pointing toward $\tilde{x}$. Again, under reasonable continuity assumptions for Φ, this converges (almost everywhere) to a measurement that we call $L_{\vec{n}}(\vec{w}, \tilde{x})$, where $\vec{w}$ is now a single direction vector, and not a wedge (see figure 21.3).

We can now drop the dependence on $\vec{n}$ by converting our measurement $L_{\vec{n}}(\vec{w}, \tilde{x})$ to that of $L_{-\vec{w}}(\vec{w}, \tilde{x})$. In other words, we consider what the measurement would have been had the X plane been perpendicular to the incoming beam. To do this, we have to account for the ratio between the areas of sensor surfaces as they are tilted. This can be calculated as

$$L(\vec{w}, \tilde{x}) := L_{-\vec{w}}(\vec{w}, \tilde{x}) = \frac{L_{\vec{n}}(\vec{w}, \tilde{x})}{\cos(\theta)},$$

where θ is the angle between $\vec{n}$ and $-\vec{w}$. We now drop the normal parameter, writing this simply as $L(\vec{w}, \tilde{x})$ instead of $L_{-\vec{w}}(\vec{w}, \tilde{x})$. We call this measurement *incoming radiance* (see figure 21.3). In summary,

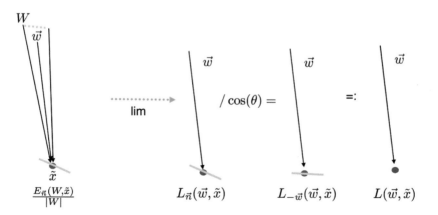

Figure 21.3
We can divide an irradiance measurement by $|W|$ to obtain a measurement $L_{\vec{n}}(W, \tilde{x}) = \frac{E_{\vec{n}}(W, \tilde{x})}{|W|}$. This converges to $L_{\vec{n}}(\vec{w}, \tilde{x})$. By dividing out by $\cos(\theta)$, we can convert this to $L_{-\vec{w}}(\vec{w}, \tilde{x})$. Dropping the subscript gives us the radiance measurement $L(\vec{w}, \tilde{x})$ used for a ray.

$$L(\vec{w}, \tilde{x}) := \frac{1}{\cos(\theta)} \lim_{W \to \vec{w}} \frac{1}{|W|} \left(\lim_{X \to \tilde{x}} \frac{\Phi(W, X)}{|X|} \right). \tag{21.1}$$

Going the other way, given a spatially and angularly varying $L(\vec{w}, \tilde{x})$, we can compute the radiant flux over a large sensor (W, X) as

$$\Phi(W, X) = \int_X dA \int_W dw \, L(\vec{w}, \tilde{x}) \cos(\theta),$$

where dw is a differential measure of steradians. Radiance measurements allow us to measure light at a point and direction without keeping track of the size and orientation of the measurement device. Moreover, even though our radiance notation includes a 3D point, $\tilde{x}$, as one of its variables, in fact (see later for an argument), radiance remains constant along a ray in free space. That is,

$$L(\vec{w}, \tilde{x}) = L(\vec{w}, \tilde{x} + \vec{w}).$$

For a point on a surface, it is also useful to have a measurement $L(\tilde{x}, \vec{w})$ of *outgoing radiance* from the point $\tilde{x}$ in the direction $\vec{w}$. (We reverse the order of the arguments to L to distinguish incoming from outgoing radiance.) We can define this as

$$L(\tilde{x}, \vec{w}) := \frac{1}{\cos(\theta)} \lim_{W \to \vec{w}} \frac{1}{|W|} \left(\lim_{X \to \tilde{x}} \frac{\Phi(X, W)}{|X|} \right),$$

where $\Phi(X, W)$ is the radiant flux of photons *leaving* a finite surface X and going out along vectors in the wedge W (again, note the order of the arguments).

In free space, it is clear that $L(\vec{w}, \tilde{x}) = L(\tilde{x}, \vec{w})$.

Radiance is the most useful quantity needed for computational light simulation. Indeed, we can go back to chapters 14 and 20 and interpret those methods using these units. For example, when we calculate the color of some 3D point $\tilde{x}$ in an OpenGL fragment shader, we can interpret this as computing the outgoing radiance $L(\tilde{x}, \vec{v})$, where $\vec{v}$ is the "view vector." This outgoing radiance value is also the incoming radiance value at the corresponding sample location on the image plane and is thus used to color the pixel. Likewise, in ray tracing, when we trace a ray along the ray $(\tilde{x}, \vec{d})$, we can interpret this as calculating the incoming radiance value, $L(-\vec{d}, \tilde{x})$.

21.1.3.1 Constancy of Radiance Along a Ray (Optional)

Suppose, in free space, that we slide our sensor (W, X) along the vector $\vec{w}$ to obtain the shifted sensor (W, X') where $X' = X + \vec{w}$ (see figure 21.4). In this case, our measured fluxes will not agree, $\Phi(W, X) \neq \Phi(W, X')$. But if we compute radiance, in the limit we will get agreement. In particular,

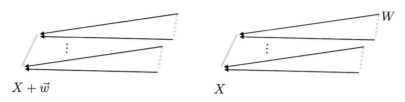

Figure 21.4
We can shift a sensor along a central direction $\vec{w}$. In the limit for small wedges, they will be measuring mostly the same photons. From this we can conclude that radiance is constant along a ray.

$$L(\vec{w}, \tilde{x}) := \frac{1}{\cos(\theta)} \lim_{W \to \vec{w}} \frac{1}{|W|} \left(\lim_{X \to \tilde{x}} \frac{\Phi(W, X)}{|X|} \right)$$

$$= \frac{1}{\cos(\theta)} \left(\lim_{X \to \tilde{x}} \frac{1}{|X|} \lim_{W \to \vec{w}} \frac{\Phi(W, X)}{|W|} \right)$$

$$= \frac{1}{\cos(\theta)} \left(\lim_{X \to \tilde{x}} \frac{1}{|X|} \lim_{W \to \vec{w}} \frac{\Phi(W, X + \vec{w})}{|W|} \right)$$

$$= \frac{1}{\cos(\theta)} \left(\lim_{X' \to \tilde{x}+\vec{w}} \frac{1}{|X'|} \lim_{W \to \vec{w}} \frac{\Phi(W, X')}{|W|} \right)$$

$$= \frac{1}{\cos(\theta)} \lim_{W \to \vec{w}} \frac{1}{|W|} \left(\lim_{X' \to \tilde{x}+\vec{w}} \frac{\Phi(W, X')}{|X'|} \right) = L(\vec{w}, \tilde{x} + \vec{w}).$$

In the third line, we use the fact that in the limit for very small wedges, our sensor and shifted sensor will be measuring the same set of photons, and thus

$$\lim_{W \to \vec{w}} \frac{\Phi(W, X')}{\Phi(W, X)} = 1.$$

As a result of this, we say that radiance is constant along a ray.

Fundamentally, we can think of this constancy as arising from the combination of two facts. First, our physical assumptions imply that, in free space, the measured flux, Φ, depends only on the set of directed lines that are measured, not where they are measured. Second, for any set of lines, say called S, if we parameterrize the lines by direction $\vec{w}$ and by where they hit some plane X, then the *line measurement* $\int_S dw\, dA_X \cos(\theta)$ will, in fact, not depend on the choice of plane X. Using this terminology, radiance is simply the *density* of flux over the line measure, and the choice of $\tilde{x}$ is not relevant.

21.2 Reflection

When light comes in from W, a wedge of incoming directions about the vector $\vec{w}$, and hits a point $\tilde{x}$ on a physical surface, then some of that light can get reflected off the surface.

We make the simplifying approximation/assumption that all reflection is pointwise (i.e., light hitting a point bounces out from that single point only). Let us measure the light that is reflected out along V, some wedge of outgoing directions around an outgoing vector $\vec{v}$. The particulars of this bouncing are governed by the physical properties of the material. We wish to represent the behavior of this bouncing with some function f describing the ratio of incoming to outgoing light. What kind of units should we use for this ratio? Our governing principle is that we want **a ratio that converges** as we use smaller and smaller incoming and outgoing wedges. This implies our second principle (that is desirable in and of itself): We want a ratio that (for small enough wedges) **does not actually depend on the size of the wedges**.

In this section, we will derive the primary way to describe reflection, called the bidirectional reflection distribution function. For special materials, like pure mirrors and refractive media, we will use a slightly different representation.

21.2.1 Bidirectional Reflection Distribution Function

We can verify experimentally that most materials (excluding pure mirrors or lenses, see later) have the following diffusing behavior. For any fixed incoming light pattern, the outgoing light measured along any outgoing wedge changes continuously as we rotate this wedge. Thus, if we double the size of a small outgoing measurement wedge V, we will see roughly twice the outgoing flux. Therefore, to set the numerator of our ratio f in a way that does not depend on the size of V, we should use units of radiance. Let us call this outgoing measurement $L^1(\tilde{x}, \vec{v})$. We place a superscript on L^1 to make clear that we are referring here to the measurement of bounced photons.

Similarly (but possibly surprisingly) we can verify that, for most materials (again mirrors and lenses excluded), if all of the light is coming in from a single small wedge W, and we double the width of this incoming wedge, the amount of flux reflected along a fixed outgoing wedge, and thus the amount of radiance reflected along a fixed outgoing direction, will roughly double as well. Thus, to get a ratio that does not depend on the size of the W, we need the denominator to double in this case. We accomplish this by measuring the incoming light in units of irradiance.

Putting this together, we see that we should measure reflection as

$$f_{\tilde{x},\tilde{n}}(W, \vec{v}) = \frac{L^1(\tilde{x}, \vec{v})}{E^e_{\tilde{n}}(W, \tilde{x})}$$

$$= \frac{L^1(\tilde{x}, \vec{v})}{L^e_{\tilde{n}}(W, \tilde{x})|W|},$$

where we use the superscript L^e to refer to photons that have been *emitted* by some light sources and have not yet bounced. Once again, by making the incoming wedge smaller and

smaller around a fixed $\vec{w}$, this quantity converges to a measurement denoted $f_{\tilde{x},\vec{n}}(\vec{w}, \vec{v})$.
This function, f, is called the *bidirectional reflection distribution function*, or BRDF. It is
a function that can vary with both incoming and outgoing directions (see figure 21.5).

The simplest BRDF is the constant BRDF $f_{\tilde{x},\vec{n}}(\vec{w}, \vec{v}) = 1$. This represents the behavior of
a diffuse material. In this case, the outgoing radiance at a point does not depend on $\vec{v}$ at all.
(Subtlety: This does not mean that incoming photons are scattered equally in all outgoing
directions. In fact, on a diffuse surface, more of the photons are scattered in the direction
of the surface normal, and the amount of scattered photons drops by a cosine factor to zero
at grazing angles. In contrast, the outgoing *radiance* does not depend on outgoing angle, as
the definition of radiance includes its own cosine factor that cancels this "drop-off" factor.
Intuitively speaking, when looking at a diffuse surface from a grazing angle, fewer photons
are coming toward you per unit of surface area, but you are also seeing more surface area
through your sensor.)

More complicated BRDFs can be derived from a variety of methods.

• We can simply hack up some function that makes our materials look nice in pictures. This
is essentially what we did in chapter 14.

• We can derive the BRDF using various physical assumptions and statistical analysis. This
involves a deeper understanding of the physics of light and materials.

• We can build devices that actually measure the BRDF of real materials. This can be stored
in a big tabular form or approximated using some functional form (see figure 21.6).

Suppose we want to compute the outgoing $L^1(\tilde{x}, \vec{v})$ at a point on a surface with normal $\vec{n}$, due to light coming in from the hemisphere, H, above $\tilde{x}$. And suppose H is broken up into a set of finite wedges W_i. Then, we can compute the reflected light using
the sum

$$L^1(\tilde{x}, \vec{v}) = \sum_i |W_i| \; f_{\tilde{x},\vec{n}}(W_i, \vec{v}) \; L_{\vec{n}}^e(W_i, \tilde{x}).$$

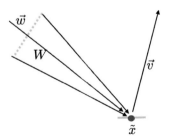

Figure 21.5
A BRDF measures the ratio of incoming irradiance to outgoing radiance.

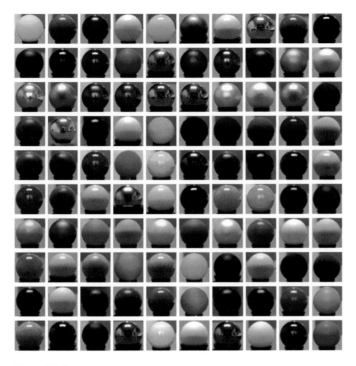

Figure 21.6
An array of BRDFs captured by a measuring device. (From [47], copyright ACM.)

Likewise, using $f_{\tilde{x},\vec{n}}(\vec{w}, \vec{v})$ and $L^e(\vec{w}, \tilde{x})$, we can compute the reflected light using the integral

$$L^1(\tilde{x}, \vec{v}) = \int_H dw \; f_{\tilde{x},\vec{n}}(\vec{w}, \vec{v}) \; L^e_{\vec{n}}(\vec{w}, \tilde{x}) \tag{21.2}$$

$$= \int_H dw \; f_{\tilde{x},\vec{n}}(\vec{w}, \vec{v}) \; L^e(\vec{w}, \tilde{x}) \; \cos(\theta). \tag{21.3}$$

This is called the *reflection equation*, and it is the basis for most of our models for light simulation (see figure 21.7).

21.2.2 Mirrors and Refraction
Pure mirror reflection and refraction are not easily modeled using a BRDF representation. In a mirrored surface, $L^1(\tilde{x}, \vec{v})$, the bounced radiance along a ray, depends **only** on $L^e[-B(\vec{v}), \tilde{x}]$, the incoming radiance along a single ray. Here, B is the bounce operator of equation (14.1).

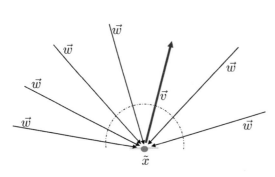

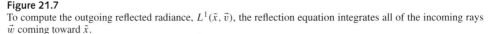

Figure 21.7
To compute the outgoing reflected radiance, $L^1(\tilde{x}, \vec{v})$, the reflection equation integrates all of the incoming rays $\vec{w}$ coming toward $\tilde{x}$.

Doubling the size of an incoming wedge that includes $-B(\vec{v})$ has no effect on $L^1(\tilde{x}, \vec{v})$. Thus, for mirror materials, we represent the reflection behavior as

$$k_{\tilde{x},\vec{n}}(\vec{v}) = \frac{L^1(\tilde{x}, \vec{v})}{L^e[-B(\vec{v}), \tilde{x}]}, \tag{21.4}$$

where $k_{\tilde{x},\vec{n}}(\vec{v})$ is some material coefficient. We replace the reflection equation with

$$L^1(\tilde{x}, \vec{v}) = k_{\tilde{x},\vec{n}}(\vec{v})\ L^e[-B(\vec{v}), \tilde{x}].$$

No integration is required in this case. For this reason, mirror reflection is easy to calculate algorithmically and easily done in a ray tracing program.

When light passes between mediums with different indices of refraction, such as when light passes into or out of glass, the rays bend using an appropriate geometric rule. Like mirror reflection, at the material interface, the radiance along each outgoing light ray is affected by the radiance of a single incoming light ray. Once again, it is easiest here to use "ratio of radiance" units, as in equation (21.4).

21.3   Light Simulation

The reflection equation can be used in a nested fashion to describe how light bounces around an environment multiple times. Such descriptions typically result in definite integrals that need to be calculated. In practice, this computation is done by some sort of discrete sampling over the integration domain.

In this section, we will start with the simple light simulation of our shading model from chapter 14 and then build up to more complicated models.

We use the symbol L with no arguments to represent the entire distribution of radiance measurements in a scene due to a certain set of photons Such an L includes all incoming and outgoing measurements anywhere in the scene. We use L^e to represent unbounced (emitted) photons and L^i to represent the radiance of photons that have bounced exactly i times.

21.3.1 Direct Point Lights

In our basic OpenGL rendering model, our light comes not from area lights but from *point lights*. Such point lights do conform to our continuity assumptions and are not so easily represented with our units. In practice, for point lights we simply replace the reflection equation with

$$L^1(\tilde{x}, \vec{v}) = f_{\tilde{x}, \tilde{n}}(-\vec{l}, \vec{v}) \; E^e_{\tilde{n}}(H, \tilde{x}),$$

where E^e is the unbounced irradiance coming into $\tilde{x}$ due to the point source, and $\vec{l}$ is the "light vector" pointing from $\tilde{x}$ to the light. We are free to calculate E^e any way we want. For example, in the real world, the irradiance at a point $\tilde{x}$ due to a very small spherical light source is proportional to $\frac{\cos(\theta)}{d^2}$, where d is the distance between the light and the surface. This is because the solid angle of the small light source drops off with $\frac{1}{d^2}$. (However, this distance drop-off term tends to make pictures too dark and so is often not used.) Also note that, in the language of Chapter 14, we have $\cos(\theta) = \vec{n} \cdot \vec{l}$.

21.3.2 Direct Area Lights

Suppose our light sources have finite area, then we really do need the integral of the reflection equation. In this case, the integrand over H in equation (21.2) is only non-zero for incoming directions $\vec{w}$ that "see" the light.

If we approximate the integral using some finite number of incoming directions, $\vec{w}_i$, we can use a ray tracing approach to calculate these $L^e(\vec{w}_i, \tilde{x})$ values. When randomness is used to select the directions, this is called distribution ray tracing [13]. As ray intersection is an expensive operation, these integrals can be very expensive to compute accurately.

When the light source is partially occluded by other geometry, this integration will produce shadows that have soft boundaries. This happens because nearby points on a light-receiving surface may see different amounts of the area light source (see figure 21.8).

21.3.3 Two Bounces

We can compute L^2, the light distribution of twice-bounced photons, by using the reflection equation but replacing the "input" L^e with L^1:

Figure 21.8
Integration over area lights causes soft shadows. (From [69], copyright ACM.)

$$L^2(\tilde{x}, \vec{v}) = \int_H dw \; f_{\tilde{x}, \vec{n}}(\vec{w}, \vec{v}) \cos(\theta) L^1(\vec{w}, \tilde{x})$$

$$= \int_H dw \; f_{\tilde{x}, \vec{n}}(\vec{w}, \vec{v}) \cos(\theta) \int_{H'} dw' \; f_{\tilde{x}', \vec{n}'}(\vec{w}', \vec{w}) \cos(\theta') L^e(\vec{w}', \tilde{x}')$$

$$= \int_H dw \int_{H'} dw' \; f_{\tilde{x}, \vec{n}}(\vec{w}, \vec{v}) \cos(\theta) \; f_{\tilde{x}', \vec{n}'}(\vec{w}', \vec{w}) \cos(\theta') \; L^e(\vec{w}', \tilde{x}').$$

In this expression, $\tilde{x}'$ is the point first hit along the ray $(\tilde{x}, -\vec{w})$. At the intersection point, $\vec{n}'$ is the normal, H' is the upper hemisphere, and $\vec{w}'$ is an incoming direction, making an angle of θ' with $\vec{n}'$ (see figure 21.9).

Once computed, we can add together $L^e(\tilde{x}, \vec{v}) + L^1(\tilde{x}, \vec{v}) + L^2(\tilde{x}, \vec{v})$ and use this as the point's observed color at the image plane.

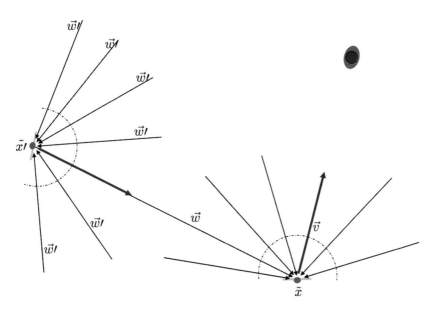

Figure 21.9
To compute L^2, we need two nested integrals. For each direction $\vec{w}$ coming into $\tilde{x}$, there we find the point $\tilde{x}'$ hit by the ray as shown. We then need to integrate the hemisphere above $\tilde{x}'$.

As suggested by the second line in the above equation, one way to compute L^2 is by recursively evaluating these nested integrals using distribution ray tracing. That is, an outer loop integrates the hemisphere above $\tilde{x}$. For each sampled direction $\vec{w}$, we hit some point, $\tilde{x}'$. We then use a recursive distribution ray tracing call to integrate the hemisphere above it (see figure 21.9).

Alternatively, as suggested by the third line in the equation above, there are also other ways to organize this integration. Let us denote by $\tilde{x}''$ the point first hit along the ray $(\tilde{x}', -\vec{w}')$. Then, in the integral, each setting of the variables $(\vec{w}, \vec{w}')$ corresponds to a *geometric path of length two*: $(\tilde{x}, \tilde{x}', \tilde{x}'')$. We can think of this integrand as calculating the light emitted at $\tilde{x}''$, reflected at $\tilde{x}'$, and then reflected at $\tilde{x}$ out toward $\vec{v}$ (figure 21.10). As such, it is often convenient to think of this not as a nested integral over two hemispheres but as an integral over an appropriate space of paths. This leads to an integration algorithm known as path tracing [71].

This second bounce light L^2 is less important than direct lighting, but it is needed to properly simulate blurry reflections of the surrounding environment (see figure 21.11). It also produces the less visible effect called color bleeding (see again figure 21.11). Caustic effects can also be seen due to L^2. In this case, light bounces off mirrored or refracting objects and creates bright spots on diffuse surfaces. This light then bounces off toward the eye (see figure 21.12).

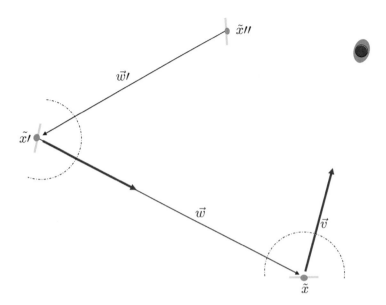

Figure 21.10
The integral that computes L^2 can be thought of as summing over paths of length two.

Figure 21.11
Second bounce light L^2 accounts for the blurry reflection in the glossy floor of the sphere as well as the color bleeding from the walls onto the ceiling. One path of length two is shown. (From [29], copyright Springer.)

Figure 21.12
Second bounce light can also create the caustic effects seen on the ground. One path of length two is shown.
(From [29], copyright Springer.)

21.3.4 And So On

In the real world, light bounces around the environment many, many times. Thus, the *total* observed light L^t is the sum of light that has come from emitters and bounced **any** number of times:

$$L^t = L^e + L^1 + L^2 + L^3 + ...$$

Some light is absorbed at each bounce, making the higher bounce terms become small and the sum convergent.

Higher bounces account for the overall distributions of lightness and darkness in the environment (see figure 21.13). In most cases, this can be done with low accuracy and at a low spatial resolution.

In software rendering, such integrals can be computed using sampling and summing. Successful methods here include distribution ray tracing [13], path tracing [71], the "Radiance" algorithm [75], and photon mapping [30].

In OpenGL, most of these effects are simply hacked using a combination of multiple pass rendering and precomputed textures. One popular such technique is called "ambient occlusion" [39].

Figure 21.13
By computing multiple bounces, we can compute the correct distribution of light and darkness in an environment.
(From [72], copyright ACM.)

21.3.5 The Rendering Equation (Optional)

Instead of thinking of L^t as an infinite sum of L^i, we can also think of L^t as the solution to the so-called *rendering equation*. This point of view can ultimately lead to other insights and algorithmic approaches to light simulation. We include it here, as it is interesting in its own right.

Let us begin by writing the reflection equation in shorthand as

$$L^1 = \mathcal{B}L^e,$$

where $\mathcal{B}$ is the bounce operator mapping light distributions to light distributions. More generally, we can use the reflection equation and bounce operator to write $L^{i+1} = \mathcal{B}L^i$.

Putting this together, we can write

$$L^t = L^e + L^1 + L^2 + L^3 + ...$$
$$= L^e + \mathcal{B}(L^e + L^1 + L^2 + L^3 + ...)$$
$$= L^e + \mathcal{B}L^t.$$

This expresses an equation that must hold for the total equilibrium distribution L^t.

At a surface point, this can be expanded out as

$$L^t(\tilde{x}, \vec{v}) = L^e(\tilde{x}, \vec{v}) + \int_H dw \; f_{\tilde{x},\tilde{n}}(\vec{w}, \vec{v}) \; L^t(\vec{w}, \tilde{x}) \cos(\theta).$$

This last form is called the rendering equation. Note that L^t appears on both sides of the equation, so it is not simply a definite integral but is an *integral equation*.

21.4 Sensors

When we place a (virtual) camera in the scene, an image is captured of the light distribution L^t, the total equilibrium distribution of light in the scene. For a pinhole camera, we simply capture the incoming radiance at each pixel/sample location along the single ray from the pixel toward the pinhole. In a physical camera (or simulation of one), we need a finite aperture and finite shutter speed to capture a finite amount of photons at our sensor plane (see figure 21.14). Given such a camera, we can model the photon count at pixel (i, j) as

$$\int_T dt \int_{\Omega_{i,j}} dA \int_W dw \; F_{i,j}(\tilde{x}) \, L^t(\vec{w}, \tilde{x}) \cos(\theta), \qquad (21.5)$$

where T is the duration of the shutter, $\Omega_{i,j}$ is the spatial support of pixel (i, j)'s sensor, $F_{i,j}$ is the spatial sensitivity of pixel (i, j) at the film point $\tilde{x}$, and W is the wedge of vectors coming in from the aperture toward the film point.

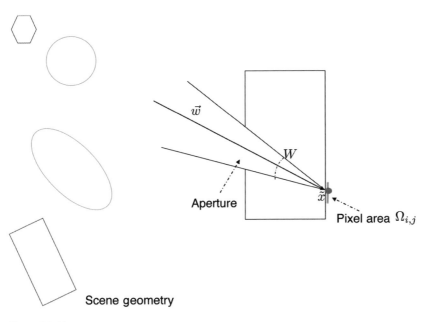

Figure 21.14
In a camera, we must integrate over the aperture and pixel footprint.

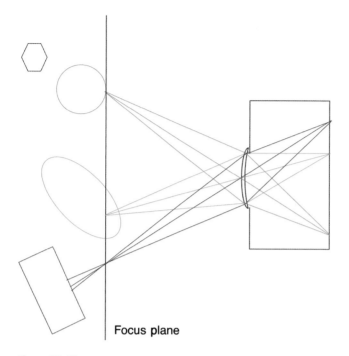

Focus plane

Figure 21.15
Here we show the effect of placing a thin lens in front of the aperture. It has the effect of focusing rays at a preferred depth plane. Objects in front of or behind this plane are out of focus and blurred.

To organize the light, a lens is placed in front of the aperture. The simplest lens model is called the *thin lens* model. Its geometry is visualized in figure 21.15. The effect of this lens is to keep objects at a particular depth plane in focus. Objects at other depths appear blurred out because of the $\int_W$ operation.

We have already seen (section 16.3) that integration over the pixel area domain produces anti-aliasing. Integration over the shutter duration produces motion blur (see figure 21.16). Integration over the aperture produces focus and blur effects, also called *depth of field* effects (see figure 21.17).

21.5 Integration Algorithms

As we have seen, starting from L^e, which is part of the scene definition, the computation of reflected light, L^1, and especially the total equilibrium distribution, L^t, requires the computation of (nested) definite integrals. Moreover, the computation of each pixel value in our sensor requires its own integrals as well. Integral computations are typically approximated by turning them into sums over some set of samples of the integrand.

Figure 21.16
One of the first published images rendered using lots of rays per pixel. (From [13], copyright Pixar.)

Figure 21.17
Integration over the lens creates focus effects. (From [38], copyright ACM.)

Much of the work in the photo-realistic rendering field is all about the best ways to approximate these integrals. Key ideas for computing these efficiently include:

• Use randomness to choose the samples [13]. This avoids noticeable patterns in the errors during approximation. Using randomness, we can also use expectation arguments to argue about the correctness of the method.

• Reuse as much computation as possible [75, 29]. If we know the irradiance pattern at a point, perhaps we can share these data with nearby points.

• Do more work where it will have the most effect on the output. For example, it may not be worth it to follow rays of light that don't carry much radiance [71].

Possibly the most important lesson to keep in mind is that there is a certain duality at work here: One the one hand more integrals means more work, but on the other hand each of the integrals is typically some kind of blurring operation. Thus, more integrals means less accuracy is needed. For efficiency, we should not spend too much effort on computing details that will get blurred out and never impact the final image. For example, we should typically spend more time on calculating direct illumination and less time on indirect lighting.

21.6 More General Effects

There are other optical effects that we have not captured in our simple model of light and reflection. Atmospheric volumetric scattering occurs when light passes through fog. Fluorescence occurs when surfaces absorb light and later re-emit this energy out (often at different wavelengths). Polarization and diffraction effects can occasionally be observed as well.

Figure 21.18
From left to right, more and more subsurface scattering is used. This can give scale cues, making the rightmost figure look smallest. (From [31], copyright ACM.)

One interesting effect that turns out to be somewhat important is subsurface scattering. In this case, light enters a material at one point, bounces around inside of the surface, and comes out over a finite region around the point of entrance. This gives an overall softening effect and can be important properly to model surfaces such as skin and marble (see figure 21.18).

Exercises

21.1 Given a diffuse wall with constant irradiance from the incoming hemisphere over all points, what is the distribution of outgoing radiance?

21.2 If we observe the above wall with a finite sensor and compute $\Phi(W, X)$, how will the flux depend on the distance between the sensor and the wall? What about its dependence on angle?

21.3 Starting with a ray tracer, use multiple rays to render depth of field effects or soft shadows from area light sources.

21.4 Learn about and photon mapping. This is an algorithm that generates photons at the light sources and sends them out along rays through the scene. The absorbed photons are stored in a *kd-tree* spatial data structure and later used to determine the colors of observed surface points.

22 Geometric Modeling: Basic Intro

In computer graphics, we need concrete ways to represent shapes. Geometric modeling is the topic of how to represent, create, and modify such shapes. Geometric modeling is a broad topic that deserves (and has) its own books (e.g., [21, 76, 7]). Here, we will simply survey the topic a bit to give you a feel for it. We spend a bit more time on the representation of subdivision surfaces, as these are becoming popular representations.

22.1 Triangle Soup

For rendering in OpenGL, the most obvious representation is *triangle soup*; a set of triangles, each described by three vertices (see, e.g., figure 22.1). These data can often be better organized to reduce redundancy. For example, in many cases, it makes sense to store each vertex only once, even when it is shared by many triangles. Additionally, the connectivity information can be represented more compactly using representations such as "triangle fans" and "triangle strips" [79].

Related representations include quad soup (using four-sided polygons) and polygon soup (for general-sided polygons). For hardware rendering, such polygons first need to be diced up into triangles and then can be drawn using the general triangle pipeline.

There are many ways that triangle-based geometry can be created. In particular, triangle geometry can be created ab initio using a geometric modeling tool, it can be obtained by tessellating a smooth surface representation (see later), or it can be obtained by directly scanning a physical object (see figure 22.2).

22.2 Meshes

In the soup representation, there is no way to "walk along" the geometry. One cannot easily (in constant time) figure out which triangles meet at an edge or which triangles surround a vertex. Walking along a mesh can be useful, for example, if one is trying to smooth the geometry or if one wishes to simulate some physical process over the geometry.

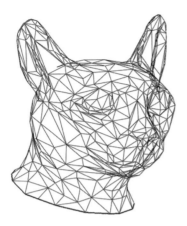

Figure 22.1
A cat head is described by a soup of triangles. (From [64], copyright Eurographics and Blackwell Publishing Ltd.)

Figure 22.2
Sophisticated scanners can be used to digitize real things. (From [44], copyright ACM.)

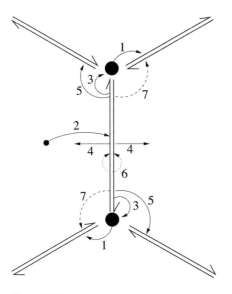

Figure 22.3
A mesh data structure, visualized here, keeps track of how the various vertices, edges, and faces fit together in the geometry. (From [8].)

A *mesh* data structure is a representation that organizes the vertex, edge, and face data so that these queries can be done easily (see, e.g., figure 22.3). There is a variety of different mesh data structures, and they can be tricky to implement. For a good reference on mesh data structures, see [63].

22.3 Implicit Surfaces

One way to represent a smooth surface is as the set of points that evaluate to zero under some given trivariate function $f(x, y, z)$. This is called an *implicit representation*. For example, simple shapes, like spheres and ellipsoids, can be represented as the zero set of a quadratic trivariate function. Additionally, we can define an implicit function as a sum of simpler elemental implicit functions: $f(x, y, z) = \sum_i f_i(x, y, z)$. Doing so, say, with a set of sphere functions creates a smoothly blended union of the individual spheres (see figure 22.4). This technique is known as *blobby modeling* and is ideal for modeling organic shapes such as sea mammals.

Implicit surfaces have some nice properties. If we define a surface as the zero set of f, then we can think of the points where f evaluates to a positive value as the volumetric interior of the surface. As such, it is easy to apply volumetric set operations, such as union, intersection, negation, and difference, to these interior volumes. For example, the intersection of the volumes defined by functions f_1 and f_2 can be defined using the new function $f(x, y, z) = \min[f_1(x, y, z), f_2(x, y, z)]$ (see, e.g., figure 22.5).

Figure 22.4
Implicit function representations are very good at representing blobby shapes such as this digital water fountain.
(From [34], copyright John Wiley & Sons.)

Figure 22.5
This surface has been extracted from a volumetric data representation using the dual-contouring method. Volume
intersection operations have been used to cut out the shown shape. (From [32], copyright ACM.)

To render an implicit surface in OpenGL, we need to create a set of triangles that approximate the implicit surface. This is a nontrivial task.

22.4 Volume

A volume representation is a specific kind of implicit representation that uses a regular 3D grid of discrete values called *voxels*. Using trilinear interpolation over each grid cell, these voxels define a continuous function in 3D. The zero set of this function can then be thought of as an implicit surface.

Volume data is often obtained as the output of a volumetric scanning process, such as magnetic resonance imaging (MRI). We can also take some general implicit function representation and then sample it along a regular 3D grid to get a voxel-based approximation.

To render the zero-set of a volume-based representation in OpenGL, one needs to extract a set of triangles that approximate the zero-set. Because of the regular pattern of the data, this can be done a bit more easily than for a general implicit function. The standard technique is called the *marching cube* method [45], but there are newer methods such as *dual contouring* [32] (figure 22.5) that may give better results.

22.5 Parametric Patches

Parametric patches represent a section of surface called a *patch* using three coordinate functions $x(s, t)$, $y(s, t)$, and $z(s, t)$. These functions are defined over some square or triangular portion of the (s, t) plane. In most cases, each coordinate function over the patch is represented as a piecewise polynomial bivariate function (see, e.g., figure 22.6).

The most common parametric representation is the *tensor-product spline surface*. Recall (section 9.5) that a spline curve can be used to represent a curve in space. Such a spline curve is defined by an input control polygon that connects a sequence of discrete points in space. This spline curve is made up of a set of smaller pieces, each having coordinate functions that are, say, cubic polynomials

For a tensor-product spline, this construction is "upgraded " from curves to surfaces. In this case, the control polygon is replaced by an m by n rectilinear *control mesh*, with vertices in 3D. By appropriately applying the spline definitions in both the s and t variables, we end up with a parametric patch. Such a patch is made up of small pieces defined over small squares in the (s, t) domain. The coordinates of each such piece are polynomials in s and t. In the case where we upgrade from a cubic spline curve construction, each square piece is defined by a bicubic polynomial in (s, t) (i.e., have terms up to the highest power: $s^3 t^3$).

For rendering, splines can easily be approximated by a quad mesh in a number of ways. For example, we can just place a fine grid of sample points over the (s, t) domain and evaluate the spline functions to obtain $[x, y, z]^t$ coordinates for each sample. These samples

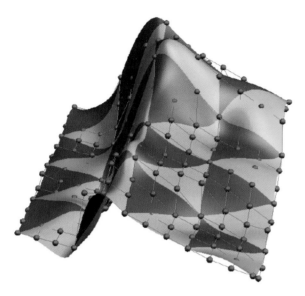

Figure 22.6
Here we show a spline patch controlled by an *m* by *n* rectilinear control mesh. (From [61], copyright IEEE.)

can be used as the vertices of a regular quad mesh. Another approach is to apply a recursive refinement process that takes in a control mesh and outputs a denser control mesh that represents the same surface. After a few steps of subdivision, the quads themselves form a dense control mesh that forms a good approximation to the underlying spline surface.

One can typically design surfaces using splines in a geometric modeling package. Spline surfaces are very popular in the computer-aided design community. In particular, because of their explicit parametric polynomial representation, it is easy to apply various calculations to such shapes.

Modeling with splines is not without a number of difficulties. To model a closed (say ball-like) surface, we have to stitch together some number of patches. Doing the stitching in a smooth manner is tricky. Additionally, if we want patches to meet up along specific creased curves, we need to explicitly do something called "trimming" to each of the patches. One interesting book about the spline representation is [59].

22.6 Subdivision Surfaces

The subdivision surface is a simple representation that solves many of the difficulties associated with parametric patches. The basic idea is to start with a single control mesh. This mesh need not be rectilinear; it can represent a closed surface and can have vertices of any valence. We then use a set of rules to refine the mesh, resulting in a higher-resolution

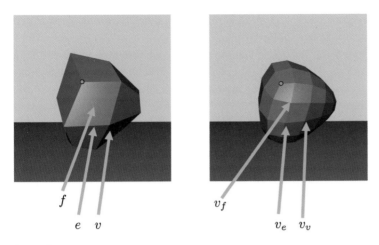

Figure 22.7
On the left we show a low-resolution mesh. On the right we show one level of subdivision. A vertex v on the left gives rise to a vertex v_v on the right. An edge e on the left gives rise to a vertex v_e on the right. A face f on the left gives rise to a vertex v_f on the right. An extraordinary vertex is shown in red. The number of such vertices remains fixed through subdivision.

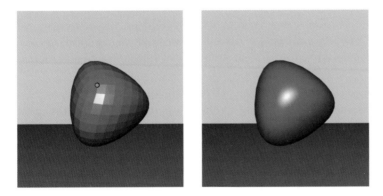

Figure 22.8
On the left, we show one more level of subdivision. On the right, the same mesh has been smooth shaded.

control mesh. By applying this process recursively some number of times, we obtain a very-high-resolution mesh that can be directly rendered as an approximation to a smooth surface (see, e.g., figures 22.7 and 22.8). Subdivision surfaces do not require any patching steps. Additionally, special rules can be applied along certain portions of the control mesh to achieve creases in the surface where desired.

The subdivision rules are defined such that the meshes arising after more and more levels of subdivision converge to a smooth *limit-surface* (a C^1 immersed submanifold in $\mathbb{R}^3$). In many cases, such as in regions where the mesh is rectilinear, the subdivision steps match those used to refine a tensor-product spline surface.

One drawback of a subdivision surface is that the surface representation is defined by a procedure and not by a formula. Thus, such surfaces are more difficult to analyze mathematically. Additionally, away from the rectilinear regions (at so-called extraordinary points), the limit surface can be somewhat poorly behaved [55] and harder to control. But, for casual use (movies and games), these are not big issues, and subdivision surfaces have proved to be simple, useful, and general.

22.6.1 Catmull–Clark

Here we describe in more detail a specific subdivision representation due to Catmull and Clark. One starts with some input mesh M^0 (which we will assume is a watertight "manifold with no boundary"). This mesh has connectivity information describing its vertex, edge, and face structure. The mesh also has geometric information, mapping each abstract vertex to a point in 3D.

Now we apply a set of connectivity updates to get a new refined mesh M^1, with its own connectivity and geometry. The connectivity of M^1 is defined as follows (and shown in figure 22.7). For each vertex v in M^0, we associate a new "vertex-vertex" v_v in M^1. For each edge e in M^0, we associate a new "edge-vertex" v_e in M^1. For each face f in M^0, we associate a new "face-vertex" v_f in M^1. These new vertices are connected up with new edges and faces as shown in figure 22.7. We can easily verify that in M^1, all faces are quads. In M^1, we call any vertex of valence four "ordinary" and any vertex of valence different from four "extraordinary."

We apply this subdivision process recursively. Given M^1, or more generally, M^i, for any $i \geq 1$, we apply the same subdivision rules to obtain a finer mesh M^{i+1}. In the new mesh, we have roughly four times the number of vertices. But importantly, we can verify that the number of extraordinary vertices stays fixed (see figure 22.7)! Thus, during subdivision, more and more of the mesh looks locally rectilinear, with a fixed number of isolated extraordinary points in between.

Now all we need are rules to determine the geometry for the new vertices as they are created during each subdivision step. First, let f be a face in M^i surrounded by the vertices v_j (and let m_f be the number of such vertices). We set the geometry of each new face-vertex v_f in M^{i+1} to be

$$v_f = \frac{1}{m_f} \sum_j v_j \tag{22.1}$$

(i.e., the centroid of the vertices in M^i defining that face). (Again, for any subdivision level $i \geq 1$, we have $m_f = 4$.) See figure 22.9.

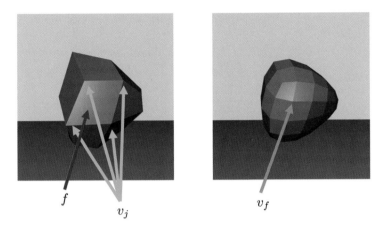

Figure 22.9
A face f on the left gives rise to v_f on the right. The geometry of v_f is determined by the v_j on the left.

Next, let e be an edge in M^i connecting the vertices v_1 and v_2 and separating the faces f_1 and f_2. We set the geometry of the new edge-vertex in M^{i+1} to be

$$v_e = \frac{1}{4}(v_1 + v_2 + v_{f_1} + v_{f_2}). \tag{22.2}$$

See figure 22.10.

Finally, let v be a vertex in M^i connected to the n_v vertices v_j and surrounded by the n_v faces f_j. Then, we set the geometry of the new vertex-vertex in M^{i+1} to be

$$v_v = \frac{n_v - 2}{n_v}v + \frac{1}{n_v^2}\sum_j v_j + \frac{1}{n_v^2}\sum_j v_{f_j}. \tag{22.3}$$

For an ordinary vertex, with valence $n_v = 4$, this becomes

$$v_v = \frac{1}{2}v + \frac{1}{16}\sum_j v_j + \frac{1}{16}\sum_j v_{f_j}. \tag{22.4}$$

See figure 22.11.

There has been much study into the development of these subdivision rules and understanding of their convergence properties. The first complete analysis of the first-order behavior at extraordinary points is found in Reif [60].

In practice, you don't need to know any of this; all you need to do to use subdivision surfaces is to implement equations (22.1), (22.2), and (22.3). The hardest part is simply getting a mesh data structure set up so that you can implement this computation.

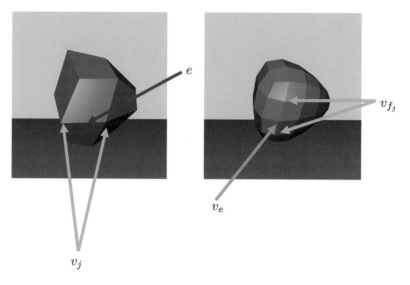

Figure 22.10
An edge e on the left gives rise to v_e on the right. The geometry of v_e is determined by the v_j on the left and v_{f_j} on the right.

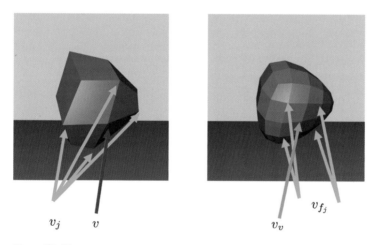

Figure 22.11
A vertex v on the left gives rise to v_v on the right. The geometry of v_v is determined by the vertices v_j on the left and v_{f_j} on the right.

Exercises

22.1 Download a mesh data structure and read in some mesh to display. If there are quad faces in the mesh, you should draw each quad as two triangles. To draw with "flat shading," compute a single normal for each face and use it for drawing.

Next, compute one "average normal" for each vertex. An average normal at a vertex will be the average of the normals of all the faces around the vertex. Draw the mesh with "smooth shading," using this average normal when drawing each vertex.

22.2 Beginning with code from the previous exercise and with a simple quad mesh describing a cube, implement subdivision. Use the Catmull–Clark rules to calculate the coordinates for the new vertices and update the mesh appropriately.

23 Animation: Not Even an Introduction

In computer graphics movies and video games, things move around. This is called animation. Once again, animation should be covered by its own full book, one that we are not qualified to write. In this chapter, we will give you a feel for some of the techniques used in computer animation (and show a lot of pictures). The interested reader may wish to check out the course notes in [4]. Computer animation is arguably the subarea of computer graphics with the most challenges remaining. Important improvements in this area are going on even today.

23.1 Interpolation

The simplest way to do animation is to have the artist do most of the hard work by hand. The computer can be used to simply interpolate, or fill in, various kinds of data as needed.

23.1.1 Keyframing

The idea behind keyframing is to have the animator sketch out the animation sequence at a low-resolution set of time samples. At each such time sample, the artist describes the complete state of the scene. The computer then uses smooth interpolation methods to generate the frames that are in between the artist-specified ones. We covered such techniques in chapter 9. In keyframing, the hard work is done by the artist; computation is just used to offload some of the more tedious and gruntish work. As unglamorous as it seems, much of computer animation is done in this fashion. It gives the animator full control over the look and feel of the final output.

23.1.2 Skinning

Skinning is a simple technique used to simulate the deformation of body parts in a triangle mesh (see figure 23.1). Skinning is easy to do in the vertex shader and is commonly used in video games.

Let us assume that an artist starts with an input triangle mesh describing the object in a natural "rest pose." In this input, each vertex is described using object coordinates (i.e.,

Figure 23.1
By blending the modelview matrices near joints, one can easily produce animations of objects with deformable joints. (From [74], copyright Industrial Light & Magic.)

$\tilde{p} = \vec{\mathbf{o}}^t \mathbf{c}$). Next, in a process called *rigging*, the artist designs a geometric skeleton and fits it to the mesh. This skeleton can be thought of as a set of *bones* that are connected at *joints*. Let us, at this point, also assume that each vertex is associated to one bone by the artist.

This skeletal shape naturally gives rise to a hierarchy of subobject coordinate frames and subobject matrices, just as we saw earlier in section 5.4 (see figure 5.4). Each of these subobject matrices represents the relationship between a frame and its "parent" frame in the rest pose. Recall, for example, in section 5.4, we had $\vec{\mathbf{d}}_r^t = \vec{\mathbf{o}}_r^t A_r B_r C_r D_r$, where $\vec{\mathbf{d}}_r^t$ was the (orthonormal) right lower arm frame, and the matrices A_r, B_r, C_r, and D_r were rigid body matrices. We have added the r subscript to mean "rest pose." Let us define the cumulative matrix for this bone, $N_r := A_r B_r C_r D_r$; this matrix expresses the frame relationship $\vec{\mathbf{d}}_r^t = \vec{\mathbf{o}}^t N_r$. Let us consider some vertex, with input object-coordinates $\mathbf{c}$, that has been associated with the lower arm bone. We can write this point as $\tilde{p} = \vec{\mathbf{o}}^t \mathbf{c} = \vec{\mathbf{d}}_r^t N_r^{-1} \mathbf{c}$.

As was done in section 5.4, during animation, we manipulate the skeleton by updating some of its matrices to new settings, say A_n, B_n, C_n, and D_n, where the subscript n means "new." Let us also define the "new" cumulative matrix for this bone, $N_n := A_n B_n C_n D_n$, which expresses the relation $\vec{\mathbf{d}}_n^t = \vec{\mathbf{o}}^t N_n$. This skeletal manipulation has moved, say, the lower arm frame: $\vec{\mathbf{d}}_r^t \Rightarrow \vec{\mathbf{d}}_n^t$. If we want to move the point $\tilde{p}$ in a rigid fashion along with this frame, then we need to update it using

$$\vec{\mathbf{d}}_r^t N_r^{-1} \mathbf{c} \Rightarrow \vec{\mathbf{d}}_n^t N_r^{-1} \mathbf{c}$$
$$= \vec{\mathbf{o}}^t N_n N_r^{-1} \mathbf{c}.$$

In this case, the eye coordinates of the transformed point are $E^{-1} O N_n N_r^{-1} \mathbf{c}$, and we see that our modelview matrix for this vertex should be $E^{-1} O N_n N_r^{-1}$.

This process gives us a "hard" skinning result, where each vertex moves along with only one bone. To get *smooth skinning* near a joint of the object, we allow the animator to associate a vertex to more than one bone. We then apply the above computation to each vertex, *for each of its bones*, and then blend the results together.

More specifically, we allow the animator to set, for each vertex, an array of weights w_i, summing to one, that specify how much the motion of each bone should affect this vertex. Then, during animation, we compute the eye coordinates for the vertex as

$$\sum_i w_i E^{-1} O(N_n)_i (N_r)_i^{-1} \mathbf{c}, \tag{23.1}$$

where the $(N)_i$ are the cumulative matrices for bone i.

Skinning is easy to implement in a vertex shader. Instead of passing a single model-view matrix to the shader, we pass an array of modelview matrices as a uniform variable. The weights for each vertex are passed as attribute variables using a vertex buffer object. The sum in equation (23.1) is then computed in the vertex shader code.

23.2 Simulation

Physics gives us equations that govern the movement and evolution of objects over time. Starting from an input set of initial conditions, such equations can be computationally simulated to predict how actual physical objects in the real world would move. If done well, this can produce very realistic and convincing effects. Physical simulation in its basic form is a predictive process: You feed in the initial conditions and out comes an animation. It is much less obvious how to control such an animation. The area of physical simulation has seen a lot of improvement over the past decade, which has been crucial to the success of computer graphics in special-effects generation.

23.2.1 Particles

The physics of motion begins with the ordinary differential equation (ODE) for the time evolution of a point

$$f = ma = m\dot{v} = m\ddot{x}, \tag{23.2}$$

forces is mass times acceleration, where acceleration is the time derivative of velocity, which in turn is the time derivative of position. The force can represent something like gravity or the wind.

Starting from an initial condition, we can discretize this ODE and march forward in time using so-called *Euler steps*

$$x_{t+h} = x_t + v_t h$$

$$v_{t+h} = v_t + a_t h$$

$$a_{t+h} = f(x_{t+h}, t+h)/m.$$

This process is called *time integration*. When using Euler steps, we need to take small-enough steps to ensure that the method does not end up doing crazy things. Alternatively,

Figure 23.2
Simulation of a bunch of simple particles can be used to animate flowing water. (From [37], copyright Eurographics and Blackwell Publishing Ltd.)

there is a whole literature of more sophisticated ways to solve an ODE. For more details, see the notes in [4].

In *particle system* animation, we model our scene as a set of noninteracting point-particles evolving under equation (23.2). This can be used, for example, to model a flowing fall of water particles or a stream of smoke particles in the air (see figure 23.2). Typically, each particle is rendered as a semitransparent little blob or surface.

23.2.2 Rigid Bodies
To model the time evolution of rigid bodies (such as dice rolling on a table), things get much more complicated right away. First of all, because our objects are not points, we need to deal with rotations and angular momentum. There are a number of other difficult issues that need to be addressed. For more details, see the notes in [4].

In rigid body simulations, we typically want to model bodies colliding with each other and bouncing in response. Computing collisions requires us to keep track of all pairs of bodies and determine when they intersect (see figure 23.3). To do this efficiently, we typically use a dynamically evolving, spatial bounding hierarchy. Another problem is that once we have found an intersection, this means that the bodies have already interpenetrated, which must be properly undone. Another subtlety is that real objects are not truly rigid; they actually bounce by very slightly deforming on contact. Because we do not wish to simulate this, we need to come up with new approximating equations of motions.

Other (surprisingly) difficult issues come from properly modeling friction as well as contact forces. When an object is at rest on the floor, we need properly to model the physics that keeps the object from falling through the floor or endlessly bouncing and twitching around.

23.2.3 Cloth
One kind of phenomenon that is important to model is cloth. In this case, the surface is either modeled as a grid of particles or as a mesh of triangular elements. In a particle-based approach, forces are added to this system to avoid stretching, shearing, as well as excessive

Figure 23.3
To simulate rigid objects, we must compute collisions and deal with momentum, friction, and contact forces. (From [27], copyright ACM.)

Figure 23.4
Cloth can be simulated using a variety of algorithms. There are many subtleties in getting the behavior "just right." (From [24], copyright ACM.)

bending. *Damping* is also added to model internal friction; this kills off oscillation. In a triangle-based approach, one writes down an expression E for the energy of the cloth state due to stretching, shearing, and bending. Force is then computed as $f = \frac{\partial E}{\partial \bar{x}}$. For more on cloth, see [24] and references therein. To model cloth, we also need to calculate collisions within the cloth, as well as between the cloth and its environment (see figure 23.4).

Hair modeling is also often similarly dealt with as a mass-spring model. For more on hair, see [67] and references therein (see figure 23.5).

Figure 23.5
Hair can be animated as a mass-spring system. (From [67], copyright ACM.)

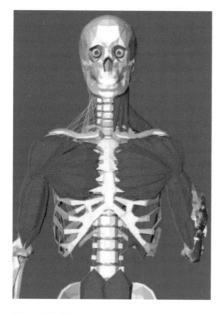

Figure 23.6
To model deformable models, we need to represent the volumes in question. (From [57], copyright Springer.)

23.2.4 Deformable Materials

Many objects in the real world are visibly deformable. This can be modeled with the appropriate physical equations and integrated over time as well. To model the physics of deformation, we need to model the internal volume of the object, often as a discrete tetrahedral mesh. Besides novelty items like Jello, this is important to produce realistic models of human bodies (see figure 23.6).

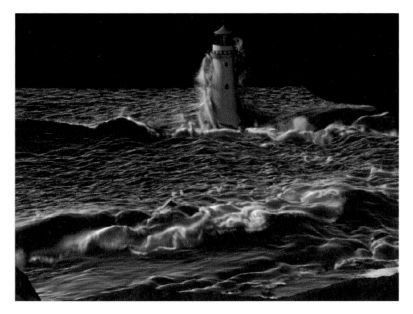

Figure 23.7
A stunning image of simulated water. (From [46], copyright IEEE.)

Figure 23.8
A man and a horse. (From [41], copyright Sian Lawson.)

23.2.5 Fire and Water

It can be important to model and animate physical phenomenon like fire and water (see figure 23.7). These are often modeled using both particle and 3D grid-based techniques. The evolution of the whirls and eddies in a volume of fluid is governed by something called the *Navier–Stokes* partial differential equation. Its numerical simulation requires its own numerical methods, such as the very popular method of "stable fluids" [70]. For more on fluid simulation, see the recent book by Bridson [9].

23.3 Human Locomotion

Humans are not simple passive objects, and their simulation by computer has proved to be much more difficult than that of passive objects like water and dirt. Moreover, in computer animation, we clearly want to carefully control what is done by the virtual creature and not simply simulate what results from some set of initial conditions.

There was a time when researchers were hopeful that concepts from robotics, control theory, and optimization would ultimately be able to produce realistic looking human animation completely *ab initio*. This goal has been elusive, and much of the current promising techniques rely heavily on the use of motion capture. In motion capture, a real human acts out various motions while being viewed by a calibrated camera/sensor setup. The captured subject often wears dots to help with the capture process (see figure 23.8). These data can then be transferred onto virtual actors, and the data can also be modified and controlled to some degree.

Exercise

23.1 Implement a basic particle-based animation system.

APPENDIXES

A Hello World 2D

In this appendix, we will describe the basic programming model used in OpenGL. In the rest of this book, we will use this programming model to do actual 3D computer graphics. For readability, some of the helper code used in this appendix is not transcribed here but can be found on the book's website. In the remainder of the book, we will be able to study the conceptual material needed to program 3D computer graphics and, with this simple programming model in mind, will be able to implement these ideas in OpenGL.

There is, unfortunately, lots of gobbledygook involved in setting up even the simplest OpenGL program; it is not pretty. Luckily, once you get this setup right, you can copy and paste these basic building blocks to your heart's content.

A.1 APIs

In this book, we will use OpenGL with the GLSL shading language to do our graphics programming. We have chosen OpenGL because it is cross-platform. On an MS Windows system, you could alternatively use DirectX with the HLSL shading language; translating the concepts of this book from OpenGL to DirectX should not be too difficult. We have chosen to use the most recent version of OpenGL so that your programs will be supported going forward into the future. As such, we do not use many of the older features of OpenGL that have been deprecated. We also stay quite minimal in our use of OpenGL and GLSL and do not use many of its advanced features. We do not document here all of the parameters for each API call shown. For that you should consult the main pages and OpenGL documentation. For more advanced OpenGL information, you may want to look at [79] and [62]. Additionally, for any of the API calls that we use here, you can easily get its specification by simply Googling the name of the call. We will also use something called the GLEW library to gain access to the latest features of OpenGL.

In this book, we will use the GLUT library to open windows and to allow our program to respond to mouse and keyboard events. Our main motivation for using GLUT is that it is cross-platform (MS Windows, Mac OS, Linux, and so forth). For hardcore development, you would probably not use GLUT and would need to learn a richer platform-dependent windowing interface. The way you use GLUT is to register *callback* functions. A callback function is code that you write and that is called whenever an associated windowing "event" has occurred. Such events may include things like mouse movement or keys being pressed on the keyboard. It is through these callback functions that you manage and update what is drawn on the screen. For details on the entire GLUT API, see [36].

To get started, you should be sure to download the latest drivers for your graphics/video card. You will also need to download and install the GLUT or freeGLUT library and the GLEW library.

Our C++ file starts by including the necessary libraries.

```
#include <GL/glew.h>
#ifdef __APPLE__
# include <GLUT/freeglut.h>
#else
# include <GL/freeglut.h> // or glut.h
#endif
```

A.2 Main Program

Our main program consists of the following:

```
int main()
{
  initGlutState();
  glewInit();
  initGLState();
  initShaders()
  initVBOs();
  glutMainLoop();
  return 0;
}
```

In the first five lines, we set up the various aspects of our program. In the last line, we hand over control to GLUT. We will only regain control of the program when a windowing event occurs, causing GLUT to call one of our registered callback functions (described next).

During the initialization, we allocate various OpenGL resources such as shaders, vertex buffers, and textures. In a full-blown program, we should also take care to free these resources properly at suitable points. For our simple program, however, we neglect this step, as the resources will be freed by the operating system after our program exits.

A.2.1 initGlutState

The first thing we need to do is set up the window and callback functions.

```
static int g_width= 512;
static int g_height= 512;

void initGlutState()
{
  glutInit();
  glutInitDisplayMode(GLUT_RGBA|GLUT_DOUBLE|GLUT_DEPTH);
  glutInitWindowSize(g_width, g_height);
  glutCreateWindow("Hello World");
  glutDisplayFunc(display);
  glutReshapeFunc(reshape);
}

void reshape(int w, int h)
{
  g_width = w;
  g_height = h;
  glViewport(0, 0, w, h);
  glutPostRedisplay();
}
```

In the line `glutInitDisplayMode`, we request that our window be made up of pixels with colors each described with red, green, blue and alpha values. The use of red, green, and blue for color is described in chapter 19. Alpha is used to represent opacity and is discussed in section 16.4. We also request that the window can do *double buffering*. This means that all of the drawing is done into a hidden "back" buffer. Only after the entire frame drawing is done do we request that this hidden buffer be *swapped* into the "front" buffer and thus appear on the screen. If double buffering is not done, the screen will be updated immediately, as each part of the scene is drawn, and this can result in distracting "flickering" effects. We also request that our window can handle depth, or z-buffering. When multiple objects attempt to update some pixel in common, OpenGL uses z-buffering to determine which object is front-most. The topic of z-buffering is discussed in chapter 11.

We also register the functions called `display` and `reshape`. A reshape event occurs whenever the window size is changed. In the reshape function, we record the width and height of the new window in our global variables `g_width` and `g_height`. We pass this information on to OpenGL with the call to `glViewport`. The viewport processing is discussed more in section 12.3. We call `glutPostRedisplay` to have GLUT (when it is good and ready) trigger a redisplay event, which will then call our display function. We describe the `display` function below.

Contrary to what you may have been taught in school, in a GLUT-based program we need to keep around global variables to record information that we will need to use when our callback functions are called.

A.2.2 glewInit

The call to glewInit is a magic call to the GLEW library that gives us access to the latest API interface in OpenGL.

A.2.3 initGL

In this procedure, we set up the desired state variables in OpenGL.

```
void InitGLState()
{
  glClearColor(128./255,200./255,1,0);
  glEnable(GL_FRAMEBUFFER_SRGB);
}
```

In this case, all we are doing is setting up the background color for the window and enabling the use of the sRGB color space when drawing. The sRGB color space is described in chapter 19.

A.2.4 initShaders

In initShaders, we upload the text of the shaders from a file to OpenGL and compile them in OpenGL. We then ask OpenGL for *handles* to the input variables for these shaders. A handle is an index that OpenGL uses (like a pointer) to keep track of various items. It is not a C++ pointer and cannot be de-referenced by your code.

```
//global handles
static GLuint  h_program;
static GLuint  h_aTexCoord;
static GLuint  h_aColor;

initShaders()
{
  readAndCompileShader("./shaders/simple.vshader",
  "./shaders/simple.fshader",  &h_program);

  h_aVertex = safe_glGetAttribLocation(h_program, "aVertex");
  h_aColor = safe_glGetAttribLocation(h_program, "aColor");
  glBindFragDataLocation(h_program, 0, "fragColor");
}
```

A GLSL program is made up of one vertex shader and one fragment shader. In most applications, you may have many different GLSL programs compiled and used for different objects that are being drawn. In our case, we have but one. Our code readAndCompileShader (see the book's website) reads the two named files, gives the code to OpenGL, and saves a handle to the GLSL program.

Next, we get handles to the attribute variables in our vertex shaders called aVertex and aColor. Attribute variables are the inputs sent per vertex to our vertex shader. We also tell OpenGL that the variable named fragColor should be used as the output of our fragment shader as the actual drawn color.

We have wrapped safe_ versions of many of the shader calls in OpenGL (see the book's website). These safe calls check that the handle is valid before following it. This can be useful during debugging when we are disabling certain parts of our shaders. In this case, the shader's compiler may optimize away an unneeded variable, and then if we try to set this variable in our C code, it will cause an error. By using the "safe" wrapper, we avoid such errors.

Note that OpenGL has its own basic numerical data types (such as GLuint for unsigned integer), which may translate to different representations on different platforms.

A.2.5 initVBOs

In this procedure, we are loading the information about our geometry into OpenGL vertex buffer objects. These will be drawn later as needed.

Our scene consists of one square in 2D with its lower left corner at $(-0.5, -0.5)$ and upper right corner at $(0.5, 0.5)$. The square is described by two triangles, each triangle with three vertices. This gives us the sequence of six vertex coordinates in sqVerts. We color each of these vertices with the associated red, green, and blue (RGB) values shown in sqCol.

```
GLfloat sqVerts[6*2]=
{
  -.5, -.5,
   .5,  .5,
   .5, -.5,

  -.5, -.5,
  -.5,  .5,
   .5,  .5
};

GLfloat sqCol[6*3] =
{
  1, 0, 0,
  0, 1, 1,
  0, 0, 1,

  1, 0, 0,
  0, 1, 0,
  0, 1, 1
};
```

```
static GLuint sqVertBO,  sqColBO;

static void initVBOs(void){
  glGenBuffers(1,&sqVertBO);
  glBindBuffer(GL_ARRAY_BUFFER,sqVertBO);
  glBufferData(
      GL_ARRAY_BUFFER,
      12*sizeof(GLfloat),
      sqVerts,
      GL_STATIC_DRAW);

  glGenBuffers(1,&sqColBO);
  glBindBuffer(GL_ARRAY_BUFFER,sqColBO);
  glBufferData(
      GL_ARRAY_BUFFER,
      18*sizeof(GLfloat),
      sqCol,
      GL_STATIC_DRAW);
}
```

The call to glGenBuffers asks OpenGL to create one new "name" for a vertex buffer. The call to glBindBuffer makes the named buffer into the "current" OpenGL buffer. (Later we will see a similar gen/bind sequence of API calls for textures.) Finally, the call to glBufferData allows us to pass data into the current OpenGL buffer. We need to pass the size of the data and its pointer. We also specify using GL_STATIC_DRAW that we will not be modifying the data and that we will be using this data for drawing.

A.2.6 Display
Our display function is called by GLUT whenever it decides that we need to redraw the window.

```
void display(void){
  glUseProgram(h_program);
  glClear(GL_COLOR_BUFFER_BIT | GL_DEPTH_BUFFER_BIT);
  drawObj(sqVertBO, sqColBO,6);
  glutSwapBuffers();

  // check for errors
  if (glGetError() != GL_NO_ERROR){
    const GLubyte *errString;
    errString=gluErrorString(errCode);
    printf("error: %s\n", errString);
  }
}
```

In our code, we first tell OpenGL which shaders to use. Then we clear the screen, draw our object, and then tell GLUT that we are done and it is free to swap our drawing into the displayed window. Finally, we check for OpenGL errors.

To draw the square, we do the following:

```
void drawObj(GLuint vertbo, GLuint colbo, int numverts){
  glBindBuffer(GL_ARRAY_BUFFER,vertbo);
  safe_glVertexAttribPointer2(h_aVertex);
  safe_glEnableVertexAttribArray(h_aVertex);

  glBindBuffer(GL_ARRAY_BUFFER,colbo);
  safe_glVertexAttribPointer3(h_aColor);
  safe_glEnableVertexAttribArray(h_aColor);

  glDrawArrays(GL_TRIANGLES,0,numverts);

  safe_glDisableVertexAttribArray(h_aVertex);
  safe_glDisableVertexAttribArray(h_aColor);
}
```

The pair of calls to `glVertexAttrbPointer` and `glEnableVertexAttribArray` tells OpenGL to use the data in the current vertex buffer for the shader attribute variable pointed to by our handle.

Finally, the call to `glDrawArrays` tells OpenGL to draw the triangles defined by this data.

A.2.7 Vertex Shader

Our vertex shader is written in GLSL, a special shader language (consult [62] for a precise specification of this language). GLSL is a C-like language but has built-in vector types as well as a host of special functions. Data are passed in and out of the shader through the variables labeled `in` and `out`.

Our very simple vertex shader is the following:

```
#version 330
in vec2 aVertex;
in vec3 aColor;

out vec3 vColor;

void main()
{
  gl_Position = vec4(aVertex.x,aVertex.y, 0,1);
  vColor = aColor;
}
```

The `version` directive tells the GLSL compiler which version of the language we are using. This shader does nothing more than pass the input attribute color out the other end as a varying variable to be interpolated over the pixels inside the triangle. We use the attribute aVertex to directly set gl_Position. This is a reserved output variable, which is used to determine where in the window the triangle will be drawn. gl_Position is actually a vec4, and we set its third and fourth coordinates as shown here. The full use of all four coordinates will be made clear in chapters 11–13.

A.2.8 Fragment Shader

Finally, our very simple fragment shader is the following:

```
#version 330

in vec3 vColor;
out vec4 fragColor;

void main(void)
{
  fragColor = vec4(vColor.x, vColor.y, vColor.z, 1);
}
```

All we are doing here is passing the interpolated input color data on to an output variable fragColor. The first three coordinates are for red, green, and blue, and the fourth is for opacity, with 1 meaning fully opaque. We have already instructed OpenGL to use this output variable as the displayed color for the pixel.

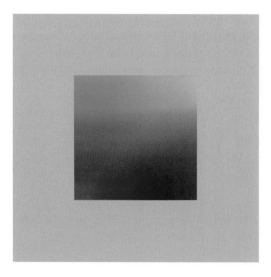

Figure A.1
A colored square is drawn in our first OpenGL program.

Ta-da: we are done. After all this work, if we were successful, we get the colorful image
of figure A.1 .

A.3 Adding Some Interaction

Next, we augment our program by adding a bit of user interaction. We use the mouse movement to set a horizontal scaling variable. This scaling is applied in the vertex shader to
change the geometry of the drawn square. For this purpose, we create a uniform variable
uVertexScale. A uniform variable can be read in both vertex and fragment shaders but can
only be updated in between OpenGL draw calls.

In this case, our vertex shader becomes:

```
#version 330

uniform  float uVertexScale;


in vec2 aVertex;
in vec3 aColor;

out vec3 vColor;

void main()
{
  gl_Position = vec4(aVertex.x*uVertexScale,aVertex.y, 0,1);
  vColor=aColor;
}
```

In initShaders, we add the line

```
h_uVertexScale = safe_glGetUniformLocation(h_program,
                                "uVertexScale");
```

to obtain a handle to our new uniform variable.

In void initGlutState, we register two more functions:

```
glutMotionFunc(motion);
glutMouseFunc(mouse);
```

The registered mouse function is called whenever a button on the mouse is clicked
down or up. The motion function is called whenever the mouse is moved within the
window.

```
void mouse(int button, int state, int x, int y){
  if (button == GLUT_LEFT_BUTTON)
  {
```

```
    if (state == GLUT_DOWN)
    {
      // left mouse button has been clicked
      g_left_clicked = true;
      g_lclick_x = x;
      g_lclick_y = g_height - y - 1;
    }
    else
    {
      // left mouse button has been released
      g_left_clicked = false;
    }
  }
}


void motion(int x, int y)
{
  const int newx = x;
  const int newy = g_height - y - 1;
  if (g_left_clicked)
  {
    float deltax = (newx - g_rclick_x) * 0.02;
    g_obj_scale += deltax;

    g_rclick_x = newx;
    g_rclick_y = newy;
  }
  glutPostRedisplay();
}
```

Here, we keep track of the mouse's position whenever the user moves it while holding down the left mouse button. [Although we are not using the y coordinate, we also show here how it is properly handled. In particular, it needs to be flipped using (g_height - 1) - y because GLUT considers the uppermost pixel row to be 0, whereas OpenGL considers the *y* direction to be pointing up.] The change in desired horizontal scale is saved in a global variable g_obj_scale.

In our display function, we add the line

```
safe_glUniform1f(h_vertex_scale, g_obj_scale);
```

to send these data to our shaders.

A.4 Adding a Texture

Finally, we show how a texture image can be accessed in the fragment shader to be used in color computation.

To set up the texture, we add the following lines to `initGLState`.

```
...
glActiveTexture(GL_TEXTURE0);
glGenTextures(1, &h_texture);
glBindTexture(GL_TEXTURE_2D, h_texture);
glTexParameteri(GL_TEXTURE_2D, GL_TEXTURE_WRAP_S, GL_CLAMP);
glTexParameteri(GL_TEXTURE_2D, GL_TEXTURE_WRAP_T, GL_CLAMP);
glTexParameteri(GL_TEXTURE_2D, GL_TEXTURE_MIN_FILTER, GL_LINEAR);
glTexParameteri(GL_TEXTURE_2D, GL_TEXTURE_MAG_FILTER, GL_LINEAR);
int twidth, theight;
packed_pixel_t *pixdata = ppmread("reachup.ppm",
    &twidth, &theight);
assert(pixdata);
glTexImage2D(GL_TEXTURE_2D, 0, GL_SRGB,
    twidth, theight, 0,
    GL_RGB, GL_UNSIGNED_BYTE, pixdata);
free(pixdata);
...
```

First, we set `GL_TEXTURE0` as the active hardware texture unit. (There are multiple units, letting our fragment shader have access to multiple texture images simultaneously.) We generate a name texture and bind it as the "current 2D texture." Then, we set a number of the parameters on the current 2D texture. The `WRAP` parameters tell OpenGL what to do if we attempt to look for data off of the end of the texture. The `FILTER` parameters tell OpenGL how to blend colors when we attempt to look for data "in between" pixels of the texture (see chapter 17 for more). Then, we read an image from the file `reachup.ppm` (in ppm format) and load that data into the texture.

In `initShaders`, we add the line

```
h_texUnit0 = safe_glGetUniformLocation(h_program, "texUnit0");
h_aTexCoord = safe_glGetAttribLocation(h_program, "aTexCoord");
```

In our `display` function, we add the line

```
safe_glUniform1i(h_texUnit0, 0);
```

after the call to `glUseProgram`. The second argument is `0` to refer to the texture unit named `GL_TEXTURE0`. This allows the fragment shader access to this texture unit. If we want to use more than one texture in our shader, then we would use multiple texture units.

Next, we need a vertex buffer object that stores texture coordinates associated with each vertex. These are x, y coordinates that point into the stored texture. We wish to map the lower left vertex of our square to the lower left corner of the texture. This texture location is addressed as (0, 0). We wish to map the upper right vertex of our square to the upper right corner of the texture. This texture location is addressed as (1, 1). Thus, we encode these data with the following attribute list:

```
GLfloat sqTex[12] =
  {
     0, 0,
     1, 1,
     1, 0,

     0, 0,
     0, 1,
     1, 1
  };
```

These data need to be loaded in initVBOs and passed to the vertex shader variable aTexCoord as part of drawObj.

The vertex shader does nothing surprising:

```
#version 330

uniform  float uVertexScale;

in vec2 aVertex;
in vec2 aTexCoord;
in vec3 aColor;

out vec3 vColor;
out vec2 vTexCoord;

void main()
{
  gl_Position = vec4(aVertex.x*uVertexScale,aVertex.y, 0,1);
  vColor=aColor;
  vTexCoord=aTexCoord;
}
```

As varying variables, the texture coordinates are interpolated from their vertex values to appropriate values at each pixel. Thus, in the fragment shader, we can use the texture coordinates to fetch the desired colors from the texture. This is accomplished in the following fragment shader:

```
#version 330

uniform float uVertexScale;
uniform sampler2D texUnit0;
```

Figure A.2
We have now added a texture. Using mouse interaction, we change the size of the drawn rectangle and alter the blending factor.

```
in vec2 vTexCoord;
in vec3 vColor;

out vec4 fragColor;

void main(void)
{
  vec4 color0 = vec4(vColor.x, vColor.y, vColor.z, 1);
  vec4 color1 = texture2D(texUnit0, vTexCoord);

  float lerper = clamp(.3 *uVertexScale,0.,1.);
  fragColor = (lerper)*color1 + (1.-lerper)*color0;
}
```

The data type `sampler2D` is a special data type that refers to an OpenGL texture unit. In this code, `color1` is fetched, using the special GLSL function `texture2D`, from the texture unit pointed to by `texUnit0`, using the texture coordinates passed in as `vTexCoord`. Next, we use `uVertexScale` to determine the mixing factor between the two computed colors. Finally, these are mixed together and output to the window. As a result, as we move the mouse, the drawn rectangle is stretched and the texture image is blended in more strongly (see figure A.2)

A.5 What's Next

These are the basic ingredients in the OpenGL programming model. Ultimately, we will want to use this model to draw pictures of 3D shapes in space. This will require us to learn the appropriate geometric concepts covered over the first few chapters of the book. By chapter 6, we will be ready to write a simple 3D OpenGL program.

Exercises

A.1 In this appendix, we have explained the basics of an OpenGL 2D "Hello World" program. The complete program is at the book's website. Download the program and set up your computing environment so that you can compile and run this program.

• **Hardware support.**   You will need hardware that supports OpenGL 4.0.

• **Driver support.**   Even if you have a new or up-to-date graphics card installed in your machine, your programs may not be able to utilize the advanced features unless you have installed new drivers. OpenGL is a continually evolving standard, and the various graphics chip vendors make regular releases of drivers exposing more and more advanced features (as well as fixing bugs in previous versions).

• **Installing GLUT and GLEW.**   GLUT and GLEW are cross-platform libraries that make interfacing with OpenGL and OS-specific tasks easier. GLUT handles windowing and message control. GLEW loads the various advanced extensions that have come out since OpenGL's conception. You will need to download and install the headers (.h), and binaries (.lib, .dll/so/a) for them.

A.2 In our "Hello World" program, when the window is made wider, the rendered geometry appears wider as well. Modify the program so that when the window is reshaped, the aspect ratio of the object drawn does not change (i.e., if a square is rendered, resizing the window should not make it look like a rectangle with different edge lengths), and it doesn't crop the image. Making the window uniformly larger should also make the object uniformly larger. Likewise for uniform shrinking. There are some important constraints:

• Your solution should not change the vertices' coordinates that are sent by your program to the vertex shader.

• Your solution should not modify the call to `glViewport` (which is in the `reshape` function in `HelloWorld2D.cpp`).

• **Hint:** You can modify the vertex shader, as well as change uniform variables that are used in the vertex shader.

A.3 Browse through the documentation for OpenGL Shading Language (GLSL) and get familiar with some of the built-in operations available. Edit your vertex and/or fragment programs to achieve novel effects. Examples might be using the built-in sine and cosine functions to create undulating patterns or perhaps reading in multiple texture files and combining them in some interesting way. Have fun!!!

B   Affine Functions

In chapters 12 and 13, we discuss linear interpolation of varying variables. To understand that material, we first need to learn some simple concepts about affine functions.

B.1   2D Affine

We say a function v is an *affine function* in the variables x and y if it is of the form

$$v(x, y) = ax + by + c \tag{B.1}$$

for some constants a, b, and c. This can also be written as

$$v = \begin{bmatrix} a & b & c \end{bmatrix} \begin{bmatrix} x \\ y \\ 1 \end{bmatrix}.$$

Such a function is often called "linear," but we use the term affine because there is an additive constant term ($+c$) included. The same term, affine, is used for the affine transformations of chapter 3, as those transformations allow for an additive constant term, which, in that context, represents a translation.

Obviously, one way to evaluate such a v at some (x, y) is simply to plug (x, y) into equation (B.1). It is also easy to march in evenly spaced steps along some line in the plane (say along an edge of the triangle or along a horizontal line) and quickly evaluate v at each step. In particular, because the function is affine, each time we move along a fixed unit vector, the function v changes by some fixed amount.

We have already seen examples of 2D affine functions. Recall from chapter 11 that a 3D projective transform maps planar objects in 3D to planar objects in 3D. As such, given a triangle in 3D and a selected eye frame and projection matrix, the value z_n at a point on a 3D triangle is an affine function of the (x_n, y_n) values at that point.

If we are given v_i, the values of v for three (noncollinear) points in the (x, y) plane, say the vertices of a triangle, this determines v over the entire plane. In this case, we say that

v is the *linear interpolant* of the values at the three vertices. The process of evaluating the linear interpolant of three vertices is called *linear interpolation*.

Computing the v_i at the three vertices $[x_i, y_i]^t$, we have

$$
\begin{bmatrix} v_1 & v_2 & v_3 \end{bmatrix} = \begin{bmatrix} a & b & c \end{bmatrix} \begin{bmatrix} x_1 & x_2 & x_3 \\ y_1 & y_2 & y_3 \\ 1 & 1 & 1 \end{bmatrix}
$$

$$
=: \begin{bmatrix} a & b & c \end{bmatrix} M.
$$

By inverting this expression, we see how to determine the (a, b, c) values given the v_i and $[x_i, y_i]^t$:

$$
\begin{bmatrix} a & b & c \end{bmatrix} = \begin{bmatrix} v_1 & v_2 & v_3 \end{bmatrix} M^{-1}. \tag{B.2}
$$

B.2   3D Affine

We say a function v is affine in variables x, y, and z if it is of the form

$$
v(x, y, z) = ax + by + cz + d \tag{B.3}
$$

for some constants a, b, c, and d. Such a function can be uniquely determined by its values at the four vertices of a tetrahedron sitting in 3D.

B.3   Going Up

Given a triangle in 3D, suppose we specify the value of a function at its three vertices. There may be many functions that are affine in (x, y, z) that agree with these three values. But all of these functions will agree when restricted to the plane of the triangle. As such, we can refer to this restricted function over the triangle as the linear interpolant of the vertex values. We can still write it in the form of equation (B.3), though the constants will no longer be unique.

Getting back to 3D computer graphics and varying variables, in our vertex shader of section 6.3, when we associate a color with each vertex of a triangle, the most natural interpretation is that we wish for the color of the interior points of the triangle to be determined by the unique interpolating function over the triangle that is affine in the object coordinates, (x_o, y_o, z_o).

In computer graphics, we can glue a texture onto a triangle using texture mapping. In this process, we associate two values, called texture coordinates, x_t y_t, to every point in the triangle. If we specify this gluing by associating texture coordinates with each vertex of a triangle, the most natural interpretation is that we wish for the texture coordinates of the interior points to be determined using their corresponding unique interpolating functions over the triangle that are affine in (x_o, y_o, z_o).

As a rather self-referential example, we can even think of each of the three object coordinates of a point on some triangle in 3D as affine functions in (x_o, y_o, z_o). For example, $x_o(x_o, y_o, z_o) = x_o$ (i.e., $a = 1$ and $b = c = d = 0$). This means that in our vertex shader, the three coordinates in vPosition should be interpreted as three functions that are affine in (x_o, y_o, z_o).

For this reason, the default semantics of OpenGL is to interpolate all varying variables as functions over triangles that are affine in (x_o, y_o, z_o). As we will see in section B.5, this is equivalent to a function being affine over eye coordinates, (x_e, y_e, z_e), but it is not equivalent to a function being affine over normalized device coordinates, (x_n, y_n, z_n).

B.4 Going Down

If we have a function v that is affine in (x, y, z) when restricted to a triangle in 3D, then we can use the fact that the triangle is flat to write v as a function that is affine in only two variables. For example, suppose the triangle has non-zero area when projected down to the (x, y) plane. Then, at each point of the triangle in 3D, the value of z is itself an affine function of (x, y), say $z = ex + fy + g$. One can take this expression for z and plug it into the affine expression for v. This gives us a function of the form

$$v = ax + by + c\,(ex + fy + g) + d$$
$$ = hx + iy + j$$

for some constants (h, i, j). After this is done, the dependence on z goes away and what remains is some affine function over (x, y). Knowing this, we can directly compute the appropriate (h, i, j) coefficients using equation (B.2).

B.5 Going Sideways

Suppose we have some matrix expression of the form

$$\begin{bmatrix} x' \\ y' \\ z' \\ w' \end{bmatrix} = M \begin{bmatrix} x \\ y \\ z \\ 1 \end{bmatrix} \tag{B.4}$$

for some 4 by 4 matrix M (where M does not even have to be an affine matrix). Then, just looking at the four rows independently, we see that x', y', z', and w' are all affine functions of (x, y, z).

If we have a function v that is affine in (x, y, z), then, given the relation of equation (B.4), we can see that v is also affine (in fact linear) in (x', y', z', w'). To see this, note that:

$$v = \begin{bmatrix} a & b & c & d \end{bmatrix} \begin{bmatrix} x \\ y \\ z \\ 1 \end{bmatrix} \tag{B.5}$$

$$= \begin{bmatrix} a & b & c & d \end{bmatrix} M^{-1} \begin{bmatrix} x' \\ y' \\ z' \\ w' \end{bmatrix} \tag{B.6}$$

$$= \begin{bmatrix} e & f & g & h \end{bmatrix} \begin{bmatrix} x' \\ y' \\ z' \\ w' \end{bmatrix} \tag{B.7}$$

for some values of e, f, g, and h.

The only time we have to be careful is when division is done. For example, given the relation

$$\begin{bmatrix} x'w' \\ y'w' \\ z'w' \\ w' \end{bmatrix} = M \begin{bmatrix} x \\ y \\ z \\ 1 \end{bmatrix},$$

it will generally not be the case that a function v that was affine in (x, y, z) will be affine in (x', y', z') or (x', y', z', w'). In chapter 13, we will see how this non-affine function can be evaluated efficiently.

Exercises

B.1 Assume that a triangle is not seen "edge on." Are the four clip coordinates of the points on the triangle affine functions of (x_o, y_o)? What about its normalized device coordinates?

B.2 Let v be an affine function in (x, y). If we are given the values v_1, v_2, and v_3 of v for three (noncollinear) points in the (x, y) plane, this determines v over the entire plane.

What happens to the determined interpolating function if we replace these three values by kv_1, kv_2, and kv_3 for some constant k?

References

[1] Adelson, E. Web page on checkershadow illusion. Available at: http://persci.mit.edu/gallery/checkershadow.

[2] Akenine-Moller, T., and Haines, E. *Real-Time Rendering*. AK Peters Ltd., 2002.

[3] Arvo, J. *Analytic Methods for Simulated Light Transport*. Ph.D. thesis, Yale University, 1995.

[4] Baraff, D. Physically based modeling: Rigid body simulation. *SIGGRAPH Course Notes*. ACM SIGGRAPH, 2001.

[5] Blinn, J. *Jim Blinn's Corner: A Trip Down the Graphics Pipeline*. Morgan Kaufmann, 1996.

[6] Blinn, J. *Jim Blinn's Corner: Dirty Pixels*. Morgan Kaufmann, 1998.

[7] Botsch, M., Kobbelt, L., Pauly, M., Alliez, P., and Lévy, B. *Polygon Mesh Processing*. AK Peters Ltd., 2010.

[8] Botsch, M., Steinberg, S., Bischoff, S., and Kobbelt, L. Openmesh: A generic and efficient polygon mesh data structure. In *OpenSG Symposium 2002*, 2002.

[9] Bridson, R. *Fluid Simulation for Computer Graphics*. AK Peters Ltd., 2008.

[10] Buss, S., and Fillmore, J. Spherical averages and applications to spherical splines and interpolation. *ACM Transactions on Graphics (TOG) 20*, 2 (2001), 95–126.

[11] Cohen-Or, D., Chrysanthou, Y., Silva, C., and Durand, F. A survey of visibility for walkthrough applications. *IEEE Transactions on Visualization and Computer Graphics 9*, 3 (2003), 412–431.

[12] Cook, R. Stochastic sampling in computer graphics. *ACM Transactions on Graphics (TOG) 5*, 1 (1986), 51–72.

[13] Cook, R., Porter, T., and Carpenter, L. Distributed ray tracing. *ACM SIGGRAPH Computer Graphics 18*, 3 (August 1984), 137–145.

[14] Cook, R. L., and Torrance, K. E. A reflectance model for computer graphics. *ACM SIGGRAPH Computer Graphics 15*, 3 (August 1981), 307–316.

[15] Debevec, P. E., Taylor, C. J., and Malik, J. Modeling and rendering architecture from photographs: A hybrid geometry- and image-based approach. In *Proceedings of the 23rd Annual Conference on Computer Graphics and Interactive Techniques*, ACM, 1996, pp. 11–20.

[16] DeRose, T. *Three-Dimensional Computer Graphics: A Coordinate-Free Approach*. Unpublished manuscript, 1992.

[17] Dorsey, J., Rushmeier, H., and Sillion, F. *Digital Modeling of Material Appearance*. Morgan Kaufmann, 2008.

[18] Fattal, R., Carroll, R., and Agrawala, M. Edge-based image coarsening. *ACM Transactions on Graphics (TOG) 29*, 1 (2009), 1–11.

[19] Fernando, R., and Kilgard, M. *The CG Tutorial: The Definitive Guide to Programmable Real-Time Graphics*. Addison-Wesley Longman, 2003.

[20] Feynman, R. *The Feynman Lectures on Physics: Volume 1*, vol. 3 of *The Feynman Lectures on Physics*. Addison-Wesley, 1963.

[21] Gallier, J. *Geometric Methods and Applications: For Computer Science and Engineering.* Springer-Verlag, 2001.

[22] Ge, Q. J., and Ravani, B. Computer aided geometric design of motion interpolants. *Journal of Mechanical Design 116*, 3 (1994), 756–762.

[23] Glassner, A. *An Introduction to Ray Tracing.* Academic Press, 1991.

[24] Goldenthal, R., Harmon, D., Fattal, R., Bercovier, M., and Grinspun, E. Efficient simulation of inextensible cloth. *ACM Transactions on Graphics (TOG) 26*, 3 (2007).

[25] Greene, N. Environment mapping and other applications of world projections. *IEEE Computer Graphics and Applications 6* (1986), 21–29.

[26] Grenspun, P. How to photograph architecture. Availbale at: http://photo.net/learn/architectural/exterior.

[27] Guendelman, E., Bridson, R., and Fedkiw, R. Nonconvex rigid bodies with stacking. *ACM Transactions on Graphics (TOG) 22*, 3 (2003), 871–878.

[28] Heckbert, P. S. Fundamentals of Texture Mapping and Image Warping. Tech. Rep. UCB/CSD-89-516, EECS Department, University of California, Berkeley, June 1989.

[29] Jensen, H. Global illumination using photon maps. In *Proceedings of the eurographics Workshop on Rendering Techniques*, Springer-Verlag, 1996, pp. 21–30.

[30] Jensen, H. *Realistic Image Synthesis Using Photon Mapping.* AK Peters, Ltd., 2009.

[31] Jensen, H., Marschner, S., Levoy, M., and Hanrahan, P. A practical model for subsurface light transport. In *Proceedings of the 28th Annual Conference on Computer Graphics and Interactive Techniques*, ACM, 2001, pp. 511–518.

[32] Ju, T., Losasso, F., Schaefer, S., and Warren, J. Dual contouring of hermite data. *ACM Transactions on Graphics (TOG) 21*, 3 (2002), 339–346.

[33] Kajiya, J. T., and Kay, T. L. Rendering fur with three dimensional textures. *ACM SIGGRAPH Computer Graphics 23*, 3 (July 1989), 271–280.

[34] Kanamori, Y., Szego, Z., and Nishita, T. Gpu-based fast ray casting for a large number of metaballs. *Computer Graphics Forum 27*, 2 (2008), 351–360.

[35] Kavan, L., Collins, S., Žára, J., and O'Sullivan, C. Geometric skinning with approximate dual quaternion blending. *ACM Transactions on Graphics (TOG) 27*, 4 (2008), 1–23.

[36] Kilgard, M. The opengl utility toolkit. Available at: http://www.opengl.org/resources/libraries/glut/spec3/spec3.html.

[37] Kipfer, P., Segal, M., and Westermann, R. Uberflow: A GPU-based particle engine. In *Proceedings of the ACM SIGGRAPH/EUROGRAPHICS Conference on Graphics Hardware*, ACM, 2004, pp. 115–122.

[38] Kolb, C., Mitchell, D., and Hanrahan, P. A realistic camera model for computer graphics. In *Proceedings of the 22nd Annual Conference on Computer Graphics and Interactive Techniques*, ACM, 1995, pp. 317–324.

[39] Landis, H. Production-ready global illumination. *SIGGRAPH Course Notes*, ACM SIGGRAPH, 2002.

[40] Lang, S. *Linear Algebra.* Springer-Verlag, 1989.

[41] Lawson. Web page on equine mocap. Available at: http://research.ncl.ac.uk/crest/projects_equinebiomechanics. html.

[42] Lengyel, J., Praun, E., Finkelstein, A., and Hoppe, H. Real-time fur over arbitrary surfaces. In *Proceedings of the 2001 Symposium on Interactive 3D Graphics*, ACM, 2001, pp. 227–232.

[43] Levin, A., Lischinski, D., and Weiss, Y. A closed-form solution to natural image matting. *IEEE Transactions on Pattern Analysis and Machine Intelligence 30*, 2 (2007), 228–242.

[44] Levoy, M., Pulli, K., Curless, B., Rusinkiewicz, S., Koller, D., Pereira, L., Ginzton, M., Anderson, S., Davis, J., Ginsberg, J., Shade, J., and Fulk, D. The digital Michelangelo project: 3d scanning of large statues. In *Proceedings of the 27th Annual Conference on Computer Graphics and Interactive Techniques*, ACM, 2000, pp. 131–144.

[45] Lorensen, W., and Cline, H. Marching cubes: A high resolution 3D surface construction algorithm. In *Proceedings of the 14th Annual Conference on Computer Graphics and Interactive Techniques*, ACM, 1987, pp. 163–169.

[46] Losasso, F., Talton, J., Kwatra, N., and Fedkiw, R. Two-way coupled SPH and particle level set fluid simulation. *IEEE Transactions on Visualization and Computer Graphics 14*, 4 (2008), 797–804.

[47] Matusik, W., Pfister, H., Brand, M., and McMillan, L. A data-driven reflectance model. *ACM Transactions on Graphics (TOG) 22*, 3 (2003), 759–769.

[48] McNamara, R., McCormack, J., and Jouppi, N. Prefiltered antialiased lines using half-plane distance functions. In *Proceedings of the ACM SIGGRAPH/EUROGRAPHICS Workshop on Graphics Hardware*, ACM, 2000, pp. 77–85.

[49] Mitchell, D. Consequences of stratified sampling in graphics. In *Proceedings of the 23rd Annual Conference on Computer Graphics and Interactive Techniques*, ACM, 1996, pp. 277–280.

[50] Mitchell, D., and Netravali, A. Reconstruction filters in computer-graphics. *ACM SIGGRAPH Computer Graphics 22*, 4 (1988), 221–228.

[51] Ngan, A., Durand, F., and Matusik, W. Experimental analysis of BRDF models. In *Proceedings of the Eurographics Symposium on Rendering*, Eurographics Association, 2005, pp. 117–126.

[52] Olano, M., and Greer, T. Triangle scan conversion using 2d homogeneous coordinates. In *Proceedings of the ACM SIGGRAPH/EUROGRAPHICS Workshop on Graphics Hardware*, ACM, 1997, pp. 89–95.

[53] OpenGL.org. Web page on fbos. Available at: http://www.opengl.org/wiki/GL_EXT_framebuffer_object.

[54] Parilov, E., and Zorin, D. Real-time rendering of textures with feature curves. *ACM Transactions on Graphics (TOG) 27*, 1 (2008), 3:1–3:15.

[55] Peters, J., and Reif, U. Shape characterization of subdivision surfaces–basic principles. *Computer Aided Geometric Design 21*, 6 (2004), 585–599.

[56] Pharr, M., and Humphreys, G. *Physically Based Rendering: From Theory to Implementation*. Morgan Kaufmann, 2004.

[57] Porcher Nedel, L., and Thalmann, D. Anatomic modeling of deformable human bodies. *The Visual Computer 16*, 6 (2000), 306–321.

[58] Poynton, C. Charles Poynton's color FAQ. *Electronic Preprint* (1995). Available at: http://www.poynton.com /colorFAQ.html.

[59] Ramshaw, L. *Blossoming: A Connect-the-Dots Approach to Splines*. Digital Systems Research Center, 1987.

[60] Reif, U. A unified approach to subdivision algorithms near extraordinary vertices. *Computer Aided Geometric Design 12*, 2 (1995), 153–174.

[61] Reis, G., Zeilfelder, F., Hering-Bertram, M., Farin, G., and Hagen, H. High-quality rendering of quartic spline surfaces on the GPU. *IEEE Transations Visualization Computer Graphics 14*, 5 (2008), 1126–1139.

[62] Rost, R. *OpenGL (R) Shading Language,* 3rd ed. Addison Wesley Longman, 2009.

[63] RTWH. Openmesh web page. Available at: http://www.openmesh.org.

[64] Sander, P., Gortler, S., Snyder, J., and Hoppe, H. Signal-specialized parametrization. In *Proceedings of the 13th Eurographics workshop on Rendering Techniques*, 2002 Eurographics, pp. 87–98.

[65] Sander, P., Snyder, J., Gortler, S., and Hoppe, H. Texture mapping progressive meshes. In *Proceedings of the 28th Annual Conference on Computer Graphics and Interactive Techniques*, ACM, 2001, pp. 409–416.

[66] Schlag, J. Using geometric constructions to interpolate orientation with quaternions. In *GRAPHICS GEMS II* (J. Arvo, ed.). Morgan Kaufmann, 1991, p. 377.

[67] Selle, A., Lentine, M., and Fedkiw, R. A mass spring model for hair simulation. *ACM Transactions on Graphics (TOG) 27*, 3 (2008), 1–11.

[68] Shoemake, K. Animating rotation with quaternion curves. *ACM SIGGRAPH Computer Graphics 19*, 3 (1985), 245–254.

[69] Soler, C., and Sillion, F. Fast calculation of soft shadow textures using convolution. In *Proceedings of the 25th Annual Conference on Computer Graphics and Interactive Techniques*, ACM, 1998, pp. 321–332.

[70] Stam, J. Stable fluids. In *Proceedings of the 26th Annual Conference on Computer Graphics and Interactive Techniques*, ACM, 1999, pp. 121–128.

[71] Veach, E. *Robust Monte Carlo Methods for Light Transport Simulation*. Ph.D. thesis, Stanford University, 1997.

[72] Veach, E., and Guibas, L. Metropolis light transport. In *Proceedings of the 24th Annual Conference on Computer Graphics and Interactive Techniques*, ACM, 1997, pp. 65–76.

[73] Wald, I., Boulos, S., and Shirley, P. Ray tracing deformable scenes using dynamic bounding volume hierarchies. *ACM Transactions on Graphics (TOG) 26*, 1 (2007), 6.

[74] Wang, X., and Phillips, C. Multi-weight enveloping: Least-squares approximation techniques for skin animation. In *Proceedings of the 2002 ACM SIGGRAPH/Eurographics Symposium on Computer Animation*, ACM, 2002, pp. 129–138.

[75] Ward, G. The RADIANCE lighting simulation and rendering system. In *Proceedings of the 21st Annual Conference on Computer Graphics and Interactive Techniques*, ACM, 1994, pp. 459–472.

[76] Warren, J., and Weimer, H. *Subdivision Methods for Geometric Design: A Constructive Approach*. Morgan Kaufmann, 2002.

[77] Whitted, T. An improved illumination model for shaded display. *Communications of the ACM 23*, 6 (1980), 343–349.

[78] Williams, D. Aliasing in human foveal vision. *Vision Research 25*, 2 (1985), 195–205.

[79] Wright, R., and Lipchak, B. *OpenGL Superbible, 4th ed.* Addison-Wesley Professional, 2007.

Index